ASSASSINS' DEEDS

ASSASSINS' DEEDS

A HISTORY OF ASSASSINATION FROM ANCIENT EGYPT TO THE PRESENT DAY

JOHN WITHINGTON

REAKTION BOOKS

For Anne

Published by Reaktion Books Ltd
Unit 32, Waterside
44–48 Wharf Road
London N1 7UX, UK
www.reaktionbooks.co.uk

First published 2020
Copyright © John Withington 2020

Printed and bound in Great Britain by TJ Books Limited, Padstow, Cornwall

A catalogue record for this book is available from the British Library

ISBN 978 1 78914 351 5

CONTENTS

PROLOGUE

In the dead of night, <u>the assassin</u> creeps into the hotel room, and is immediately confronted with a dilemma. The man he is there <u>to murder</u>, <u>an arms dealer supplying the enemy</u>, is lying under a mosquito net. Should he lift it, running the risk of waking the sleeper, or should he just stab through it? In the darkness, his target is an indistinct shadow, apart from a foot protruding from the net right next to where he stands. This small corner of the dealer's body is illuminated by light from a window. A sudden noise startles the assassin. Is he discovered? No. It is just car horns in the street outside. He reflects that they seem to belong to a different world to this one in which he is about to commit murder.

Then fear of being caught, tortured, executed evaporate. All that matters is that he should kill the arms dealer before he can fight back or cry out. He fumbles in his pockets. In the right is a razor, and in the left, a dagger. Another dilemma. Which should he use? He feels the razor is more dependable, but for some reason it disgusts him. The profound silence in the room makes him freeze, as though he is terrified that something might topple over and wake his target. But nothing does.

He wonders: when he strikes with the dagger, will it penetrate the victim's flesh easily, or will it meet resistance? He cannot help pressing its point into his own arm. The sleeper's foot, by now almost touching him, suddenly moves. To add to his horror, he feels an insect run across his skin. No, it is the trickle of blood! His blood. The assassin's eyes begin to adjust to the gloom, and he can see the arms dealer is wearing just a pair of shorts and lying on his side, making his heart a more difficult target. He is too chubby for the assassin to make out the ribs, which means he will need to use the victim's nipples as markers to guide him to a fatal strike. As he toys with the dagger, working out the best angle of attack, a death rattle rasps in the arms dealer's throat, but he carries on breathing and the rattle turns into a snore. Then all at once he moves. With a blow that would have split a plank, the assassin drives the dagger down through the net and into the arms dealer.

The victim leaps up towards him, his body rebounding from the bed springs. The assassin fights to hold him down. The arms dealer's legs jack-knife towards his chest, then jerk out straight and stiff. The assassin thinks he needs to stab him again to be sure, but can he pull the blade out? He does not dare let go of the dagger, and now his shoulder is starting to hurt. The blood running down his own arm is mixing with the blood running from the wound in the victim's chest just as it seems his own anguish is merging with the arms dealer's. Both are motionless. It appears to the assassin that the only thing moving in the room is his furiously pounding heart. He feels sure now the man must be dead, but as he holds on to the knife, his arm starts to tremble. He feels overwhelmed by revulsion but also by a taste for blood. His revulsion grows as a mysterious figure with pointed ears begins to take form on the sheet beside the dead man. Is it an evil spirit? The assassin is not superstitious, but now he is paralysed with fear. Then a miaow. It is an alley cat, which has somehow slipped in. Now it flees out on to the balcony. The assassin follows and finds himself back on the city streets.

Ten minutes later, the killer realizes he has left behind a crucial document he was meant to steal, and he has to go back. Returning to the room feels like going to prison. But in spite of the terrible deed he has done, nothing seems to have changed. The man's clothes are still hanging by the bed; just as before there is the solitary rectangle of light, which he sees is coming from a late-night gambling den. He thinks the document will be under the pillow, but is he certain he has really killed the man? The assassin has to close his eyes before he can steel himself to extract the paper. Once he has it, he sees the arms dealer is dead all right. Eyes open. No breathing. Blood on the sheets. The assassin finds the key, goes out of the room, double-locks the door, and takes the lift down. He checks in the mirror to make sure the deed has not put some dreadful mark of guilt on his face. No. He looks the same as ever, perhaps a bit tired.

The assassin was a young Chinese revolutionary, the city Shanghai, the year 1927 and the murder the opening of André Malraux's award-winning novel *La Condition humaine* (1933). When it comes to real assassins, we do not have the benefit of the novelist's all-seeing eye to peer into their souls. But we can examine whether Malraux's nervous, self-doubting, rather bungling young man is closer to their profile than those cool, assured fictional killers who are better known, like James Bond or the Jackal. That is one of the puzzles this book will try to unravel as it tells the story of more than 4,000 years of assassination.

Even though Malraux's assassin is operating in the twentieth century, he chooses a weapon that would have been available 4,000 years before. How much has the practice of assassination been changed by the many ingenious developments in ways to kill people that those forty centuries have seen? Then there is motivation. Malraux's character is driven by determination to advance a political cause. How common is that among real assassins, and how does it compare with other motives – religion, personal ambition, financial or other reward, revenge, fear? What sort of people are assassins? Malraux's is a rebel, but how prominent have rulers and governments been in assassination projects?

The victim in Malraux's novel appears to have taken few precautions. Is that typical? Down the centuries, how careful have

novel

been those who might be targets, and how effective have been the measures they put in place? Do assassinations work? In spite of the problems he encounters, Malraux's character dispatches his target, but how often is this the case? And do killers usually get caught or do they more often escape? What about the broader consequences? Over a longer term, do assassinations tend to deliver the assassin's objective? How often do they have unintended consequences, and how serious are these? And what do theologians, philosophers and political theorists have to say about when, if ever, assassination is justified?

Malraux's young assassin, incidentally, successfully escapes after killing the arms dealer, and then tries to murder the Chinese Nationalist leader Chiang Kai-Shek. He decides the only way to achieve this is a suicide mission. So he discovers the route Chiang's car takes each day and waits for it, clutching a bomb. As the car appears, the assassin throws himself at it, detonating the device. After a few moments he comes round, to find his body mutilated, his legs blown off. Dimly he spots a policeman approaching. Dreadfully injured though he is, he manages to take a pistol from his pocket and put it in his mouth. It goes off and kills him when the policeman kicks him. But Chiang is not dead. As a precaution, he has a number of identical cars that he travels in. He was not in the one the assassin blew up.

Finally we need a definition. All assassinations may be murders, but the converse is not true. So what qualifies as an assassination? The *Cambridge Dictionary* offers a commendably concise answer: 'the murder of someone famous or important', while the *Oxford English Dictionary* adds that it involves 'a planned attack, typically with a political or ideological motive, sometimes carried out by a hired or professional killer'. I have on the whole followed these as a guide to what qualifies as an 'assassin's deed'. So I have generally excluded execution after some kind of legal process, however unsatisfactory critics might consider it to be. Nor do I include the killing of people held captive. So, for example, I do not regard the Princes in the Tower as having been assassinated (assuming they were murdered, about which there are one or two doubts). I have also omitted victims killed by a mob. Underworld killings motivated by rivalries between gangs are sometimes described as 'assassinations', but they find no place in the book either.

At the end of each chapter, there is an analysis of some of the assassinations that happened during the era in question, but these are not intended to be a representative sample. I have examined those about which we have enough information to address questions such as who were the assassins, what motivated them, what methods did they use, what happened to them, what were the consequences of their deeds, and were they successful? Plainly all were successful in the sense that the victim died, but I have tried to reach a conclusion on whether the assassin would have been satisfied with the overall outcome. Obviously, this often depends on a highly subjective and speculative judgement. Finally, there is a chapter on the celebrated figures who survived assassination attempts.

1

THE ANCIENT WORLD

Humans being what they are, it is probably reasonable to assume that assassinations have been happening ever since there was any kind of organized society. Lawrence Keeley, an anthropologist from the University of Chicago, investigated how violent ancient communities were, and decided the answer was: 'very'. Excavating a prehistoric Californian Indian village, he discovered the percentage of inhabitants who appeared to have suffered violent deaths was four times what you would find in modern America and Europe, while in an ancient Egyptian cemetery dating back 12,000 to 14,000 years he found that 40 per cent of those buried had evidence of wounds from sharp stones, with a number having multiple injuries to their heads or necks.

Egypt

A good candidate for 'first known victim of an assassination' is an Egyptian pharaoh named Teti (sometimes known as Othoes) who died in 2333 BC. The ancient Egyptian historian Manetho, writing around 300 BC and probably drawing on materials that have since been lost, says Teti was 'murdered by his bodyguard'. The pharaoh was dubbed 'He who pacifies the Two Lands', and this is seen by some historians as implying that he came into his kingdom at a time of strife. Certainly he was the first pharaoh of a new dynasty, the sixth, and his predecessor, Unas, had died without leaving a male heir. Teti took Iput, Unas' daughter, as one of his wives, and while he ruled there is evidence of Teti trying to tighten up security. He greatly increased the number of guards and sentries and introduced a new job entitled 'overseer of the protection of every house of the king'.

Estimates of the length of Teti's reign range from 12 to 23 years, and not all historians are convinced he was assassinated. After all, Manetho was writing about 2,000 years after the event, but there is other evidence. A number of senior officials including a vizier, the chief physician and the overseer of weapons had their memorials defaced. Some had their names erased, their images chiselled away or their remains moved. This was a dreadful fate usually meted out to hated criminals, because it meant that in the afterlife they would be homeless and condemned to endless wandering. Do these punishments suggest there was a major conspiracy? Were the plotters emboldened by the fact that Teti's claim to the throne was rather shaky, based as it was on his wife's lineage rather than his own? As usual for a pharaoh, he had a number of wives and children, spawning plenty of family rivalries and jealousies that ambitious would-be usurpers might exploit. We know that he was succeeded for a short time by a man named Userkare. Some have suggested he may have been Teti's son by a wife other than Iput. Was he the chief conspirator? Or was he actually on Teti's side, keeping the dead king's throne warm for Pepy I, the son he had with Iput? Certainly, Pepy did eventually follow his father and ruled for forty years or more.

A similar 'was he murdered or wasn't he?' mystery used to surround another pharaoh who reigned more than a millennium after Teti. Ramesses III met his end in 1155 BC, after thirty years on the throne, and thanks to the survival of 3,000-year-old papyrus court records, we know that more than thirty 'great criminals' from his court were put on trial over their part in a conspiracy against him. We also know that before then, Ramesses had had his share of trouble, with economic and political problems building up as his reign went on. Towards its end, Egypt experienced the earliest known strike when skilled workers at the Royal Necropolis at Deir el-Medina downed tools because they had not been paid for two months. Ramesses had other difficulties too. He had taken a Syrian wife, which may have stirred up discord, and he had no designated principal, or Great Royal Wife, throwing the question of which son would succeed him up in the air.

The assassination plot took place at the time of a major celebration, the Festival of the Valley at Medinet Habu, near Luxor. The leading instigator appears to have been one of Ramesses' wives, Queen Tiye, and her objective to kill Ramesses and secure the throne for her son Pentawere. A whole swathe of the royal household was accused of being involved, including the royal butler, Mesedsure, and the 'Chief of the Chamber', Pebekkamen. The names used in the court documents, incidentally, were terms of abuse, so Mesedsure means 'Re [the sun god] hates him'. Pebekkamen subverted the overseer of the royal herds, getting him to supply magic wax figures that were supposed to weaken or disable people's limbs. Similar objects were procured from two other sources. The conspirators believed these supernatural aids would neutralize Ramesses' guards. Mesedsure and Pebekkamen secured the help of ten harem officials, including an overseer of the treasury. They also turned three royal scribes and an army commander. Six wives of officers of the harem-gate were recruited to pass on messages, while relatives of the plotters outside the harem were roped in too. A harem woman named Binemwese sent a letter to her brother, who was a captain of archers from Nubia, urging him to incite people to rise against the pharaoh, so perhaps the plotters were hoping a rebellion would break out when they killed Ramesses.

By the time the conspirators came to trial, we know Ramesses was dead, but some historians argued that the court documents provided evidence only that there had been a plot, and not that it had been successful. Then, in 2012, a team of researchers from the Institute for Mummies at the European Academy of Bozen-Bolzano in Italy used CT scans to reveal that Ramesses had a wide and deep wound to the throat, probably caused by a sharp blade, which would have killed him instantly. Further investigation showed he had suffered other injuries inflicted by different weapons, suggesting there had been a number of assailants. The plotters' trial was pretty lurid. Two judges and two guards were accused of 'carousing' with some of the women prisoners. They were sentenced to having their noses and ears cut off. One committed suicide. The trial documents indict some of the accused with conspiring 'to commit hostility against their lord'. In a foretaste of modern UK anti-terrorist legislation, which makes it an offence to fail to inform the police if you know an attack is being prepared, ten, including six former inspectors of the harem and three butlers, were charged with omitting to report seditious words they had heard. Altogether more than thirty people were condemned. Their punishment, historians believe, would have been death. A number 'took their own lives' with the agreement of the court.

That appears to have been the fate of Pentawere. The researchers who found the throat wound to Ramesses examined the body of a young man aged about eighteen to twenty, who appeared from genetic evidence to be Ramesses' son. It had been buried in a 'ritually impure' goatskin, probably as a punishment. They believed the cause of his death may have been strangulation. The fate of Tiye is not recorded, but we do know that Ramesses' eldest son succeeded to the throne as Ramesses IV.

The Penn Museum in Philadelphia reckons that between 3150 BC and 31 BC, there were about 170 pharaohs, though other authorities put the figure at 190 or more. We know of only around half a dozen who were assassinated, though some murders may, of course, have been lost in the mists of ancient history, but the pace of killing seems to have picked up towards the end of the pharaohs' era. In the ninth decade before Christ, Ptolemy IX married his daughter Berenice III. This was unusual, but by no means unique as pharaohs strove to keep the bloodline pure. Ramesses the Great is said to have married at least three of his daughters. With Berenice, it is probable the arrangement was strictly business. According to the Roman scholar Cicero, who was also a statesman and orator, she was very popular in Alexandria, and Ptolemy desperately needed to shore up his position in the face of local unrest. Anyway, when he died in 80 BC, she was his only surviving legitimate child, and she succeeded to the throne, ruling alone for five months from March to August.

Queens had held power in Egypt before, but they had found it hard to gain acceptance. And now the Romans were taking a growing interest in the affairs of the kingdom, on which they depended for corn, and they decided they wanted their man installed as her husband. The only legitimate male descendant of the Egyptian royal line was Berenice's cousin, Alexander, the son of Ptolemy X, who had kept being eased on and off the throne in a series of power struggles with Ptolemy IX. Alexander was in his mid-twenties, and fortunately for Rome, very much under its influence. As a boy he had been captured on the island of Cos by Mithradates, king of Pontus in modern Turkey. Alexander was brought up a royal hostage at the Pontic court, but managed to escape and take refuge with the Romans, and it was Rome's dictator, Sulla, who sent him off to marry Berenice and become Ptolemy XI. The marriage evidently was not a great success. Perhaps Berenice wanted Alexander to play second fiddle. Whatever the reason, after a few days, he killed her and became sole ruler, but this enraged the Alexandrians, and just nineteen days later, they lynched him.

Ptolemy XI was succeeded by his cousin Ptolemy XII, but he was overthrown by a popular uprising in 58 BC and fled to Rome. His daughter Berenice IV took over. She would have her husband assassinated, but apparently for reasons of personal disgust rather than dynastic ambition. After two matches had fallen through, she was married off to an illegitimate Syrian princeling, Seleucus, whom the Alexandrians nicknamed 'seller of salt-fish'. Whether the problem was his smell or just general crassness, Berenice had him strangled after only a few days of matrimony. But in 55 BC, Ptolemy XII bribed the Romans to provide an army to reinstate him, and he had Berenice put to death. The Roman cavalry commander, incidentally, was Mark Antony, who, during the operation, caught his first glimpse of Berenice's sister, the great femme fatale Cleopatra.

Persia, Syria and Other Parts of the Middle East

Assassination may have been relatively rare in Egypt, but if you were a Persian king of the Achaemenid dynasty, you had a more than fifty-fifty chance of meeting your end that way. Between 550 and 330 BC, out of thirteen, seven were murdered and five died of natural causes, while Cyrus the Great died peacefully in his bed or in battle; we are not sure which. This same Cyrus, though, thought a good deal about the danger of assassination. The ancient Greek historian Xenophon recorded that the emperor 'realized men are nowhere an easier prey to violence than when at meals, or at wine, or in bed and asleep'. And it was while he was asleep that one of Cyrus' successors was shuffled off this mortal coil.

His grandson, Xerxes the Great, ruled half a century after him, and was remembered for his ambitious but unsuccessful attempt to conquer Greece, during which his huge army was held up by three hundred Spartans. Xerxes met his end in the great imperial capital, Persepolis, which he had played an important part in building. Ancient sources differ on the details of his murder, but the story seems to go something like this. The commander of the royal bodyguard, Artabanus, who came from Hyrcania on the southern shores of the Caspian Sea, had become very powerful and influential. So powerful that he perhaps began to have ambitions of overthrowing Xerxes' dynasty and replacing it with his own family. By 465 BC, he had managed to place his seven sons in important positions at court, and working with them and Xerxes' chamberlain, the eunuch Aspamithres, he had the king assassinated in his bedroom. (In spite of Cyrus' strictures and the opening of Malraux's *La Condition humaine*, few assassination victims seem to meet their end in their sleep. Imad ad-Din Zengi, a Muslim leader who fought hard against the Crusaders, was killed as he lay in a drunken stupor in 1146, while Alessandro de' Medici in 1537 and Albrecht von Wallenstein in 1634 were both attacked while they slept but awoke before breathing their last.)

According to some accounts, Artabanus managed to persuade Xerxes' son, Artaxerxes, that his elder brother, the Crown Prince Darius, was guilty of the king's murder, and Artaxerxes then had Darius put to death. Others have Artabanus killing Darius before he had Xerxes murdered. Either way, Artabanus remained a dominant force. Some say he became king himself, others that he remained the power behind the throne as Artaxerxes reigned as King Artaxerxes I. Whatever the truth, after a few months Xerxes' son learned what had really happened to his father. At this point, Artabanus decided to mount a coup, but an important general betrayed the plot, and Artaxerxes survived. Artabanus was then either executed, killed by Artaxerxes or dispatched by his fellow conspirators as they fell out among themselves.

Artaxerxes ruled for forty years. He left seventeen sons by his many concubines, but just one legitimate heir, who in 425 BC became Xerxes II. While his father lasted forty years, Xerxes barely managed forty days. A Greek historian from the fifth century BC, Ctesias, was also physician to the Persian king Artaxerxes II, grandson of Artaxerxes I. He records that six and a half weeks after his accession, while he 'lay drunk in his palace', Xerxes II was killed by a couple of assassins on the orders of his younger half-brother Sogdianus, the son of Artaxerxes and a Babylonian woman named Alogyne, which means 'rose-coloured'. Sogdianus then became king. When this news reached another half-brother, Ochus, the governor of Hyrcania, he was incensed, believing he had a much better claim to the throne than Sogdianus. Not only was he Artaxerxes I's son, by another Babylonian concubine, but he was also married to one of his half-sisters, the daughter of yet another of Artaxerxes' Babylonian concubines. Ochus put together a formidable army and within six months he had deposed Sogdianus. Having promised his half-brother that he would not be killed by the sword, poison or starvation, Ochus had him smothered in ashes, and became the emperor Darius II, ruling for nineteen years.

Apart from the murder of Seleucus, who may have been assassinated because of his smell, the thread that runs through all these ancient killings is personal ambition, the wish to seize power for oneself or one's protégé. So, as the warning of Cyrus the Great suggests, it would be wise to keep a close eye on those who had easy access to you, such as your household staff or your bodyguards, who ironically had been recruited to protect you from assassination. But very often the ones to be most afraid of were your closest loved ones – spouses, children, siblings. Indeed, in the Assyrian empire, patricide appears to have been a favoured means of regime change.

The emperor Tukulti-Ninurta I was a highly cultured man who commissioned an epic poem about his exploits, the only one of its kind to survive from ancient Assyria. He also founded a great library, much of it stocked with loot from his wars because Ninurta was a formidable conqueror who greatly extended the Assyrian Empire. When he took Babylon he sacked the city and plundered the temple, enslaved prisoners, and said in an inscription that he had 'filled the caves and ravines of the mountains with the corpses' of those who resisted him. As for the Babylonian king, Ninurta 'trod on his royal neck with my feet like a footstool', then marched him 'naked and in chains' to the Assyrian capital.

The Assyrians and the Babylonians shared the same gods and the same cuneiform alphabet, and they had once been part of the same empire. This had led to Assyrian kings observing a measure of restraint when there was conflict, so many at Ninurta's court now felt he had overstepped the mark. In 1208 BC, the Babylonian Chronicles report that 'his son and the nobles of Assyria revolted'. They 'cast him from his throne . . . and then killed him with a sword'. His son Ashur-Nadin-Apli is generally believed to have been his assassin, or at least one of the leading conspirators, and the murder plunged the empire into a period of civil war from which Ashur emerged as the new emperor to restore order.

In 681 BC, one of Ninurta's successors was also to fall victim to his son – Sennacherib, the Assyrian, who in Byron's famous poem 'came down like the wolf on the fold'. The verses tell of a mysterious catastrophe that destroyed Sennacherib's army. The emperor's first campaign in Palestine in 701 BC had been a great success as he plundered a number of towns, but when he invaded again, some time after 689 BC, something very odd happened. Though 'unsmote by the sword', his soldiers died en masse in their sleep. The Bible talks of the 'Angel of the Lord' killing more than 5,000 in the Assyrian camp. Was it cholera that struck down so many? Whatever it was, it forced Sennacherib to withdraw in confusion, and his prestige never recovered.

'And it came to pass,' continues the Bible, as Sennacherib, 'was worshipping in the house of Nisroch his god, that Adrammelech and Sharezer his sons smote him with the sword', though a more colourful version has it that the emperor was crushed under a huge

This c. 1300 miniature from Sicily shows Sennacherib being stabbed by his two sons as he prays to his pagan god.

statue of a winged bull. Sennacherib had designated his son
Esarhaddon as his successor even though Adrammelech and Sharezer
were older, perhaps thanks to the machinations of Esarhaddon's
mother, who had risen to be chief lady in the royal harem. An
inscription written by Esarhaddon about ten years after the event
said his brothers began plotting against him and bad-mouthing him
to his father, forcing the heir to flee. The Babylonian Chronicle
tells of the emperor's death being followed by a 42-day war that
ended with Esarhaddon defeating his brothers, taking the crown
and ruling for the next eleven years, though some historians believe
it was actually Esarhaddon who murdered Sennacherib when he
feared he had lost his father's favour.

China and an Advocate for Assassination

Around 500 BC, assassination got perhaps its first theoretician. In
the earliest known work on military tactics, *The Art of War*, the
Chinese general Sun Tzu sang its praises, declaring: 'Raising a host
of a hundred thousand men and marching them great distances
entails heavy loss on the people and a drain on the resources of the
State.' A better alternative, whenever possible, was to recruit well-
paid 'spies', one of whose tasks would be 'to assassinate an individual',
presumably a crucial one, perhaps by bribing 'attendants, aides-
de-camp, and door-keepers and sentries' among the enemy. This
was much more cost-effective than war. There are those who question whether Sun Tzu really was the author of *The Art of War*, but
he does appear to have been a fine general, and one of the rulers
he served was Prince Guang, who reigned over the Chinese kingdom of Wu. In a dispute over the succession to its throne, Guang
claimed he had been cheated by his uncle, King Liao. He was
desperate to get his crown back, but Liao made sure he was always
well protected. Everywhere he went he took his army, which
included a hundred highly efficient bodyguards, and he invariably
wore a suit of armour made up of three layers. In 515 BC Guang's

right-hand man, another general, Wu Zixu, told him he had found just the person to remove Liao. The assassin he recommended was a mountain of a man named Zhuan Zhu. Zhuan thought the world of his mother, and Guang promised that if he killed Liao, she would live like a queen for the rest of her days.

That clinched the deal, but while the assassin was making his preparations, his mother hanged herself, leaving word that she had done it so nothing would distract her son from his task. This devastating turn of events only made Zhuan more determined, but he knew he would need more than his brute strength to eliminate Liao. So he mastered the art of cuisine, and managed to worm his way into the king's household as a chef. For a banquet he prepared a magnificent fish. As he came to present it, he was searched thoroughly by the guards. Having found nothing amiss, they stepped back while Liao took in the delicious aroma rising from this culinary masterpiece. With the king and his entourage momentarily mesmerized, Zhuan thrust his hand into the fish and pulled out a dagger which, in the blink of an eye and with dreadful force, he plunged through Liao's multi-layered armour and into his heart. Dozens of royal guards immediately descended on Zhuan, making mincemeat of him, but Guang regained his throne, taking the title King Helu.

With tales like this to tell, or embellish, it is no wonder that assassins commanded a section all of their own in the works of the great Chinese historian from the second century BC, Sima Qian. He was perhaps the first person to glamorize them, stressing their self-sacrifice and sense of honour. Zhuan Zhu knew he would receive no reward for his mission and that carrying it out would mean almost certain death, but that did not stop him. As it happened, King Helu had not occupied his throne for long when he found he needed the services of an assassin once more, as he heard that Liao's son, Qing Ji, was building an army to regain his father's crown. Helu's response is described in *Stratagems of the Warring States*, a collection of anecdotes compiled by an unknown author in the third century BC. Wu Zixu, who had recommended Zhuan Zhu, once again said he knew just the man. Helu was a bit surprised when in walked a scrawny, rather ugly-looking fellow named Yao Li who was barely four feet tall, but Wu was able to assure him that whatever the little man might lack in stature, he made up for in attitude, and that his stoic courage would carry him through all the perils and hardships that would no doubt stand between him and his goal.

Any doubts Helu might have had about Yao's determination were immediately dispelled when the young man asked the king to cut off his hand and kill his entire family. The assassin argued that once Qing had learned of these dreadful crimes committed against him by Helu, he would have no doubt that the king was Yao's sworn enemy, and sure enough when Yao turned up and offered his services, Qing hired him. So as Helu's rival embarked on his invasion by crossing the Yangtze River, Yao stood behind him on his ship. A gale was blowing, and while Qing closed his eyes against the fierce wind, Yao used his one hand to plunge his spear into his leader's back. Qing realized immediately that the game was up. He calmly congratulated Yao on his daring, then as he pulled the spear from his body, he ordered his troops not to punish his killer, and fell dead. But in his moment of triumph, Yao was overcome with remorse. He had committed three terrible betrayals: against his family members who had been killed at his request, against Qing, whom he had promised to serve, and against his parents, because allowing himself to be mutilated was an insult to them. So he threw himself into the churning waters of the Yangtze and was never seen again.

Another celebrated Chinese assassin who embodied self-sacrifice appeared in the early years of the fourth century BC. After killing a man, Nie Zheng had to go into hiding, working as a butcher. Then an old friend, government official Yan Zhongzi, reported a leading politician, Xia Lei, to his lord for treachery. Feeling certain that Xia would retaliate and fearing for his safety,

Yan tracked down Nie Zheng and offered to pay him handsomely if he would kill the politician, but Nie declined, saying he needed to look after his mother. When, a little later, his mother died, he presented himself to Yan and announced that he was now available. Nie's method did not rely on finesse. He simply barged into Xia's residence and stabbed anyone in his way before dispatching his victim. Nie would like to have been remembered as a hero, but he did not want to cause embarrassment to his family, so he slashed at his face with his knife until he was unrecognizable, then killed himself. The authorities laid his body in the marketplace, offering gold to anyone who could identify it. Nie's sister, Nie Rong, guessed her brother was the assassin and decided he deserved a place in history. So she set off to the marketplace, boldly declared the dead man was her brother and told the story of how he had at first refused to do his deed because of his filial duty, but that once that had been discharged, he performed it out of loyalty to Yan Zhongzi. Then, stricken with grief, she fell dead beside her brother.

The first woman ruler of China made a career of assassination, but self-sacrifice and honour had nothing to do with it. In 206 BC, after a civil war, a peasant emerged to become the first emperor of the Han dynasty, taking, with a hint of irony, the name Gaozu, meaning 'Exalted Ancestor'. His wife – who was also low-born, though less so than her husband – became the prodigiously dangerous Empress Lü. In those days in China, a man kept as many wives as he could afford, with one being the principal wife, or, in imperial circles, the empress, but this was a precarious position, belonging to the mother of whichever son was at the time regarded as heir apparent. New heir apparent meant new empress. At first, Gaozu named Lü's son as his heir, but as her charms faded he had a rethink, and toyed with the idea of replacing him with the son of his new favourite, Lady Qi. Lü kept intriguing, winning over learned men and palace advisers to argue against it, and somehow the emperor had still not got around to making the change when he died in 195 BC. The empress promptly had Qi's son poisoned, and any other woman in the household that Gaozu had been too fond of was also killed off. As for Qi herself, according to Sima Qian, Lü cut off her hands and feet, gouged out her eyes, burned off her ears, gave her a potion that struck her dumb, then threw her into a pigsty, where she was turned into a freak show for people invited to see the 'human pig'. Lü then became effectively the first woman ruler of China, exercising power on behalf of her young son. When he died, apparently from natural causes, she engineered it so another infant ascended the throne. As soon as he was old enough to be a potential threat, she murdered him and had him replaced by someone younger so she could continue to run the show, and all the while she promoted and enriched her own relatives, having wealthy men killed off so she could hand out their estates. After she died in 180 BC, Gaozu's surviving sons joined together to annihilate her entire clan.

The Chinese assassinations above were prompted by the dominant motives from this era of dynastic ambition or fear, but another was provoked by a reform programme. When he was a boy, it is said that Wu Qi bit his arm and swore on his own blood that he would leave his village and not return until he was rich and famous. He went on to have a distinguished career as a general, winning many battles and becoming celebrated for his stress on discipline and organization. Once, as his troops were lining up for battle, a soldier ran from the ranks, killed two men in the enemy's front line and then trotted back. Wu Qi ordered his immediate execution. When his officers protested that he was a fine soldier, Wu Qi replied: 'He is indeed a fine warrior, but he disobeyed my orders.' Later the general went on to serve as prime minister to King Dao of the state of Chu, where he fought corruption, reformed the government's finances and concentrated power and money in the hands of the king at the expense of the aristocracy, but in 381 BC, Dao died, and the nobles who had been slighted decided to assassinate Wu Qi at the king's funeral. They cornered him by Dao's corpse and peppered him with arrows, but some of their shafts also hit the dead king, and his son was so incensed by this desecration of his father's body that he hunted down the culprits and had them executed.

India and Another Theorist

During the same century, the Indian teacher, philosopher and royal adviser Chanakya (sometimes known as Kautilya) developed a new and more elaborate theory of assassination. Echoing Sun Tzu, he writes: 'An assassin, single-handed, may be able to achieve his end with weapon, poison and fire. He does the work of a whole army or more.' The philosopher offers a whole quiver of assassination methods, such as using beautiful women to stir up rivalries and discord among an enemy's leaders. Then the assassin can strike and people will assume the victim has been killed by a jealous rival. Or how about getting a fake doctor to administer poison to an infatuated enemy leader, pretending it is a love potion? And what if a king has a general of suspect loyalty in his service? Chanakya suggests infiltrating assassins into his army so they can murder him during a battle and pretend he was killed in action. The philosopher argues that assassination is preferable to arrest and trial because it avoids the risk of the victim's supporters causing trouble when he is detained.

These methods may sound devious and underhand, but Chanakya also plants the seed of a moral justification for assassination. It is better, he says, to murder an enemy general than to fight his army in battle, or to kill a king than mount a long siege of his city. Building on this, later theorists would argue that assassination is more humane than war or revolution. It is likely to cost fewer lives, and its victims will be the powerful rather than the humble rank and file. One of those Chanakya taught was Chandragupta Maurya, who built a great empire in India and Pakistan in the fourth century BC, rolling back the conquests of Alexander the Great. Chandragupta organized the assassination of Macedonian

Statue of
Chandragupta
Maurya, Laxminarayan
Temple, Delhi, India.

governors installed by Alexander, an approach described as cutting
down the 'tall poppies' of Greek rule.

Greece

Most assassinations in ancient times were the product of power
struggles in or between dynasties, though nationalism and liberation were also motives in those instigated by Chandragupta.
The first we come across that looks like the result of ideological
differences over a political system happened in Athens in the fifth
century BC. Ephialtes, 'a man with a reputation for incorruptibility
and public virtue', according to Aristotle writing a century later,

led the radical democratic faction in the city. In 462 BC he took advantage of the absence of the leader of the aristocratic faction, Cimon, who had gone to Sparta to help the local powers-that-were put down a serfs' rebellion. Ephialtes stripped the Athenian aristocratic council, the Areopagus, of most of its powers, handing them to more democratic bodies such as the Popular Assembly, the Council of Five Hundred and the law courts. In the view of the great historian and biographer Plutarch, writing more than five hundred years later, this helped 'transform the city into a thoroughgoing democracy'. When Cimon returned, he was not able to reverse the changes, and the new regime banished him.

But Ephialtes did not enjoy the triumph of democracy for long. Shortly afterwards he was assassinated. Aristotle writes that the killer was a man named Aristodikos from Tanagra, a town to the north of Athens. Another source refers to 'killers', suggesting that more than one person was involved, while Antiphon, writing closer to the event than the others, also uses the plural, saying the killers 'have remained undiscovered', adding the detail that they made no attempt to conceal the body. We know nothing more about Aristodikos than his name and the town where he lived, and neither he nor anyone else was ever tried for the murder. But whatever the identity of the killer or killers, what was the motive?

The obvious explanation is that Ephialtes was a victim of the Athenian aristocratic faction, and the Sicilian Diodorus Siculus, who wrote a monumental forty-volume universal history in the first century BC, describes his death as a 'punishment' for having 'provoked the masses to anger' against the aristocracy. But earlier, about 150 years after Ephialtes' death, in perhaps the first example of an assassination conspiracy theory, a Greek historian named Idomeneus claimed Ephialtes was actually a victim of infighting in the democratic party, and that his murder was organized by one of its leading members, Pericles, who was jealous of Ephialtes' popularity. And Pericles did become the leading light in Athens as it entered a golden age after Ephialtes, with the building of the

Parthenon and the city's emergence as a centre for education, art, culture, philosophy and medicine. So pervasive was his influence that the era was dubbed the 'Age of Pericles'. Idomeneus is not regarded as particularly reliable, and Plutarch rejected his Pericles theory as a 'poisonous accusation', but, as with so much about Ephialtes' death, who exactly did instigate it remains uncertain. What is clear is that it did not undermine the pro-democratic political changes the politician had made, and Pericles went on to develop them further.

Half a century before Ephialtes' murder, Athens was the scene of an assassination that echoed down the centuries, giving birth to the notion that tyrannicide – killing a tyrant – was justifiable. This is not quite as straightforward as it seems because 'tyrant' had two meanings. It could be the modern one of someone who uses power in a cruel, unjust way or it might mean someone who had taken power by unconstitutional means. Aristotle classified the first kind as tyrants by oppression and the second as tyrants by usurpation. Anyway, the story went that in 514 BC, two aristocrats, Harmodius and Aristogeiton, decided to kill Hipparchus, the tyrant of Athens, at a public festival. They succeeded, but they were captured and put to death by Hipparchus' brother, Hippias. Before long, they became heroes. A statue of them was placed on the Acropolis, they appeared on coins, and more than 2,000 years after their deed the American writer Edgar Allan Poe was celebrating them as 'avengers of liberty's wrongs' whose names would endure for 'endless ages'.

It is an inspiring tale of brave self-sacrifice for the common good, but in the century following their deed, the great ancient Greek historian Thucydides, who prided himself on taking a strict, evidence-based approach, debunked much of it. Athens had suffered a long period of instability and in 546 BC the city let the tyrant (by usurpation) Pisistratus take power. He rewarded them with twenty years of law and order, and his regime, wrote Thucydides, was not in the least 'odious'. He 'cultivated wisdom and virtue as much as any, and without exacting from the Athenians more than a twentieth of their income, splendidly adorned their city, and carried on their wars, and provided sacrifices for the temples'. In addition, Athens 'was left in full enjoyment of its existing laws'. When he died, he was succeeded by his son Hippias, Hipparchus' brother. So, flaw number one in the story. Thucydides pointed out that it was not the tyrant who was killed, but his brother – a junior partner in his government. The assassins had planned to kill both brothers, but they panicked when they saw one of their small group of co-conspirators chatting in a friendly way with Hippias, thinking their plot had been betrayed. As Hipparchus was close by, Harmodius and Aristogeiton immediately killed him with their

Harmodius and Aristogeiton, casting, Pushkin Museum, Moscow.

daggers. Harmodius was then slain on the spot by Hipparchus' guards, while Aristogeiton was soon caught 'and dispatched in no merciful way'.

Thucydides also says the assassins' main motive was not political, but personal. Harmodius, then 'in the flower of youthful beauty', and Aristogeiton, 'a citizen in the middle rank of life', were lovers, but Hipparchus tried to steal the young man away. It was the fear that he would misuse his powerful position as Hippias' brother to take Harmodius by force that prompted the assassination. There is an old saying: 'never let the facts get in the way of a good story', and certainly the inconvenient ones Thucydides advanced did not damage the legend of the two tyrannicides. Indeed, it appeared to gain additional credibility because after the assassination Hippias did become tyrannical by oppression, putting many people to death, and after three years he was deposed and exiled.

While Sun Tzu and Chanakya wrote about how assassination could be used *by* rulers, others considered the morality of using it *against* them, as Harmodius and Aristogeiton did. In the fifth century BC Socrates is said to have believed tyranny released those living under it from any obligation to obey, and that, in extreme circumstances, tyrannicide was justified. Socrates' great pupil Plato developed this idea further. A tyrant, through his corruption, contaminated the whole political system and so forfeited his right to live. One of Plato's pupils, Chion, became court philosopher to Clearchus, the tyrant by usurpation and oppression of Heracleia on the Black Sea in the fourth century BC. In 352 BC he led a group who killed Clearchus. It seems Chion, who was related to his victim, had been hoping the people would rise up against the tyranny, but he and his associates had made no attempt to forge links with others who were discontented with Clearchus' rule. So the upshot was that Chion and his associates were killed on the spot by Clearchus' bodyguards while power passed smoothly to the dead tyrant's brother, who some claimed was even worse than Clearchus.

Taking the view that man is a political animal, Aristotle, who was also a pupil of Plato, believed people could achieve their full potential only within a political system, and that the rule of a tyrant prevented this, because the system was then run solely in the interests of the ruler. The philosopher said that tyrannicide was therefore justified, provided there was no other solution. He thought it should be the job of the elite because they had better access to the ruler, though he recognized there was a danger they might act from motives other than trying to promote the public good. Xenophon remarked that Greek states 'bestow great honour on him who kills a tyrant', and in China too tyrannicide won support from philosophers such as Mencius, regarded by many as second in importance only to Confucius, in the fourth century BC. He said a tyrant became an 'outcast' because he 'mutilated' benevolence and righteousness. Then in the first century BC, Cicero, perhaps the greatest of all Roman orators, said tyranny was like a plague that corrupts the whole political system, and that it needed to be cut out by tyrannicide. He would spend his life defending the Roman Republic against what he saw as the tyranny threatening it.

Julius Caesar

In 48 BC Julius Caesar had been made dictator in Rome, a formal office giving the holder sweeping powers that was normally reserved for times of national crisis and allowed to last no more than six months. But Caesar was appointed first for ten years, then in 44 BC, at the age of 56, for life. His birthday became a public holiday, statues of him were put up in every temple and he took to wearing purple robes and a crown of laurel leaves like Rome's early Etruscan kings. Before he took the reins, Rome had indeed suffered many years of turmoil, with civil war and Spartacus' slave rebellion, but the adulation surrounding the dictator began to alarm supporters of the republic. Caesar was an astute politician as well as a great general, and he spent lavishly on popular policies, such as expanding the Circus Maximus so it could hold 150,000 spectators. He led a fairly modest life compared with most wealthy Romans, and he was generous, but also cunning, lustful, cruel and highly ambitious. Still, Caesar appeared to draw the line at taking the title of king. It was still something of a dirty word in Rome even though it was more than 450 years since the last king, the tyrant Lucius Tarquinius Superbus, had been driven out. He had allegedly murdered his predecessor, then launched a reign of terror against the senate, putting many senators to death.

Plutarch's account of the events of 44 BC, on which Shakespeare draws heavily for his famous tragedy *Julius Caesar*, was written a century-and-a-half later. The historian says that at a public festival Mark Antony offered Caesar a royal diadem three times, and that Caesar refused it three times, but that the dictator's statues were decked with royal diadems, and that Caesar dismissed the tribunes who removed them. And there was scepticism about how sincere his rejection of Antony's diadem was. Had the dictator's friend actually been testing the political temperature when he made the offer?

A soothsayer had warned Caesar to beware the Ides of March – or 15 March, a traditional deadline for settling debts in ancient Rome – and Plutarch mentions some of the portents that figure so graphically in Shakespeare's *Julius Caesar* in the days leading up to it: violent storms, men on fire who remained miraculously unhurt, the animal without a heart that Caesar sacrificed, his wife Calpurnia's dream that she was holding her dead husband's body. On 15 March 44 BC the dictator was due to attend a meeting of the senate. Calpurnia tried to persuade him not to go, and Caesar himself 'was in some suspicion and fear', having perhaps heard whispers about a plot against him, but Decimus Brutus (not the famous Brutus), whom Caesar trusted, mocked these misgivings. He said the senate was planning to heap further honours on Caesar, but 'if someone should tell them at their session to be gone now, and to come back again when Calpurnia should have better dreams, what speeches would be made by his enemies?'

In fact, Decimus Brutus was one of a group conspiring against Caesar, and while they talked, he took the dictator's hand and began leading him out of the house. A philosophy professor passed a warning to Caesar, but in the crush of people, he never had a chance to read it. On the way to the senate, they passed the sooth-sayer. Plutarch says Caesar greeted him 'with a jest' and remarked 'Well, the Ides of March are come.' Softly the seer replied: 'Ay, they are come, but they are not gone.' When they reached the building where the senate was meeting, Decimus Brutus buttonholed Caesar's great friend Mark Antony, 'a robust man', and engaged him in a 'lengthy conversation'. The dictator went in and the senate rose in his honour. Then the conspirators gathered around him, ostensibly to support a petition from Tullius Cimber on behalf of his exiled brother. Caesar 'repulsed' their entreaties. They crowded in on him, growing more insistent. Caesar got angry, then 'Tullius seized his toga with both hands and pulled it down from his neck. This was the signal for the assault.' Casca struck the first blow, in Caesar's neck: 'not a mortal wound, nor even a deep one, for which he was too much confused, as was natural at the beginning of a deed of great daring'. Caesar even managed to grab the knife as he shouted at Casca, while the conspirator called on his comrades to join in.

Those not privy to the plot were transfixed, daring neither to flee nor to go to Caesar's aid. The dictator was hemmed in on all sides; 'whichever way he turned confronting blows of weapons aimed at his face and eyes, driven hither and thither like a wild beast . . . for all had to take part in the sacrifice and taste of the slaughter.'

Enter Brutus, the famous one – Marcus Junius Brutus. He was a descendant of another Brutus who had helped depose the tyrant Lucius Tarquinius Superbus all those centuries before. He was also one of Caesar's most trusted friends, whose career the dictator had helped to advance. His mother was Caesar's favourite mistress. Some even said, probably wrongly, that he was Caesar's son. Up

Vincenzo Camuccini, *The Assassination of Julius Caesar*, 1804–5, oil on canvas.

Marble bust
of Brutus, Roman, 30–15 BC.

to this point, the dictator had tried to defend himself against the blows, but it is said that when he saw Brutus too had a dagger drawn, he gave up and covered his face with his toga, allowing his friend to stab him. Then Caesar sank dying at the foot of the statue of Pompey the Great, who had once been his friend and son-in-law, but who became his rival and was killed after losing a civil war to him. It was as though, wrote Plutarch, 'Pompey himself was presiding over this vengeance upon his enemy'. There were 23 conspirators, all senators, and every one landed a blow. Indeed, in the mayhem a number of them wounded each other.

Brutus then tried to address the senate, but the senators burst out of the building and ran for it, spreading panic through the city. People locked their houses. Businesses shut up shop. Caesar's friends hid in other people's homes. The conspirators marched off to the Capitol, still brandishing their bloody daggers, says Plutarch, 'not like fugitives, but with glad faces and full of confidence, summoning the multitude to freedom', though other accounts say they had to flee for their own safety. According to Plutarch, the next day the senate trod warily, honouring Caesar, but also rewarding his killers. The target might have been successfully dispatched, but, oddly for assassins, the conspirators seemed to lack the killer instinct. They had wanted to throw Caesar's body in the Tiber, but instead they allowed Mark Antony to hold a public funeral. Brutus' brother-in-law, Cassius, had said they should kill Antony too, but Brutus thought that once Caesar was dead the Roman Republic would somehow miraculously reassert itself. Like Chion three hundred years before, they had failed to make alliances with others opposed to their enemy, and, like the Greek philosopher, they paid the price. The turning point came with the reading of Caesar's will, which bequeathed three pieces of gold to every citizen. Then 'when the multitude saw his body carried through the forum all disfigured with its wounds, they no longer kept themselves within the restraints of order and discipline' and ran off to try and catch the conspirators and 'tear them to pieces'. The only person they actually managed to dismember was a man named Cinna, who was a friend of Caesar and completely innocent. Brutus fled the city along with Cassius.

The assassination sparked off fourteen years of civil war. Brutus and Cassius were soon defeated. Both killed themselves, and, in Plutarch's words, the conspirators were hunted down 'until not one of them was left, but even those who in any way soever either put hand to the deed or took part in the plot were punished'. Some argue that Caesar's assassination should not be seen as a blow struck against tyranny so much as a fight between factions within the Roman elite. Whoever is right, instead of the revival of the Roman Republic, it led to the birth of the Roman Empire, with Caesar's adopted son Octavian becoming the first emperor – Augustus. The plotters must have been turning in their graves. Cicero lamented: 'the tyranny survives though the tyrant is dead.' He was executed in 43 BC after speaking out against Octavian.

Although his grand project failed, Brutus became perhaps the most famous assassin in history. Plutarch argued that Cassius had 'private grounds' for hating Caesar, whereas Brutus acted against the dictator in spite of the genuine friendship between them in order, as he saw it, to save Rome. He wrote that Brutus 'objected to the rule, but Cassius hated the ruler'. Writing 1,600 years later, Shakespeare has Mark Antony describing his mortal enemy Brutus as 'the noblest Roman of them all', and asserting that while the other conspirators acted out of 'envy', Brutus was genuinely motivated by belief in the 'common good'. During the next two millennia, Brutus' name would often be invoked to justify or condemn assassination, and the debate would ebb back and forth as to whether he was hero or villain.

REGARDING the assassinations of the ancient world, there are many known unknowns – killings that we are aware of, but do not have enough information to analyse – and, no doubt, many more unknown unknowns – murders of which all record has been lost – but there are nineteen where I have found enough detail to draw some statistical conclusions. More than half (ten) happened in what we would now call the Middle East, while there were also four in China, two each in India and Athens and one in Rome. Seven of the victims were kings or pharaohs, and there was also an emperor, a queen (the only woman among the nineteen), a queen's husband and a prince. In addition, three politicians, two tyrants, two governors and a general lost their lives. The most common motive, seen in at least ten of the murders, was dynastic ambition, while two were committed in the cause of national liberation, helping to expel a foreign invader. Three or four appear to have been prompted by political principles that went wider than just an argument over which individuals should be in charge, while on one occasion those losing out through a clamp-down on corruption were behind the plot. At least a dozen of the assassinations involved a conspiracy, and with dynastic ambition being the strongest motive, it is not surprising that many of the killers or those directing them came from within the victims' families – three sons, two wives (the only women to be found among the assassins or instigators), a husband, a brother and a nephew. Hired assassins were used up to five times, while on three occasions members of the nobility or elite did the assassin's work with their own hands. Cyrus the Great would not have been surprised to learn that in two instances the assassins were bodyguards. On each occasion when the motive was national liberation, the lower orders did the killing – one of the satraps of Alexander the Great in India was assassinated by his native mercenaries, and the other by his subjects. Perhaps the most unusual perpetrator was Chion, the court philosopher.

Of the ten assassinations where we know something of the method used, stabbing was the favourite, employed in seven or eight, with bows and arrows, strangling, and perhaps crushing by a heavy statue featuring in the others. As for the dozen cases in which we know the fate of the assassins, in at least seven they were killed at the time of, or soon after, their deeds. Two were despatched in mass executions, while the Chinese assassins Yao Li and Nie Zheng killed themselves. As to longer-term consequences, two groups of murderers became regarded as martyrs, while five of the assassinations were followed by serious disorder or civil war – in the case of Julius Caesar, a conflict that lasted fourteen years – and Chion's tyrannicide of Clearchus saw a worse tyrant take over. On the other hand, the killing of Qing Ji helped prevent a war, and two murders appear to have advanced a national liberation struggle. We know of only one case of collateral damage, when Nie Zheng stabbed anyone in his way as he closed in on his victim. So, finally, did the assassinations work? Would the perpetrators have been satisfied with the ultimate outcome? Of the fourteen where I felt able to make a judgement, my assessment is that six succeeded, but eight failed.

2

THE ROMAN EMPIRE
AND THE DARK AGES

The Roman Empire

In the early nineteenth century, a Russian nobleman is supposed to have described the country's political system as 'despotism tempered by assassination'. But if that applied to the Russian Empire, it was true in spades of the Roman. The pattern was soon established. As we saw, the aftermath of Julius Caesar's assassination was fourteen years of civil war, at the end of which his adopted son, Octavian, emerged as Rome's first emperor, taking the name 'Augustus'. In that civil war, the husband of a woman named Livia Drusilla had supported Augustus' enemies. So had her father, a senator who killed himself after Augustus' decisive victory at Philippi in 42 BC. Livia had to flee from Italy, but returned with her family three years later under an amnesty. It was then that the emperor met her for the first time. He was very taken with her dignified beauty and even though she was pregnant with her second son, Drusus, he was determined to marry her. Her husband, probably wisely, agreed to a divorce.

Augustus' union with Livia produced no offspring, and he had only one child, Julia, a daughter from a previous marriage. In this new empire, there were no proper rules for the succession, but Augustus felt he needed to name a male heir to secure an orderly transfer of power when he died. His first choice was his nephew, Marcus Claudius Marcellus, to whom Julia was married, but in 23 BC he died in mysterious circumstances. Livia, who was known to be friendly with experts on poisons and thought to be hoping one of her own sons might inherit the purple, was suspected of murdering him. Julia's second husband was Agrippa, for a time Augustus' deputy, and in 17 BC the emperor adopted his two young sons, Gaius and Lucius, just as Julius Caesar had adopted him. Meanwhile, Livia's two sons, Drusus and Tiberius, also took on significant offices, and after Agrippa died in 12 BC, Tiberius was designated as regent if Augustus should die before Gaius or Lucius were old enough to take the throne. The succession seemed secure, but then Gaius and Lucius died mysteriously in AD 2 and AD 4. The Roman historian and senator Tacitus, writing about a century later, said their deaths were caused by 'fate, or the treachery of their stepmother Livia'. So by this point, there is a potential body count of three laid at Livia's door.

At his wife's prompting, Augustus now adopted her son Tiberius (Drusus had been killed when he fell off a horse in 9 BC) but he did the same with Agrippa Postumus, Agrippa's last surviving son, born, as his name suggests, after his father's death. Once again, the curse of being named as Augustus' potential successor struck, and within a couple of years, Postumus was sent into exile. Some say it was because he was feckless and thuggish, showing little interest in anything apart from fishing, others that he had been involved in a plot against Augustus, while Tacitus again thought he detected the hand of Livia, who had firmly 'riveted her chains upon the aged Augustus'. Disturbingly for Livia, though, a rumour arose in AD 14 that Augustus had made a secret visit to the island where Postumus was exiled, and, according to Tacitus, 'tears and signs of affection on both sides had been plentiful enough' to suggest a reconciliation might be on the cards. After that, wrote the historian, the emperor's health went into decline and 'some suspected foul play on the part of his wife'. Livia got an urgent message to Tiberius who raced to the imperial estate at Nola, near Naples, where Augustus lay ill. It is not clear whether he arrived before or after the emperor breathed his last, because Livia maintained a ruthless news blackout, revealing Augustus' death only when she could announce at the same moment that Tiberius had succeeded him.

According to the historian Cassius Dio, writing about a century after Tacitus, Augustus had voiced to Livia his fears that he might meet his end at the hand of those closest to him, saying rulers have a 'most serious disadvantage . . . that we have not only our enemies to fear, as have other men, but also our friends. And a far greater number of rulers have been plotted against by such persons than by those who have no connexion with them.' So, in an echo of Cyrus the Great, he added that the ruler is always vulnerable 'day and night, when he takes his exercise, when he sleeps, and when he takes the food and drink' that those around him have prepared, and 'although he can protect himself from his enemies by arraying his friends against them, there is no corresponding ally on whom he may rely to protect him from these very friends.' And, indeed, wrote Cassius Dio, some people said Livia had killed Augustus by smearing poison on the figs he loved to pick at Nola.

Not all modern historians believe Livia was a serial killer. There is no evidence Augustus was murdered, Gaius had been wounded in war, and some say Marcellus died of typhoid, but Cassius Dio wrote that soon after Tiberius took the throne, Postumus was dispatched, with some difficulty, by a centurion who, the new emperor claimed, was acting on orders left by Augustus. The historian, though, believed Tiberius and Livia were actually behind the deed.

Tiberius does not seem to have been overjoyed at becoming emperor. He had already retired from public life once, in 6 BC, partly because of the blatant philandering of Augustus' daughter Julia who had been married off to him after Agrippa's death. (Tiberius had been forced to divorce a wife he genuinely loved to wed her.) After Augustus' death, he stalled for a month before finally allowing the senate to name him emperor. Hard-working but shy, some would say sullen, he resented Livia's continued interference once he had ascended the throne, so much so that when she died, he refused to attend her funeral. Increasingly the show was run by Lucius Aelius Sejanus, commander of the Praetorian Guard, the troops who formed the emperor's personal bodyguard. Before Tiberius came to power, they had been stationed all over Italy, but he concentrated them around Rome. After twelve years on the throne, Tiberius retired again – to Capri where, according to the rather sensationalist historian Suetonius, he indulged in 'secret orgies' in which members of both sexes 'selected as experts in deviant intercourse . . . copulated before him to excite his flagging passions', while boys were trained to 'get between his legs and nibble him' as he swam. But noting the number of learned men who accompanied him to the island, some historians have suggested he went to pursue more scholarly interests.

Sejanus had seduced Livilla, the wife of Tiberius' only son, Drusus, and allegedly conspired with her to poison her husband. Certainly Drusus died, like other imperial family members before him, in mysterious circumstances. With Tiberius tucked away on Capri, Sejanus began to look more and more like the real emperor. His birthday was declared a holiday. Golden statues were erected to him. But suddenly Tiberius denounced him, and had him arrested and strangled. Livilla killed herself soon after. The emperor then devoted his final years to a reign of terror while he adopted as his son his great-nephew Gaius Caesar, who had been with him on Capri and allegedly shared his debaucheries from a young age, and who would become known to history as Caligula. Tiberius acknowledged that he was 'nursing a viper in Rome's bosom', but seems to have regarded his adopted son as the best of a bad lot. In AD 37 the viper struck. As Tiberius lay in a coma after injuring his shoulder, and perhaps close to death anyway, Caligula is said to have ensured his departure by smothering him with a pillow. In another version of the story, it was the commander of the Praetorian Guard who did away with Tiberius when he inconveniently recovered consciousness after the guard had proclaimed Caligula emperor. Tiberius was one of eight consecutive rulers of the empire who, it was suspected, had met violent ends.

'Power tends to corrupt, and absolute power corrupts absolutely.' The historian Lord Acton's remark could have been written for Caligula. Tiberius, perhaps lacking confidence that the 24-year-old was up to the job of emperor, had decreed he should rule jointly with his cousin Tiberius Gemellus, but within a year Caligula had disposed of his kinsman. Whether Gemellus was killed or forced to commit suicide is not clear. According to Suetonius, during his time with Tiberius on Capri, Caligula 'could not control his natural cruelty and viciousness'. He was 'a most eager witness of the tortures and executions of those who suffered punishment, revelling at night in gluttony and adultery, disguised in a wig and a long robe'. Thanks to Suetonius, we are well informed about Caligula's more outlandish stunts such as making his horse a consul and getting his troops to gather sea shells on the shore to demonstrate his victory over Neptune, the god of the sea. He replaced statues of the gods with statues of himself, and was said to have appeared in the circus as singer, gladiator and charioteer. When he went bald, he made it an offence for anyone to look at him. He developed ingenious tortures – such as covering people in honey and setting swarms of bees loose on them. If eminent citizens had the temerity to criticize one of his shows, they could be branded, thrown to wild beasts, sent to work in the mines or caged on all fours. He was supposed to have had an incestuous affair with his sister Drusilla, got her pregnant, then, because he could not wait to see his child, ripped it from her womb. Suetonius happily related gossip, but even according to historians more scrupulous about the provenance and accuracy of stories, Caligula's reign was a triumph of excess. Knowing which side his bread was buttered, he pampered and increased the number of the Praetorian Guard, while replenishing his coffers by putting rich Romans on trial for treason so he could confiscate their assets.

By the end of AD 40, Caligula had come up with another crazy scheme. He would retire to Egypt to be worshipped as a living god. Around the same time it is said he started making fun of the

Roman statue of
Caligula, c. AD 40.

Praetorian Guard commander, Cassius Chaerea, whom he thought
had an effeminate voice. This was a particularly cruel jibe as Chaerea
had suffered a wound to his genitals while in the service of Caligula's
father. For much of the time, if Suetonius is to be believed, the
emperor behaved like a naughty schoolboy: 'when Chaerea had
occasion to thank him for anything, he would hold out his hand
to kiss, forming and moving it in an obscene fashion', but, of
course, most naughty schoolboys cannot have you put to death
just because they feel like it. Caligula had received what he believed
was a warning from the goddess of fortune to beware of 'Cassius',
so he immediately ordered the death of the proconsul of Asia, one
Cassius Longinus, but he had picked on the wrong Cassius.

If there is doubt about whether Augustus or Tiberius were
assassinated, there is none about Caligula. On 24 January AD 41,

the emperor was debating whether to get up for lunch as he was still rather full from the previous night's gluttony. Suetonius says he eventually decided to rise and was chatting to some 'boys of good birth who had been summoned from Asia to appear on the stage' and were rehearsing, when Cassius Chaerea came up behind the emperor, shouted: 'Take that!' and cut deep into his neck. Then a fellow conspirator stabbed him in the chest. In another version, in a scene reminiscent of Julius Caesar's murder, a whole crowd of assassins dispatched Caligula, inflicting thirty wounds; 'some even thrust their swords through his privates'. His bearers tried to defend him with their poles, and then some loyal German guards rushed up. They were too late to save him, though they killed 'several' of his assassins as well as 'some inoffensive senators'. Caligula was still just 28 and had reigned less than four years. For good measure, the conspirators also killed his wife and dashed out his baby daughter's brains against the wall. Some senators thought Caligula's death would mean the end of the empire, and the restoration of the republic, but the Praetorian Guard quickly named his uncle Claudius the new emperor. They had found him hiding behind a curtain shaking with fright. Chaerea was sentenced to death, and chose to be executed with the sword he had used to kill Caligula.

An attack of paralysis while he was a child had left Claudius a grotesque figure with a pot belly. He stammered, slobbered, twitched and kept banging into things. But he was astute enough to keep a low profile during Caligula's time, devoting himself to learning, and studiously avoiding looking like a candidate for emperor. Claudius did not have much luck with his wives. In AD 48, when he had occupied the throne for seven years, his third, the promiscuous Valeria Messalina, tried to mount a coup against him in cahoots with her latest lover, the senator Gaius Silius. When it failed, Messalina killed herself and Silius was executed. A few months later, the emperor married his niece, Caligula's sister, the beautiful Agrippina, who was 25 years younger than him, and no angel. She had been married twice, as well as being her brother-in-law's mistress, and was rumoured to have had an incestuous relationship with Caligula and to have poisoned her second husband. She already had a twelve-year-old son, Nero, three years older than Britannicus, Claudius' son by Messalina. (Britannicus was given his name in celebration of Claudius' conquest of Britain.) Agrippina got Claudius to adopt Nero, promoting him above Britannicus in the line of succession, and to marry him to the emperor's daughter Octavia, after the man she was betrothed to had been forced to kill himself.

Claudius believed one of the reasons Caligula had been such a disaster as emperor was that Tiberius had not prepared him properly, so he made sure Nero got plenty of experience of government. At first everything seemed to be going swimmingly, but by October AD 54, when Nero was sixteen, Agrippina began to have misgivings, fearing that Claudius was toying with the idea of making Britannicus his heir, or perhaps she was just anxious to see Nero on the throne while he was still young enough to control. Either way, according to Tacitus, she hired a woman named Locusta, an 'artist' in poisons, who was serving a gaol sentence because of her 'vast reputation for crime'. Locusta provided a 'potion' to the eunuch Halotus, whose job was to taste the emperor's food before he ate it. Halotus sprinkled the noxious substance on an 'exceptionally fine mushroom' before Claudius consumed it. But to Agrippina's consternation, though the poison had made the emperor feel sick, it did not look as though it would kill him, so she called in a doctor, who was also part of the plot, and was 'well aware that crimes of the first magnitude are begun with peril and consummated with profit'. Ostensibly to help Claudius vomit, the physician put a feather treated with a 'quick poison' down his throat, and this time the toxin worked.

While the Praetorian soldiers stood guard, a crisis meeting was held to sort out the succession. As had happened after Augustus' death, the royal widow kept a tight grip on information, even releasing fake news that Claudius was getting better. When

Agrippina and the astrologers judged the moment right, she is supposed to have embraced her stepson Britannicus so long and so tightly that he was unable to leave the room. So it was Nero who emerged accompanied by the guard commander, who was a protégé of Agrippina. Some of the soldiers cheered, but others asked: where was Britannicus? Then, seeing no sign of Claudius' son, they decided it was prudent to join in the cheering. The young Nero promised a generous cash hand-out to the guard, and they proclaimed him emperor.

If not preparing the new emperor failed with Caligula, preparing him worked no better with Nero. The young man was more interested in singing, acting and chasing women than governing. For a time, Agrippina was so important that her face appeared on coins, but when she felt her star waning, Tacitus reports stories that she tried to seduce her son. She also started to cultivate Britannicus. The upshot was that Nero pressed Locusta into service again, under pain of death, to eliminate Claudius' son. When the first attempt did not work, Nero personally flogged her, and the second dose did the job. Locusta was rewarded with a pardon and 'large estates in the country', according to Suetonius. (She would have fourteen years to enjoy them before Nero's successor Galba had her led in chains through Rome, then executed.) Other potential rivals to Nero also met sticky ends, while Agrippina was banned from the imperial palace. But Nero's mother could not help it. She just kept plotting. The story went that astrologers had once told her that Nero would rule the empire, but kill his mother. She is supposed to have replied: 'Let him kill me, provided he becomes emperor.' The first part of the prophesy had come true in AD 54. The second followed in 59.

Nero had fallen head over heels in love with a woman named Poppaea, the wife of one of his friends. When the emperor was dilatory about divorcing his own wife and making a reasonably honest woman of her, Poppaea started to taunt him, saying he was 'a mere ward' under Agrippina's thumb. Eventually the emperor did banish the virtuous and popular Octavia, before having her murdered. Next it was time to deal with his mother. He decided that having her poisoned so soon after Britannicus had departed that way might stir up trouble, and anyway, according to Tacitus, Agrippina 'from her familiarity with crime, was on her guard against treachery', and had even 'fortified her constitution by the use of antidotes'. Then the commander of the fleet at Misenum came up with the idea of a complicated mechanism on a ship, which would throw Agrippina into the water while they were out sailing in the Bay of Naples one night. The device misfired, letting the emperor's mother and one of her attendants down into the water more gently than planned. Thinking she was Agrippina, the plotters managed to kill the unfortunate attendant with poles, oars and whatever other improvised weapons were to hand, but the target herself escaped and was picked up by a fishing smack. It brought her back to shore where local people expressed relief that she had survived what they assumed was an accident at sea.

Fearing she might take some terrible revenge, Nero was now even more anxious to get rid of his mother. This time the fleet commander took a more basic approach. He burst into Agrippina's chamber with a couple of accomplices. First they clubbed her on the head, then as one of the conspirators drew a sword to deal the fatal blow, she demanded he stab her in the womb that had borne Nero, and that was one of the many wounds that killed her.

For nine more years, Nero got more and more like Caligula. When he appeared in public as a charioteer or musician, he would detail his thugs to flog people who applauded with insufficient enthusiasm. Nodding off at a show nearly cost the future emperor Vespasian his life. When Rome burned in AD 64, Nero did not fiddle (the musical instrument had not been invented), but he may have let slip an insensitive remark about what a great opportunity it was for redevelopment. Then when he started to run out of money for his ambitious rebuilding scheme, he had rich folk murdered so he could get his hands on their property. His most crucial error was failing to keep the army and the Praetorian Guard onside. In AD 68, after a series of revolts, he fled from Rome and got a loyal servant to kill him. His death was followed by the 'Year of the Four Emperors'. The first, Galba, was murdered by the Praetorian Guard; the second, Otho, killed himself. Vitellius was slain by his own troops, and Vespasian finally emerged as top dog. He managed to cling to the top of the greasy pole for ten years and to die of natural causes.

Vespasian was succeeded by his son, Titus, who lasted only two years. There was no love lost between him and his younger brother, Domitian, but nor is there any proof for the rumours that Domitian was behind his death. Still, he acted quickly to get himself proclaimed emperor. Domitian was not helped by an economic depression, which forced him to devalue the currency and raise taxes, but did not moderate his extravagance as he helped himself to a new palace and other goodies. It was the old story, with the emperor carrying out a series of purges of the rich so he could confiscate their wealth. The execution of his cousin in AD 96 was the last straw. It seemed proof that no one in Rome was safe, and even Domitian's wife, Domitia, of whom he was genuinely fond,

Charles-Gustave Housez, *The Death of Vitellius*, 1847, oil on canvas.

joined his chamberlain and the Praetorian Guard commander in a conspiracy against him. They arranged for him to meet a steward who seemed to have an injured arm. In fact, he was hiding a dagger in the bandages, which he used to stab the emperor eight times while the chamberlain's servants held him down. After Domitian's death the Senate ordered his name to be obliterated from Roman history, his coins to be melted and his statues torn down.

When you read about the mayhem that engulfed imperial Rome in its first century, with assassination emerging not just as the preferred method of regime change, but as a standard tactic among the ruling elite, it is surprising that the great historian Edward Gibbon did not place the start of its 'decline and fall' until nearly a century later. He blamed it on Commodus, the 'worthless boy' who succeeded his father, the philosopher-emperor Marcus Aurelius, at the age of nineteen in 180. In a now familiar tale, in spite of his father's best efforts, Commodus (the villain of Ridley Scott's epic film *Gladiator*) showed little interest in affairs of state. The arena was much more appealing, especially as he believed he was the reincarnation of Hercules. Dressed in a lion skin, he would wield a club or sword, appearing more than 730 times and drawing an 'exorbitant' gladiator's stipend that turned into an onerous tax. Gibbon acknowledges that Commodus was genuinely skilled with weapons, but even so opponents were carefully handicapped in advance to make sure the emperor was not injured; wounded soldiers and amputees were allegedly much favoured. In an echo of Tiberius' time, Gibbon writes that Commodus 'valued nothing in sovereign power except the unbounded licence of indulging his sensual appetites', and kept a harem of three hundred girls and three hundred boys to play out his fantasies. After an assassination attempt involving his elder sister, he predictably launched a reign of terror. In AD 192, fearing for their own lives, Commodus' chamberlain and the Praetorian Guard commander conspired with the emperor's favourite concubine. She gave him a doctored glass of wine and, while he was drowsy, a wrestler strangled him in his bath. The plotters had removed Commodus, but the result was more civil war and the 'Year of the Five Emperors'. (The empire's record year for mayhem was the 'Year of the Six Emperors', 238, when three were assassinated and two others met violent deaths.)

Altogether, something approaching forty Roman emperors were known or suspected to have been assassinated, and perhaps a dozen of these murders involved the Praetorian Guard. In 217, for example, Caracalla, having had his own brother killed as their mother tried desperately to protect him, was stabbed by one of his guards as he urinated by the roadside. Of the other Roman emperors who met a similar fate, perhaps the most colourful story concerns the next incumbent but one, Elagabalus, Caracalla's cousin. He came to the throne when the former head of the Praetorian Guard, the Berber Marcus Opellius Macrinus, who had got himself made emperor after Caracalla's murder, was executed. Elagabalus was fourteen. He proceeded to scandalize Rome by forcing a Vestal Virgin to become his wife and adopting the name of a Syrian sun god. Horrifyingly, the finest Roman wines were then poured away on the altars of foreign deities. But what Elagabalus really wanted was to be a woman. He painted his cheeks and eyebrows, prostituted himself to men in taverns, brothels and even the imperial palace, and, according to Cassius Dio, asked doctors 'to contrive a woman's vagina in his body by means of an incision, promising them large sums for doing so'. He was just eighteen when he was assassinated along with his mother by members of the Praetorian Guard, and his mutilated corpse was dragged through the streets and thrown in the Tiber.

With the exception of Caligula, who may have smothered Tiberius, Roman emperors who wanted someone out of the way generally delegated the task, but one of the last Western emperors, Valentinian III, was different. He had ascended the throne at the age of six in 425, and would reign for thirty years, though he never bothered much about affairs of state, instead devoting himself to what Gibbon called 'unlawful amours' and generally having a good

Commodus being murdered by a wrestler. Detail from Fernand Pelez, *The Death of Commodus*, 1879, oil on canvas glued to cardboard.

time while first his mother, and then, after she died, a fine general named Aetius performed the tiresome task of ruling. As Vandals, Goths and Huns closed in on the withering empire, Aetius resisted valiantly, even scoring a victory over the terrifying Attila the Hun. But the 'feeble and dissolute' emperor began to fear the general was getting too big for his boots, and on 21 September 454, Valentinian suddenly plunged his sword – the first time he had ever drawn it, according to Gibbon – into Aetius' breast. Eunuchs and courtiers joined in, and the general was dispatched with a hundred wounds. The assassination was followed by a bloody purge of Aetius' friends and supporters, but Valentinian did not last long. After the general's murder, the emperor foolishly recruited some of his barbarian soldiers to his own guard, and the following year, while Valentinian was watching military sports at the Field of Mars, two of them killed him 'without the least opposition from his numerous train who seemed to rejoice in the tyrant's death'.

Britain's First Assassination?

The Roman era also saw perhaps the first assassination in British history. In the third century Marcus Carausius, a Menapian from the mouth of the Rhine who, in Gibbon's words, was 'of the meanest origin' but boasted 'skill as a pilot, and valour as a soldier' had been hired by the Romans to fight Saxon pirates in the Channel. His modus operandi tended to be to let the pirates mount their raids and intercept them only when they were going home laden with booty. This made him rich, but annoyed Emperor Maximian, who ordered his death. But Carausius launched a pre-emptive strike in 286, proclaiming himself 'emperor of Britain' after using his wealth to bribe the legions and auxiliaries based in the province to support him. He ruled for seven years, defending his territory ably against Caledonian raiders from the north, but a new emperor, Constantius, started to turn the screw, capturing Carausius' continental base at Boulogne and much of his fleet. While the emperor was preparing to invade Britain, he received news that Carausius had been murdered by his treasurer, Allectus – we have no details of how – who had taken his title. Allectus lasted for three more years, until the Romans defeated and killed him, restoring control of their errant territory.

Sometimes those supporting assassinations in the Roman Empire did act from ideology, believing the killings would lead to a return of the old republic, but most of the time, dynastic ambition for oneself or one's loved ones was the ruling motive, and the outcome was usually: 'meet the new boss, same as the old boss.' There was an element of tyrannicide, when a ruler such as Caligula had gone seriously off the rails, but sometimes, as with Domitian and Commodus, for example, the assassins' motive seemed to be self-defence more than ambition, fearing that if they did not kill the emperor, the emperor would kill them. Still, the Roman Empire also saw the emergence of something new in assassination – the first group that looked like a modern terrorist organization.

The Sicarii

The Sicarii's method was literally cloak and dagger. In the words of the historian Josephus, a Jewish resistance leader turned enthusiast for Rome, they 'slew men in the day time, and in the midst of the city; this they did chiefly at the festivals, when they mingled themselves among the multitude, and concealed daggers under their garments'. Having stabbed their victim or victims, they would melt away in the crowd or join those expressing horror at the killing, 'by which means they appeared persons of such reputation, that they could by no means be discovered'. They got their name from the Latin word *sica*, meaning dagger. According to Josephus, the group had emerged from a failed rebellion against the Romans in AD 6, led by Judas of Galilee, who maintained that paying taxes to Rome was a violation of Jewish religious law, because Israel should have no king but God. With some Jews refusing to pay up, the Sicarii used terror tactics against those who submitted to the Romans 'as if they had been their enemies, both by plundering them of what they had, by driving away their cattle, and by setting fire to their houses'. The revolt failed and Judas was killed.

There were stories that Judas Iscariot was a Sicarius, but these are largely discounted by modern historians. Indeed, after Judas of Galilee's death, the group disappeared from history for half a century. Then under Judas' grandson, the religious teacher Menachem, they resurfaced using the same tactics. When they killed, it was not Romans they targeted, but 'collaborators', those seen to be cooperating with the occupying power, such as priests or the wealthy Jewish elite. Their highest profile victim was the high priest Jonathan, murdered around AD 55, though some suggested the Roman governor Antonius Felix was behind the killing. Whether that was true or not, after Jonathan's death, wrote Josephus, 'many were slain every day', so quick and cunning were the Sicarii, but the historian noted that the terror they generated was more damaging than the killings themselves, as people became paranoid, seeing enemies everywhere and distrusting their friends. When Jewish Zealots mounted a full-scale revolt against the Romans in AD 66, the Sicarii do not appear to have taken the lead, but they soon joined in, and Menachem led a raid on a Roman armoury. With the weapons they took, the insurgents were then able to drive the Romans from Jerusalem.

But the rebels soon fell out among themselves, especially when Menachem, 'puffed-up' by his success, became 'barbarously cruel' and 'no better than an insupportable tyrant'. The Sicarii's leader was captured, tortured and put to death by other rebels, as were many of his followers, and the remnants of his group fled to their stronghold at Masada, where most committed mass suicide in AD 73 rather than submit to Roman rule. By then the Romans had already retaken Jerusalem, but Josephus says that some Sicarii were able to escape to Alexandria. There they continued to kill 'Jews of reputation' and assert that Rome had no authority because people should 'look upon God as their only Lord and Master'. The Roman senate called an assembly of 'all the Jews' which roundly condemned the Sicarii, and 'with great violence', six hundred or more of them were rounded up. They were tortured to try to make them recognize the authority of the Roman emperor, but Josephus, no fan of the Sicarii, reports that 'when all sorts of torments and vexations of their bodies that could be devised were made use of to them, they could not get any one of them to comply.' Indeed, it seemed the Sicarii 'rejoiced' at their suffering. Even the children resisted. This 'courage, or whether we ought to call it madness, or hardiness in their opinions, everybody was amazed at'.

A Sicarius named Jonathan, a 'vile person' and former weaver, escaped to Libya and started to recruit among the poor, promising he would show them 'signs and apparitions'. Some of the better-off Jews denounced him to the Roman governor Catullus, who captured Jonathan and killed many of his followers. The 'vile person' then told the governor that the rich Jews had put him up to his agitation. In exchange for his life, Catullus got Jonathan to falsely accuse particular Jews the governor had a grudge against.

Other Sicarii joined in the denunciations, until in the end, according to Josephus, Catullus had more than 3,000 killed with the useful bonus that he was able to confiscate their property to enrich Rome. As the accusations continued to fly around, Josephus found himself in the firing line, but fortunately for him, the emperor Vespasian smelled a rat, called an end to the witch hunt, and had Jonathan tortured and then burned alive. After this, the Sicarii movement once again disappeared, though the name lives on in the word *sicario*, which in Latin America means a hitman or assassin.

Assassination and Christianity

While the Sicarii were stabbing away, a new faith was penetrating and would eventually conquer the Roman Empire – Christianity. Soon Christian theologians were debating the rights and wrongs of tyrannicide. In the seventh century St Isidore of Seville declared it was the job of a ruler to maintain justice, so a tyrant who failed in this duty had no claim to be obeyed. But perhaps the most significant early Christian thinker, St Augustine, two centuries earlier, had been more cautious, saying a Christian had a duty to his ruler as well as to God. Obviously the duty to God was superior, but if the two duties came into conflict, the subject should confine himself to passive resistance and accept any punishment that resulted. Augustine made a highly qualified exception to this rule if the tyrant interfered with the worship of God.

But Augustine's strictures against violence did not always help Christian rulers, not even popes, who in those days ruled over a substantial corner of Italy. In 882 John VIII became the first to be assassinated. Elected in 872, he had made a reasonable fist of being pontiff, resisting the Saracens, helping Christianize the Slavs and patching up differences with the Eastern Church. Unfortunately, the papacy had become the plaything of rival Italian aristocratic factions, and John had made some dangerous enemies, such as the future Pope Formosus, whom he excommunicated. (Formosus has the distinction of having been put on trial after his death as a corpse in full papal regalia and found guilty of perjury and other offences.) John was first poisoned, then clubbed to death, probably by members of his own household, though it is not clear whether there were grander figures behind his assassination. His death was followed by perhaps the darkest period in the history of the papacy, with the so-called 'rule of the harlots' when, as Gibbon put it, 'the bastard son, the grandson and the great-grandson' of the beautiful courtesan Marozia all occupied the throne of St Peter. It is rumoured that the son in question was sired by Pope Sergius III. Marozia also became mistress of Pope John x, whom she later had thrown into prison and suffocated with a pillow. Stephen VI in 897 and Leo V in 903 were also murdered in gaol.

Early Islam

Though the Sicarii had elements of a national liberation movement, religious fervour too was a crucial motivation in their assassinations, and assassination also played an important role in the early history of Islam. Umar, Muhammad's father-in-law, became the second caliph in 634, two years after the Prophet's death. A prosperous merchant, he had originally been a fierce opponent of the new religion and was even said to have hatched a failed plan to kill Muhammad. When Umar was converted in 616, it was regarded as a crucial breakthrough as he fought and won a series of battles against Islam's opponents. Gibbon says his life was based on 'abstinence and humility'. He ate barley-bread or dates, drank water, preached in a torn and tattered gown, and sometimes slept among the beggars on the steps of the mosque of Medina. 'Careless of his own emolument', he was generous to others. But however ascetic his private life was, Umar was also a great conqueror, taking Persia, Mesopotamia and Syria and making advances in Palestine and Egypt, though as riches flowed in from these new territories, the caliph worried about the effect they would have, saying: 'When

God grants riches to a nation, envy and jealousy grow in its people and as a result enmity and injustice is created in its ranks.' So he ordered gems and jewellery to be sold in order that the proceeds could be handed out to the whole population.

A man named Pirouz Nahavandi, also known as Abu Lulu Feroze, was taken prisoner by Umar's soldiers during the conquest of Persia. He was made to work as a carpenter, renting a house from one of the caliph's companions. Not only did Umar conquer new lands, he was also an expert jurist with a reputation as a fair and thoughtful administrator of justice. In 644 the carpenter complained to the caliph that his rent was too high. Umar carefully examined the evidence and ruled that it was fair. The next morning as he led prayers in the mosque, Abu Lulu hid in a corner, Sicarius-like, with a sword concealed beneath his long robes. Then he jumped at the caliph, stabbing him five times. Refusing to surrender, he stabbed a dozen more men. He must have been a formidable swordsman because it is said he slew up to nine of them before killing himself once Umar's bodyguards had cornered him. Umar died the next day. Some asserted that the carpenter was not motivated by personal anger, but that he was actually a Persian enemy agent, though there is no evidence for this.

On his deathbed Umar appointed a committee to decide his successor. Muhammad's sons-in-law Uthman ibn Affan and Ali ibn Abu Talib emerged as the front runners, and with Ali seen by some as too young and inexperienced, Uthman, aged about seventy, was chosen. Pious, scholarly and humble, rich but generous, he established the first official version of the Qur'ān. He continued to extend the Islamic empire, but is regarded as a less forceful and decisive character than Umar. Uthman tried to create a cohesive centralized administration, and often installed members of his family as provincial governors, but there was a feeling that too much wealth was finding its way into the pockets of those he favoured, and by 650 a series of rebellions were breaking out. In 656 armed men from Egypt arrived in Medina and demanded the dismissal of their governor. The story goes that Uthman agreed, but that on their way home, the rebels caught a messenger from the caliph, riding post haste to Egypt with an order to the governor to put the leaders of the protest to death on their return. The rebels went back to Medina and stoned Uthman as he preached in the mosque, knocking him unconscious. After he was carried to his house, they besieged him there. Uthman ordered his servants and friends not to resist, and the rebels broke in and stabbed him to death.

Medina fell into chaos and some urged Ali ibn Abu Talib, to whom those discontented with Uthman had increasingly turned, to accept the caliphate. At first he refused, not wanting to seem to be profiting from the older man's death, but after representations from prominent companions of the Prophet, he agreed. Ali was Muhammad's cousin, his closest blood relative, and also the husband of his favourite daughter. He was a formidable soldier and had saved the Prophet's life on a number of occasions. In one battle, he was said to have been wounded seventeen times. Like Umar, Ali had lived among the poor and given generously to them, and like his predecessor he was also worried about the impact of the wealth flowing into the Islamic empire, fearing it would divert people from the simple life advocated by Muhammad. He decided on a programme of reform, an important element of which would be to sack provincial governors. Not all of them were prepared to go quietly, and the empire dissolved into civil war.

Ali defeated one rebel army that was supported by 'Ā'ishāh, the Prophet's third wife, but he was unable to see off the challenge from the governor of Syria, Mu'āwiyah, a relative of Uthman. Mu'āwiyah suggested Ali was behind Uthman's murder, and waged a propaganda war against him. There was no evidence, but Ali's support began to ebb away, and a new group, the Khārijites, or 'seceders', appeared. In 661 they decided to assassinate both Ali and Mu'āwiyah, blaming both for the civil war. Mu'āwiyah escaped with a slight wound, but Ali was stabbed in the head while he was praying at the Grand Mosque of Kufa in what is now Iraq. The sword was wielded by Abd al-Rahman ibn Muljam al-Murādī, who was said to have fallen in love with the daughter of a soldier who had been killed fighting against Ali. She supposedly said she would marry her suitor if he brought her the caliph's head. After al-Rahman struck, his sword was wrestled from him by worshippers. The wound was not particularly serious, but the sword was poisoned and Ali died two days later. The assassin was killed by Ali's relatives. Muslims in Kufa pledged allegiance to Ali's son Hasan as the new caliph, but Mu'āwiyah refused to recognize him, and, rather than fight him, Hasan abdicated in exchange for a generous pension. He was allowed to live quietly in retirement until his death, though some believe he was poisoned by one of his wives on Mu'āwiyah's orders. The former Syrian governor ruled as caliph for nearly twenty years until he died from natural causes in 680. Ali remains one of the central figures of Islam, and the focus of the split between Sunnis and Shi'ites, with Shi'ites believing he should have succeeded Muhammad and that his descendants should have followed him, but that they were cheated by tyrants.

China

A century later in China, affairs of the heart sparked a spate of assassinations and worse. We saw how in the second century BC, the emperor Gaozu's transfer of his affections to a new concubine brought murder in its wake, and nine hundred years later, another emperor, Xuanzong, became the centre of a similar story. Then in his fifties, he fell madly in love with the young Yang Guifei, the wife of one of his sons and perhaps the most famous beauty in Chinese history. A modern statue of Yang emerging from her bath at Huaqing Pool, near Xi'an, shows a woman of standard modern pin-up proportions, but according to some accounts she was actually obese. Still, whatever her dimensions, a contemporary poem rhapsodized:

If she turned her head and smiled she cast a deep spell,
Beauties of Six Palaces vanished into nothing.

From the moment Xuanzong saw her, he 'neglected the world'.
He made his son divorce her and took her as his favourite concubine. She became his 'midnight tyrant . . . Those nights were too
short. That sun too quick in rising.' The resulting power vacuum
was filled by squabbling ministers, while Yang became infatuated
by a general of Uzbek descent named An Lushan, who was enor-
mously fat. He went through a mock ceremony of adoption by
Yang, and was rumoured to be sharing her bed. In 755 the general
rose in revolt and proclaimed himself emperor. At first he swept
all before him, and Xuanzong fled. On the road, his soldiers muti-
nied and demanded the execution of Yang, to which, to his
everlasting remorse, he agreed. By 757, An Lushan had become
prone to flying into furies, and he was assassinated by a eunuch
slave, perhaps with the help of his own eldest son. The son was
killed by one of An Lushan's generals, who was then murdered in
turn by his own son. The rebellion dragged on for another six years
before it was finally put down, but by then Xuanzong had died,
still mourning for his lost love. The revolt had brought widespread
famine and destruction, costing the lives, according to some estimates, of more than 30 million people.

Good King Wenceslaus

As with most human enterprises, assassination can have unintended
consequences, one of which is to turn the victim into a martyr, as
happened with Good King Wenceslaus. Actually he was only a duke,
of Bohemia, in what we now call the Czech Republic. Born about
907, he was raised as a Christian by his grandmother, Ludmilla. She
had married Borivoj, the first Bohemian prince to adopt Christianity,
but they were unable to convert the whole country, and after Borivoj
died, their Christian son Ratislav married an ambitious pagan named

St Ludmilla by Emanuel Max, c. 1844.

Drahomíra. When Ratislav was killed in battle against the Magyars, the pagan faction gained the ascendancy. Wenceslaus officially took the throne in 921, but because he was so young, his mother Drahomíra acted as regent, while Ludmilla tried to persuade him to advance the Christian cause. Relations between Ludmilla and Drahomíra became very strained and Ludmilla retired to her stronghold near Prague. But two members of Drahomíra's retinue, perhaps hired Viking assassins, broke in and strangled her with her own veil while she prayed. Some historians have questioned whether religion was the motivation for Ludmilla's assassination, pointing out that Drahomíra had been baptized so she could marry Ratislav. Anyway, Ludmilla would be made a saint.

In around 925, with the country perhaps tiring of the squabbling between Christians and pagans, Wenceslaus took over the reins of government himself, and ordered his mother into exile. He set to work as a good Christian prince, sending out missionaries far and wide in his realm. According to a biography written in the late tenth century, he lived a simple ascetic life, going among the poor to hand out alms, preparing the bread and wine for communion, perhaps even taking a vow of virginity. But in 929 the affairs of this world intruded rather roughly when Henry, Duke of Saxony, invaded Bohemia and took Prague. Wenceslaus had to agree to pay him an annual tribute. This, along with his practice of bringing German priests into Bohemia, angered some of the nobility, and Drahomíra allegedly egged on her younger son Boleslav to kill his brother.

On 28 September in either 929 or 935, Boleslav invited Wenceslaus to a banquet to celebrate a feast for a couple of saints, but the brothers had a bitter quarrel. Full of remorse, Wenceslaus set off to church to try to purge his anger, but on the way he was set on by three men from Boleslav's retinue, who killed him, some say at the church door, then cut his body to pieces. There is a story that one of Wenceslaus's servants killed one of the assassins and was then hanged on Boleslav's orders. Whatever the truth, the new duke ruled as a Christian, and also helped to spread the word in Poland. In the realm of politics, he was no more successful at defying the Saxons than Wenceslaus, though he did extend Bohemia's territories. As for the murdered duke, he soon became the patron saint of Bohemia with stories of miracles happening at his tomb, widely revered as the epitome of a righteous king, and the subject of one of the best-loved Christmas carols.

King Edward the Martyr of England

Making a martyr of Wenceslaus does not appear to have had serious political consequences, but the assassination of another Christian ruler did. The English king who became known as Edward the Martyr was not obvious saintly material. Indeed, he was prone to violent outbursts of rage that alarmed everyone around him. His father, King Edgar 'the Peaceful', died suddenly in 975, leaving Edward, as the eldest son, to take the throne while still in his teens.

Edward had a half-brother, Aethelred, born to Edgar's second wife, Aelfthryth. He was a few years younger than Edward, but Edward's temper had alienated so many of his nobles that, on Edgar's death, some lobbied for the younger son to be given the crown. Virtual civil war may have broken out. Certainly, the *Anglo-Saxon Chronicle* recorded that the nobility were plundering monasteries amid famine and 'disturbances', while 'many injustices and evil crimes flourished'.

In spite of this rivalry over the throne, Edward's personal relations with Aethelred and Aelfthryth seemed cordial enough, and on 18 March 978 he went to see them at Corfe Castle in Dorset. Aethelred's retainers rode out to meet the king and showed the utmost respect, but as Edward was getting off his horse, they surrounded him and stabbed him to death. There is no evidence that Aelfthryth or Aethelred were in on the assassination plan, but rumours to this effect soon spread. Edward was buried 'with no royal honours', no one was punished for the crime, and within a month, Aethelred was crowned. The *Anglo-Saxon Chronicle* lamented: 'No worse deed for the English was ever done than this.'

A poem declared:

> Those earthly slayers would have destroyed
> His memory upon earth;
> But the Celestial Avenger has spread his fame abroad.

Whatever his shortcomings may have been, Edward was quickly made a saint, and when his body was reburied, it was allegedly found to be free from decay. As for Aethelred, he would go down in history as 'the Unready', derided by Kipling for paying the Danegeld – a crippling tax to bribe the Vikings not to mount raids – but never getting rid of the Dane, so that by the time he died in 1016, virtually the whole of England had been conquered. Even if he had not been involved in Edward's murder, he was still tainted by the fact that he had benefited from it. The prestige of the crown

The assassination of King Edward the Martyr at Corfe Castle as depicted in a 19th-century history of England.

KING EDWARD *the* MARTYR *treacherously* ASSASSINATED *at the Gate of Corfe Castle, by order of his Step Mother* ELFRIDA.

was badly damaged, while people's loyalty was diverted from Aethelred by Edward's elevation to sainthood, and some historians believe the Unready's indecisiveness sprang from the treacherous deed that had made him king. The great Anglo-Saxon historian Sir Frank Stenton, in his volume in the *Oxford History of England*, wrote that Aethelred never escaped 'the consciousness that he had come to power through what his subjects regarded as the worst crime committed among the English peoples since their first coming to Britain'. He lost 'the instinctive loyalty of the common people, on which earlier kings had been able to rely', behaving 'like a man who is never sure of himself': indecisive in war, his relationships poisoned by mistrust.

The Ingenious Assassination of King Kenneth II of Scotland

The prize for the most inventive assassination of the Roman era and the Dark Ages must surely go to a Scots lady named Finella or Finele, who lived in the village of Fettercairn in Aberdeenshire. In 995 King Kenneth II of Scotland was trying to secure the succession for his son, Malcolm, but this meant putting a number of noses out of joint. In those days, the Scottish throne did not pass from father to son. Instead the king's successor was selected from all the adult male descendants of previous kings. The benefit was supposed to be that you did not get underage monarchs. The downside was that there were plenty of disputes. Writing in the fourteenth century, the first chronicler to attempt a full history of Scotland, John of Fordun, says many nobles opposed Kenneth, and Constantine the Bald plotted 'unceasingly' against him. Finally, he and others who were like-minded persuaded the 'wily' Finele, daughter of the Earl of Angus, to help them. She had a grudge against Kenneth because he had had her son put to death. So 'in an out-of-the-way little cottage', she set 'a kind of trap, such as had never before been seen'. 'On all sides' were crossbows armed with 'very sharp arrows'. In the middle of the room was 'a statue fashioned like a boy, and cunningly attached to the crossbows; so that if any one were to touch it, and move it ever so little, the bowstrings of the crossbows would suddenly give way, and the arrows would straightway be shot forth, and pierce him through.'

In spite of her son's fate, Finele always presented 'a cheerful countenance' to the king, and 'beguiled him by flattery and treacherous words'. One day when he was out hunting, she saw him and fell to her knees. She 'besought him with great importunity to come into her house', affirming that her son had deserved his punishment, and saying that if Kenneth did not come, she would be afraid she was out of favour with him and that he believed the tales of 'spiteful' folk who claimed she was disloyal. Then, 'tripping up to the king, she whispered in his ear' that she could name names of people plotting against him. Convinced, he went with her to the house and closed the door behind them, so she could impart her secret.

The king was immediately intrigued by the statue, and Finele said that if he touched its head, a 'marvellous and pleasant jest comes of it'. So curiosity killed the king. He could not resist laying a hand on the figure's head. This released the 'levers and handles of the crossbows; and immediately he was shot through by arrows sped from all sides, and fell without uttering another word'. Finele quickly exited by the back of the cottage and made herself scarce. The king's retinue, meanwhile, started to get worried. First they knocked on the door, then they broke it down. When they found Kenneth's body, they ran off in all directions looking for Finele, but to no avail, so they set fire to the village and 'reduced it to ashes'. When they did finally catch up with the lady, legend has it that she threw herself from 150-foot-high rocks rather than surrender. Some historians have suggested that, although Kenneth was indeed murdered, Finele was a mythical figure and that her elaborate, booby-trapped contraption was also no more than a figment of the imagination. It appears that after Kenneth's death, Constantine the Bald did ascend the throne as Constantine III, but was killed in a battle with Kenneth's son Malcolm a couple of years later. Malcolm finally became king in 1005, and reigned for 29 years.

WE HAVE ENOUGH information to analyse 34 assassinations from this era; 23 of them took place in the Roman Empire. Rome's dominance of the statistics may be less down to the fact that assassination was a favoured method of regime change in the empire than to its better historical records. The next highest totals are four in the Middle East and three in what is now the United Kingdom. There were 35 victims (two were killed in one attack). Most were royalty. Nearly half – seventeen – were emperors, and there were also two emperor's sons, and one emperor's mother. In addition, there was a de facto imperial regent, one rebel 'emperor' and a potential heir to the Roman imperial throne. From the non-Roman world came three kings (if we include Wenceslaus), a king's grandmother and two princes. Four victims exercised spiritual and temporal power – three caliphs and a pope. Another significant religious figure, a high priest, was also assassinated. Two of the 35 victims were women. Up to fifteen of the 23 Roman assassinations were carried out by the emperor's bodyguards or other troops supposedly loyal to him. Of all the 34 assassinations, perhaps three involved hired killers, and virtually all were the culmination of a plot, with only a possible two carried out by a lone assassin, and one of these was a Sicarii. Compared with the figures for the ancient world, there was a big increase in the number of women involved, with five instigating assassinations and three others doing the killing themselves.

So far as we know, all the murders were executed at close quarters, and the assassins were often intimate associates of the victims. In addition to the bodyguards, up to three of the killers were family members — one or two adopted sons and a brother — while of the instigators, another two were brothers, and there were two wives, a son, a grandmother, a stepmother and a daughter-in-law. Also involved as assassin or instigator were three chamberlains, a steward and a secretary, while Pope John VIII was perhaps killed by his own clerics. Up to eleven Roman emperors were instigators, but the only ones to do the dirty work themselves were Valentinian III and possibly Caligula, while in China in 626, Prince Li Shimin killed two of his brothers with help from his followers.

Dynastic ambition remained the main motive for assassination, featuring in seventeen, or half, of the events. The second most important reason, apparent in up to eight cases, was anger or resentment at such things as outrageous behaviour, a clamp-down on privileges, seeing an enemy paid off, or not being allowed to pillage a town. Fear was also important, being a motivation in seven episodes — fear of being murdered, punished, overthrown or, in the case of soldiers of the Roman emperor Florianus in 276, having to face superior enemy forces. In some of these instances, assassination must have seemed like a pre-emptive strike. In four cases, money was the motive for murder, in three rebellion or national liberation, while in two revenge was a factor, and in one the motive may have been religious. In the 24 cases where we can be fairly sure of the method used, two-thirds, sixteen, were by stabbing, in one case with a poisoned sword. At least three involved poisoning, two strangling and one smothering. One used poisoning and clubbing, another the bow and arrow, while the killing of King Kenneth II of Scotland, as we saw, allegedly involved an ingenious machine.

As to the fate of the assassins and instigators, when soldiers murdered the Roman emperor, they generally got away with it, though those who killed Pertinax in 193 were executed by his successor. We know of three others who got off scot-free, while another escaped with a brief banishment. Four went on to kill themselves, though in the case of Nero that did not happen until nine years after the assassination of his mother. Five were executed, but it could be a long time before justice took its course – fourteen years in the case of the poisoner Locusta. Only one was despatched on the spot, though in another five cases perpetrators were killed during the year after they committed their deed, with a further six killed or assassinated within six years. Crime sometimes paid. In China, Prince Li Shimin went on to become a great emperor and to die probably of natural causes, while Boleslav, the man behind Wenceslaus's assassination, ruled for more than thirty years. In nineteen instances where a ruler was assassinated, their successor lasted for a year or less, another five lasted four years or less, while five others lasted thirteen years or more. But a long reign was not a guarantee of success. Aethelred the Unready survived for more than 35 years, but his time as king was scarred by war and humiliation. In at least nine cases, an assassination was followed by war or serious disorder, though in at least seven of these, instability had also preceded the murder. As to whether the assassins achieved their objective, in contrast with the ancient world, where failures outnumbered successes, my assessment for the Roman era and the Dark Ages is that fifteen assassinations could be regarded as a success, and that the assassins might have been satisfied with the outcome in another five, while in thirteen they certainly failed, with one other a possible failure.

3

THE AGE OF CHIVALRY

The Hashishin

The word 'assassin' comes to us from the thirteenth century. The great traveller Marco Polo said he had heard 'from several natives of that region' about an 'Old Man of the Mountain' named Aloadin, who used to live in a country called Mulehet. He had enclosed a valley between two peaks and turned it into the 'largest and most beautiful' garden ever seen, filled with pavilions and palaces 'the most elegant that can be imagined'. The place ran with 'wine and milk and honey' and boasted 'every variety of fruit'. But perhaps the biggest attraction was the 'numbers of ladies and of the most beautiful damsels in the world, who could play on all manner of instruments, and sung most sweetly, and danced in a manner that it was charming to behold'. The old man had based the design of his valley on 'the description that Mahommet gave of his Paradise'.

The garden was also a fortress 'strong enough to resist all the world'. The only way in was at the invitation of Aloadin, and the only ones who got invited were 'those whom he intended to be his Ashishin'. The old man would take to his palace 'simple hill-folks', youths and young men 'such as had a taste for soldiering', and surreptitiously give them a sleeping draught. They would then be carried into the valley, and awake, as they thought, in paradise, where 'the ladies and damsels dallied with them to their hearts' content, so that they had what young men would have' and they never wanted to leave. Then another sleeping draught would be administered to each young man, and he would wake up back in the old man's palace, 'whereat he was not over well pleased'. He would bow to Aloadin, believing him to be a great prophet, and recount that he had been in a paradise just as Muhammad had described. Aloadin would ensure other impressionable young men were there to listen to this, and, of course, reported Polo, this gave them 'the greatest desire to enter' his paradise. The old man would then explain the price for admittance or re-admittance: 'Go thou and slay So and So; and when thou returnest my Angels shall bear thee into Paradise.' This reward, they were told, would be gained whether the 'ashishin' survived or perished. So 'there was no order of his that they would not affront any peril to execute,' and in this way, he 'got his people to murder any one whom he desired to get rid of'. Indeed, princes were so afraid of him that they submitted to his authority, while the old man sent out underlings to use the same methods in Damascus and Kurdistan.

It is a vivid and colourful tale but it has no corroboration from Islamic sources. Nowadays, it is thought to refer to an Ismaili theologian and missionary, Hassan-i-Sabbāh. In 1090 Hassan managed to win over members of the garrison of a fortress belonging to the

A 15th-century edition of *The Travels of Marco Polo* helps spread the story that the 'Old Man of the Mountain' drugged his Hashishin.

Turkish Seljuq Empire in the Alborz mountains in what is now Iran, and seize it. It was called Alamut, the Eagle's Nest. There, in spite of Polo's rather racy stories about his paradise-on-earth, Hassan led an ascetic life, and his regime was quite puritanical. For example, he had one of his sons executed for drunkenness. Nor is there any proof for the widely held belief that the 'ashishin', or 'Hashishin' as they were more generally known, were under the influence of hashish (the source of their name) when they were being recruited or performing their killings. More likely it was just a slur spread by their enemies. Still, the name stuck, and by the fourteenth century, Dante was using 'assassin' to refer to any professional murderer. By the seventeenth, the word had migrated to England, with Shakespeare putting it in Macbeth's mouth to describe the killing of Duncan. And whatever the questions about their origins, the Hashishin were real, and deadly enough.

Their *raison d'être* was the enmity between different branches of Islam. The Ismailis had broken away from other Shi'ites in the eighth century. The sect was headed by the Fatimids, who managed to set up a rival caliphate in Egypt, and were trying to wrest leadership of the Muslim world from the Sunni Abbāsid caliphs in Baghdad, but in 1094, the Ismailis split over who should succeed in Egypt, with the Nizārī Ismā'īliyyah backing the claims of the

Coin issued by the Hashishin in 12th-century Syria.

previous ruler's eldest son, Nizār. As Grand Master of this sect, Hassan expanded its power, sometimes with the help of sympathetic local rulers, perhaps impressed by his doctrines or perhaps wishing to assert their independence from the Sunni Seljuk Empire that spread across much of the Middle East, so that it commanded a chain of strongholds all over Iran and Iraq. He also placed agents in enemy camps and cities, who would often lie low for a long time reconnoitring before performing their deadly task. It was said the Hashishin were expertly trained to operate with the utmost stealth, and that they turned murder into an art.

Hassan's men killed many Muslims. Their unquestioning obedience, their willingness to risk their own lives and their readiness to travel long distances meant he could strike at his foes pretty well anywhere in the Muslim world. The first major victim was the great vizier (or first minister) Nizām al-Mulk, whose abilities had kept the Seljuk dynasty in power in Iran. A celebrated scholar famed for his generosity, he established madrassas and hospices, and gave pensions to the poor, but he was a fierce opponent of Shi'ites and Ismailis. In 1092 he was killed on his way from Eşfahān to Baghdad, near Nehāvand, by a Hashishin disguised as a Sufi mystic. Although the killer was no doubt motivated by religious fanaticism, there is also a suggestion that Hassan may have been colluding with one of Nizām's rivals at the sultan's court.

Four years later, the First Crusade was launched as Europeans tried to carve out a Christian kingdom in the Holy Land. The crusades came to be seen as a great chivalric enterprise in an age when, as Sir Walter Scott put it: 'Generosity, gallantry, and an unblemished reputation, were . . . necessary ingredients in the character of a perfect knight.' When honour was supposed to be prized above wealth and a man's word was his bond. To the Hashishin, the crusaders may have been infidels, but they seem to have considered them no more odious than Sunni Muslims. Indeed their intervention may have been a bit of a bonus, as it helped Hassan increase his power at the expense of his distracted Muslim rivals, and, by accident or design, his interventions often helped the Western invaders. So in 1103, while Count Raymond IV of Toulouse was besieging a castle belonging to the emir of Homs, three Hashishin murdered the emir as he was leaving the mosque, while in 1113, a Hashishin assassinated one of the more formidable Muslim captains, Mawdud of Mosul, at the Grand Mosque in Damascus. Once again, there were suspicions that a Muslim political rival was involved. The great historian of the Crusades, Sir Steven Runciman, said the emergence of the Hashishin was 'disastrous' for any coordinated Muslim response to the invasions. As for Hassan himself, he managed to resist Seljuk attacks on Alamut for eight successive years until 1118, when the last siege was raised, and to die peacefully in his bed six years later. But assassination was not a one-way street. In 1129 the governor of Damascus had one of the Hashishin's most important local patrons murdered, and then fomented a riot in which the mob slaughtered every member of the sect they could find.

Perhaps the most formidable of the Crusaders' adversaries was the Sunni Yusuf ibn Ayyub Salah ah-Din, known to his enemies as Saladin, who recaptured Jerusalem in 1187, ending more than eighty years of Crusader rule there. He reduced the Westerners' domain to a few coastal strongholds as he carved out an emirate that ran from the borders of modern-day Tunisia to Yemen, Turkey and Iran. Saladin was also regarded as a great chivalric hero even by his enemies. Some of the stories may have been exaggerated, but it is true that when the Crusaders conquered Jerusalem, they slaughtered the inhabitants. When Saladin captured it, he spared them. The Crusaders had defiled Islam's third holiest mosque, the al-Aqsa, using it for stables, while Saladin respected Christian churches. The great fourteenth-century Italian writer Boccaccio would describe him as a man of 'courteous deeds and sterling worth', while Dante had him sharing the afterlife with the heroes of Rome and Troy. Nearly eight centuries after his death, the British would name an armoured car after him.

Count Raymond IV
of Toulouse.

The Hashishin tried to kill Saladin on a number of occasions in the 1170s. By then the leader of the Syrian branch of the sect was Rashīd al-Dīn al-Sinān, also dubbed 'the Old Man of the Mountain'. He made his first attempt while the great general was besieging Aleppo in 1175. It was foiled when an emir recognized the Hashishin agents detailed to assassinate Saladin. They still killed the emir as well as some of the general's entourage, but they could not reach the target himself. During the siege of Azaz the following year, Hashishin managed to infiltrate Saladin's army and fought with such bravery that he was going to reward them, but as he walked among them, one tried to stab the general with his dagger. Saladin survived only because he wore a cap of chain mail under his turban and the blow glanced off. He threw his assailant to the ground where he was despatched by loyal troops. Three more Hashishin came forward, but Saladin's men overcame them all, though not before they had killed a number of emirs. It

The great Saladin as portrayed in the 19th century by Gustave Doré.

is said the general started taking the extraordinary precaution of sleeping in a wooden tower that could be reached only by a rope ladder which he could then pull up. When Saladin took the offensive, laying siege to Sinān's stronghold of Masyaf in Syria, the story goes that one night he suddenly awoke in his tent to find on his bed hot cakes of a kind only the Hashishin baked and a note pinned to his pillow by a poisoned dagger with the message: 'You are in our power.' Saladin believed it was Sinān himself who had managed to breach security so comprehensively. Unnerved, he sent a messenger to the Old Man, asking his forgiveness, and promising, in return for a guarantee of safety, not to make war on the Hashishin again. Sinān pardoned him, and Saladin kept his promise.

The first Crusader to perish at the hands of the Hashishin was Count Raymond II of Tripoli in what is now Lebanon, in 1152. He was married to the beautiful Hodierna, aunt of Baldwin III, the young king of Jerusalem. She was headstrong and he was jealous, and suspicious about the parentage of their daughter, so he tried to keep her shut away. Her sister, the king's mother Melisende, travelled to Tripoli and managed to persuade the couple to patch things up, though it was agreed that Hodierna should go with Melisende for a holiday in Jerusalem. Raymond rode south with their party for a short while and then turned for home. He had passed through the barbican but had not yet reached the main city wall, when he was set on by a group of Hashishin. They stabbed him to death and also killed two knights who were with him. It all happened in the flash of an eye so Raymond's guards were unable to catch the killers who melted away, but the garrison were so enraged they ran amok in the streets, slaughtering every Muslim they could find. It was not clear why Raymond was killed, but some argued it might be because he had given help to the Knights Templar, who the Hashishin regarded as a formidable and implacable enemy, as would be emphasized in 1169, when a force of Templar knights ambushed a group of Hashishin envoys who had been meeting the Crusader king of Jerusalem and killed them all.

Killings of Crusaders by the Hashishin remained rare, but in 1192, Conrad, marquis of Montferrat, fell victim in Tyre just after he had been told he had been elected king of Jerusalem. It is said that when Conrad heard he had been chosen, he dropped to his knees and prayed to God he should not be granted this honour if he was unworthy of it. Then he set off to dine with his friend, the Bishop of Beauvais. As he turned a sharp corner on his way home, he was approached by two men. One gave him a document to read and the second stabbed him. Conrad died soon after. His guards hacked one of the assailants to death on the spot and captured the other. Before being executed, he confessed to being a Hashishin, sent by Sinān. It transpired that the killers had been in Tyre for a while, biding their time, and even getting baptized. Some said Saladin was behind the deed, while others thought Richard the Lionheart, who had preferred another candidate for the crown, had arranged it. Another explanation offered is that Conrad had angered Sinān by seizing from a ship a rich cargo the Hashishin had bought, though doubt is cast on this too, and it may simply have been that Sinān was beginning to worry that a strong Crusader state on the Lebanese shore could be a threat.

Either way, the killing did not seem to harm the cosy relationship between the Hashishin and the Crusaders for very long. Two years later Henry of Champagne, who replaced Conrad as ruler of Jerusalem, was being regally entertained by Sinān's successor (the Hashishin leader had died peacefully in 1193), who apologized for Conrad's death and said that to make up for it they would assassinate any enemy Henry chose to name. The odd Crusader was still murdered, sometimes at the instigation of rival Christians, and by the early thirteenth century, the Hashishin were paying tribute to another military order, the Knights Hospitaller, and doing the occasional killing for them. Their chosen victims included Raymond, the eldest son of Bohemond, prince of Antioch and count of Tripoli in 1213, and Patriarch Albert of Jerusalem the following year, though some believe he was stabbed to death by another eminent Christian, the former Master of the Hospital of the Holy Spirit, while he was taking part in a religious procession. The patriarch had previously deposed the master because of his transgressions.

It was the marauding Mongol hordes who finally put paid to the Hashishin. After the death of the great Genghis Khan, his son Jagatai inherited some of his conquests, including part of Iran. There he banned Muslim practices such as the halal slaughter of

animals. In retaliation the Hashishin murdered him. The Mongols were furious and concluded that there could be no orderly government in the areas they ruled while the sect survived. In 1256 Jagatai's nephew Hulagu led a great army that took a dozen Hashishin strongholds, then laid siege to Alamut. The Grand Master agreed to surrender, but, perhaps in an indication of how successfully fanaticism had been inculcated into the sect, the governor of the castle refused to give in, and the Mongols had to take it by storm. The Grand Master meanwhile had travelled to see Hulagu's cousin, Mongu, to try to secure better terms. Mongu sent him away with a flea in his ear, and on his way home, he was murdered along with his retinue. Mongu also told Hulagu to take a tougher line. From then on, every time the Mongols took a town from the Hashishin, they massacred all the inhabitants, while members of the sect who lived in the country were ordered to assemble, supposedly for a census, and then butchered. A few senior figures were spared to be sent off to Jagatai's widow so she could have them killed in whichever way she chose. By the end of 1257, just a few members of the Iranian sect were living as fugitives in the mountains, and over the next fifteen years or so, the Hashishins' Syrian castles fell too. The group still had time for a little late flurry. In 1270 a Hashishin, again masquerading as a Christian convert, managed to murder the Crusader baron Philip of Montfort in a chapel in Tyre, while two years later the future King Edward I of England was stabbed with a poisoned dagger in his tent at Acre. The 'Hammer of the Scots' managed to kill the Hashishin, yet another supposed convert to Christianity, and to recover after being ill for many months.

But Christians were also known to use assassination against their Muslim enemies. In 1146 Imad ad-Din Zengi, ruler of Basra, Mosul and Aleppo, who led the first major Muslim counterattacks against the Crusaders, was killed by a Frankish slave named Yarankash, 'for whom', according to the contemporary chronicler Ibn al-Qalanisi of Damascus, 'he had a special affection and in whose company he delighted'. Yarankash stabbed his master to death while he lay in a drunken stupor. The killer managed to flee, but was captured and handed over to one of Zengi's sons, who had him executed. Al-Qalanisi casts doubt on whether the slave had a religious or political motive, writing that he was motivated by a 'secret grudge'. It is said he may have been angry at being told off for drinking from Zengi's glass.

United though they were supposed to be in a great chivalric Christian enterprise, the Crusaders were also quite capable of murdering each other without any help from the Hashishin. So, in 1134, Hugh du Puiset, Count of Jaffa, was stabbed in the street in Jerusalem by a Breton knight while he was playing dice, and later died of his wounds. Hugh, a handsome young man, was very friendly – some felt a little too friendly – with his cousin Melisende, the wife of Fulk, king of Jerusalem, whom we met earlier trying to patch up the quarrel between Hodierna and Raymond II. At one point relations between Hugh and Fulk got so bad that the count had fled to Egypt for a time and allied himself with the Fatimids. So had the Breton knight been put up to killing him? Although he had the assassin tried and executed, many fingers of suspicion pointed at Fulk, but the victim had no shortage of enemies. In his late teens, he married a rich widow whose twin teenage sons hated him and were constantly bad-mouthing him, and plenty of others in the Crusader camp were angry at the way he had thrown in his lot with the Egyptians.

Unchivalrous Assassinations in Europe

Many of these killings were episodes in the game of thrones that had gone on at least since the days of the pharaohs, 4,000 years or more earlier – attempts to climb the greasy pole – but this was supposed to be the Age of Chivalry, so it is striking how many of its assassinations involved betrayal and the breaking of promises.

In the early fifteenth century, during the Hundred Years War with England, Charles VI 'the Mad' was king of France. Because of

The assassination of John the Fearless on the bridge at Montereau, according to a c. 1470 chronicle from Bruges.

his incapacity, his brother Louis, Duke of Orleans, and his nephew John the Fearless, Duke of Burgundy (he had gained his nickname thanks to his valour in a battle against the Turks), became wrapped up in a power struggle for control of the kingdom. In 1405 John kidnapped the king's son, the dauphin, but Louis and the queen, who was rumoured to be Louis' mistress, managed to get him back. Louis, who had quite a reputation as a womanizer, was also supposed to have tried to seduce Burgundy's wife, and then, when she resisted, to have attempted to rape her. The antagonism between the two grew so fierce that many feared it would turn to civil war.

Then in November 1407 there was a dramatic reconciliation. Louis fell ill, and when he got better, John went to congratulate him on his recovery. They took mass together in the same church, and finally they embraced and swore their mutual friendship at a banquet, but was Louis about to be double-crossed? The previous June, John had taken a house in Paris in which he installed a gang of ruffians led by a Norman knight named Raoul d'Anquetonville. On the evening of 23 November, while Orleans was visiting the queen, he received a summons to attend her husband on urgent business. In fact, the messenger was working for John, and the invitation was fake. Louis set out with only half a dozen attendants. He was in good spirits and singing, but he had not gone more than 200 metres (650 ft) before he was set upon by about eight masked men from d'Anquetonville's gang. One of his retinue was killed, another seriously wounded, and the rest fled. The assailants cut Orleans' head in two, and as he fell from his horse, they beat him as if he were a mattress, according to an eyewitness. The assassins dispersed before they could be arrested.

John expressed horror at the killing, and was a pallbearer at the funeral, but suspicion soon fell on him and he admitted he was behind the assassination. He fled Paris and gave d'Anquetonville a handsome reward. In 1408 he produced a justification, saying the deed had been done to protect the king and the country, and accusing Louis of using black magic to try to kill Charles. The king promptly pardoned him, but the infighting at court continued, focusing on who should be the next puppet-master, with John now wrestling against the dauphin, and in 1418 it was the turn of the king's son to flee from Paris. The following year, there was another solemn vow of peace, this time between John and the dauphin. Two months later, the two men agreed to meet on a bridge at Montereau, 70 kilometres (45 mi.) from Paris. Both brought retinues the size of small armies to the area, and John plainly had considerable reservations about the encounter. Three times the dauphin sent ambassadors to the duke requesting his presence, and three times he refused to attend. At the fourth time of asking, on 10 September 1419, he came on condition that only ten men were to accompany each of the protagonists. All were sworn to be on their best behaviour. John began by kneeling before the dauphin and promising his allegiance, but a fracas soon broke out. One of the dauphin's companions, Tanguy de Chastel, felled the duke with an axe, while others helped finish him off, and two members of his retinue were also killed. Some believe the dauphin gave a signal for John to be attacked, others that it all happened without his prior knowledge, but we know Tanguy de Chastel was given a generous pension. While one motive for Burgundy's assassination was clearly political calculation, revenge may have been another, with some noting that the wounds inflicted on him were very similar to those suffered by Orleans twelve years before.

Breach of faith also featured in a fifteenth-century assassination in Scotland. King James II had an uneasy relationship with one of his most powerful nobles, the Earl of Douglas. In 1452 James invited him to dinner at Stirling Castle under safe conduct, but when he appeared the king accused him of treachery and stabbed him in the neck. James's courtiers then finished the job savagely, with one said to have dashed out Douglas's brains with an axe. James himself came to a sticky end eight years later. As he tried to fire a salute in honour of his wife, a gun exploded and killed him. Incidentally, James II's father, James I, had himself been assassinated in his palace at Perth fifteen years earlier by supporters of a rival claimant for the throne. He had tried to escape through a sewer but unfortunately it had been blocked a few days earlier because the king was fed up of losing tennis balls down it.

Another unchivalrous assassination from this era was not concerned with dynastic machinations, but with revolutionary politics. Wat Tyler was a humble tiler, probably from Kent. He may also have fought in the Hundred Years War with France, and paying for that war led King Edward III of England's government to introduce a bitterly unpopular poll tax in 1377. By 1381, discontent had risen to such a degree that mobs tens of thousands strong, many of them from Kent and Essex, began to descend on London in what became known as the Peasants' Revolt. The men of Kent chose Tyler as their leader.

In the capital, they attracted further support, and pursued other grievances, such as demanding an end to serfdom. They opened prisons and freed the inmates, they burned down palaces and brothels, which particularly annoyed the Bishop of Winchester who owned some of them. They executed those they considered enemies of the people, such as lawyers and Flemish merchants. The new king, Richard II, was only fourteen, and many of his troops were either up in Scotland or on their way to Portugal, so he took refuge in the Tower of London. On 14 June he met the rebels and agreed to all their demands: abolition of serfdom, affordable land, punishment of those in power they considered 'traitors', whatever. He had left behind in the Tower two of the rebels' particular bogeymen, his treasurer, Sir Robert Hales, and the Archbishop of Canterbury, seen as the principal architects of the poll tax. Although there were more than a thousand soldiers garrisoned at the Tower, Tyler's men entered unopposed and summarily executed the treasurer, the archbishop and a couple of other clerics, exhibiting their heads on London Bridge. Had the king deliberately sacrificed them? Whether he had or not, as Richard's clerks began writing charters setting out his promises, the Essex rebels started to disperse.

On 15 June Richard went to Smithfield for a further meeting with the Kent rebels, taking a large retinue with him. Tyler rode out with his standard bearer to meet the king. He shook Richard's hand rather roughly instead of kissing it, and said, 'Brother, be of good cheer', which was not how you were meant to speak to the king. Then he presented a new series of demands: the abolition not only of serfdom but of all the privileges of nobility, so that apart from the king, everyone would be equal, and he wanted the Church's property to be confiscated and divided among the people. True to form, Richard agreed to the lot and told Tyler to go home, but the rebel leader smelled a rat. As words were exchanged, courtiers surrounded Tyler, and the Lord Mayor of London, William

Walworth, stabbed him and dragged him from his horse, leaving another member of the royal party to finish him off on the ground.

The rebels were too far away to see exactly what was going on. At first some thought the king had knighted Tyler, but as they started to get restive, the young Richard, with extraordinary coolness, rode up to them and said: 'I am your captain. Follow me!' as he led them into nearby fields. Walworth had managed to put together a volunteer force stiffened with some regular soldiers, and as the rather confused rebels arrived, his men surrounded them. Richard told the rebels they were all pardoned, and instructed them to go home. He then knighted Walworth. As the rebels streamed over London Bridge on their way back to Kent, they passed Tyler's head on a stake. Anyone looking like a rebel still left in London was liable to summary execution as Walworth launched a reign of terror. As for the promises in the royal charters, they were not worth the paper they were written on. Richard changed his tune, now announcing to the rebels: 'You will remain in bondage, not as before, but incomparably harsher. For as long as we live and by God's grace, rule over this realm, we will strive with mind, strength, and wealth to suppress you so that the rigour of your servitude will be an example to posterity.' In terms of realpolitik, the assassination of Tyler had proved remarkably successful, but, for Richard personally, his reign was all downhill from this point, and in 1399 he was deposed, to be murdered or starved to death the following year.

Unchivalrous Assassination in Japan

It was not only in Europe that realpolitik seemed to be undermining chivalric codes. In Japan in 1441 the shogun, or hereditary military dictator, Ashikaga Yoshinori was murdered by his hosts at a theatrical evening. As a younger son in a family of high status, he had originally been destined to be a Buddhist monk, but after a run of illness and bad luck cut a swathe through the ruling class, it fell to the four Ashikaga brothers, the sons of an earlier shogun, to draw lots to decide who should be the next ruler. When Yoshinori came out as the winner, he tried to get out of it because he wanted to stay in the monastery, but eventually he persuaded himself this was the will of the gods and he must submit. Yoshinori proved himself an able administrator, but he also had a fearful temper, and by the time he had been in power for five years, he had had eighty people of high rank killed, sometimes for trivial offences. A samurai, for example, was executed for serving up tasteless food. He also became besotted with a young male entertainer and decided to make a gift to him of territories belonging to Akamatsu Mitsusuke, leader of one of the most powerful Japanese clans. In July 1441 the Akamatsu clan invited Yoshinori to a lavish banquet. As a traditional noh play was being performed, armed men rushed in. Three of them grabbed Yoshinori and one cut off his head, impaling it on a spike. Some of his retinue tried to fight back and were hacked down. Despite the shogun's cruelty, contemporary nobles condemned his assassination as an 'unspeakable act'. The murder undercut the ethic of loyalty on which the shogunate was based, and it fell into decline. The result was a long power struggle between warrior families that culminated in civil war, and eventually Mitsusuke killed himself after his forces were defeated.

Murders in Cathedrals and Churches

A church was supposed to be a place where even criminals could seek sanctuary and have their lives protected, but during the Age of Chivalry, they became a favoured venue for assassination. On Ash Wednesday in 1127 Charles the Good, Count of Flanders, was murdered in the church of St Donatian in Bruges by members of the Erembald clan who were afraid he was going to take them down a peg or two. Charles's father, King Canute IV of Denmark, St Canute, had also been killed in church, as he sought refuge from rebels in St Alban's, Odense, in 1086. In 1306, Robert the Bruce, later to be King of Scotland, met with his enemy John Comyn in

Dumfries's Greyfriars' church, and stabbed him. Bruce's companions finished Comyn off with their daggers while the friars tried to protect him. In 1478 Giuliano de' Medici was stabbed nineteen times during mass in Florence cathedral by assailants from a rival banking family egged on by the pope. Giuliano died, while his brother, Lorenzo, was wounded. The plotters had hoped to overthrow Medici rule, but instead they were themselves killed by the Florence mob.

Nor were holy days any impediment to assassination. On Christmas Day 1156 King Sverker I of Sweden was in his coach on his way to attend a service when he was stabbed to death by one of his own escorts. Two pretenders to the crown, Magnus Henriksson and Erik Jedvardsson, were suspected of being behind the murder. Sverker had reached the throne via a tortuous path. When the Swedish king Inge the Younger died in 1125, there were suspicions that he had been poisoned by his wife Queen Ulvhild and a secret lover, whom some believed was Sverker. Next Ulvhild wed the king of Denmark, who was at least twenty years older than her,

How a 19th-century Danish history saw the murder of King Canute IV of Denmark in church in 1086.

but it was not a happy marriage, and she ran off with Sverker, who by then had succeeded in being crowned king of Sweden even though he was not of royal blood. When her husband was killed in battle in 1134, Ulvhild married Sverker, and this match with a queen may have shored up his legitimacy as monarch. After Sverker's murder, Erik Jedvardsson became king, and even earned the title Erik the Holy for his promotion of Christianity (though some say he actually persecuted the Church). After four years, however, he was ambushed and killed as he left a church after celebrating mass, perhaps by Magnus Henriksson's men, and Magnus took over, only to be killed the following year by Sverker's son, Charles VII, who was himself assassinated in 1167.

Even more shocking than this tangled tale of royal murder was the fate of a senior cleric who quarrelled with his king and was cut down while he was saying mass. No, not Thomas Becket, but Bishop, now Saint, Stanislaus of Krakow, who met his end in 1079, killed perhaps by King Bolesław II of Poland himself, though some historians are sceptical about this. Stanislaus had criticized the king for immorality, while Boleslaw had accused the bishop of conspiring with rebels. Whatever the truth, after Stanislaus's death the king had to flee the country and he later died in exile. Both Church and state were rich and powerful institutions in medieval Europe, so it is not surprising that they often clashed, at times violently. Another senior churchman to be murdered was St Engelbert, Archbishop of Cologne, in 1225. He had remonstrated with his cousin, Count Frederick of Isenberg, over his unfair treatment of an abbey at Essen, and then been ambushed and killed by Frederick and his henchmen.

But even in this disreputable company, Becket's assassination stood out, horrifying the whole of Christendom and becoming one of the most infamous in history. Hailing from merchant stock in London's Cheapside, Becket was endowed with considerable abilities that propelled him upwards through the household of Theobald, the Archbishop of Canterbury. The most important position in government apart from king was chancellor, and when it fell vacant, the archbishop recommended Becket. King Henry II took up the suggestion and he and his new chancellor became great friends, with Becket demonstrating daring on the battlefield as well as administrative skills and a love of luxury and display. On one diplomatic mission to France, he took two dozen silk outfits. He was also very adept at appropriating the Church's money for the royal treasury. Like so many medieval monarchs, Henry found himself at loggerheads with the ecclesiastical authorities, and so when Theobald died in 1161, it must have seemed a master stroke to make his right-hand man archbishop as well as chancellor, even though he was not even a priest. Who better to bring the clerics to heel? At first Becket refused the job, but eventually he gave way. On 2 June 1162 he was ordained a priest, and the next day consecrated archbishop.

Almost immediately, Becket went spectacularly native. He resigned as chancellor, and instead of plundering Church property, he devoted himself to wresting back lands the crown had seized. He made public displays of his humility, inviting the poor into his palace and washing their feet, and very privately he probably started wearing the vermin-infested hair shirt that was found under his robes after his murder. But why? Did Becket experience a sudden St Paul-style conversion? Or, failing that, did he have enough religion to fear his immortal soul might be in danger if he let God down in his new position? Was it just a matter of hats? While Becket was wearing the chancellor's, his job was to do the best he could for the king, but once he exchanged it for an archbishop's mitre, was his duty then to the Church? And how much of a role did the clash of two stubborn personalities play? Certainly the new archbishop had his forebodings. Before his elevation he confided to a friend: 'if it should come about that I am promoted, I know the king so well, indeed inside out, that I would either have to lose his favour, or God forbid, neglect my duty to the Almighty.'

A running sore in relations between Henry and the Church was the issue of 'criminous clerks': should clerics accused of criminal offences be tried in ecclesiastical or secular courts? Worried that Church courts gave unduly lenient sentences, the king, an energetic reformer of government and administration, wanted clerical offenders under the jurisdiction of the crown. Becket resisted. At one point the two former friends seemed to have reached agreement, but at the last minute the archbishop refused to put it in writing. Things went from bad to worse. Henry accused the former chancellor of embezzlement, and Becket fled to France, where he was supported by King Louis VII. Henry must have found this particularly galling, being married, as he was, to Louis' ex-wife, Eleanor of Aquitaine. Becket became even more ascetic – wearing a monk's habit, starving and scourging himself, sleeping on a rough wooden pallet. Even a lot of churchmen thought he was taking things a bit far, and some people in England resented what they saw as his desertion, but the archbishop was quite unabashed, and in 1166 he excommunicated eight of his enemies, including some leading figures in the Church, as well as threatening to do the same to Henry himself. Delicate negotiations went on for four years, and eventually, on 1 December 1170, Becket was persuaded to return to England, but before leaving France he renewed the excommunications. Maddeningly for Henry, Becket got a hero's welcome, and milked it by taking a roundabout route to Canterbury, culminating in a barefoot walk to the cathedral. When the king's representatives approached him and asked him to rescind the excommunications, he refused.

Even some of those who supported Becket, such as the pope, despaired of his obstinacy, and his clerk, supporter and biographer, John of Salisbury, considered the archbishop had 'provoked' the king. When the news of Becket's latest intransigence reached Henry, who was spending Christmas in his extensive French domains, he is supposed to have torn his clothes and shouted, perhaps on Christmas Day itself: 'What miserable drones and traitors have I nourished and promoted in my household, who let their lord be treated with such shameful contempt by a low-born clerk?' Was it an unthinking outburst of exasperation from a king known to be hot-tempered, or a royal command? Four of Henry's knights took it as the latter. Richard le Breton, Hugh de Morville, William de Tracy and Reginald FitzUrse sailed for England, where, on 29 December, they made contact with a more senior figure and long-time enemy of Becket, Ranulf de Broc, hereditary doorkeeper of the royal chamber, whose responsibilities also included taking charge of the king's whores. Broc got together a small task group that included a junior cleric named Hugh of Horsea, and they headed for Canterbury. Henry had also dispatched a more ortho-dox mission to arrest Becket under the leadership of the Earl of Essex, but FitzUrse and company seem to have had better luck with the December weather in the Channel and got to the cathedral city first.

Once they arrived in Canterbury, Broc and his soldiers sur-rounded the cathedral complex while the knights went to confront Becket in his palace, demanding that he revoke the excommunica-tions. He coolly refused, saying it was a matter for the pope. As the temperature rose, the archbishop's monks dragged him off to the sanctuary of the cathedral, but when they tried to bar the door, he forbade them, saying God's house should not be turned into a fortress. In the early twilight of the December afternoon, the knights, now joined by Hugh of Horsea, came into the cathedral and again demanded Becket withdraw the excommunications, accusing him of treason. When Becket again refused, they threat-ened to kill him. FitzUrse appears to have been the knights' main spokesman. According to an eyewitness account we have from one of Becket's attendants, Edward Grim, insults were exchanged, with FizUrse calling Becket a traitor and the archbishop denouncing the knight as a pimp. It may be that Becket's anger was heightened because he considered the group of men sent to confront him to be of low social rank.

There then followed a rather undignified scene as the knights tried to get Becket out of the cathedral, with FitzUrse grabbing the archbishop by his cloak and attempting to hoist him onto de Tracy's back. Becket might not have wanted the cathedral to be turned into a fortress, but when FirzUrse grabbed him, he responded with such a hefty shove that the knight nearly fell over. Then Grim held on tight to the man of God so the knights found it impossible to shift him. By now some of the townspeople were drifting into the cathedral for vespers, and FitzUrse's group must have felt there was a danger that Becket might be rescued. At about half past four, the archbishop is said to have accepted death was near and to have struck a submissive pose, with his head bent and his hands joined in prayer, as he commended himself to God.

With Morville holding the growing congregation at a distance, the first blow was struck, probably by FitzUrse. Grim tried to block it and the sword cut through his arm almost to the bone. It also sliced off the top of Becket's head. The second strike, probably from de Tracy, felled the archbishop, and as he hit the ground, he said: 'For the name of Jesus and the protection of the church I am ready to embrace death.' The *coup de grâce,* perhaps administered by le Breton, came down with such force that it broke his sword. Finally Hugh of Horsea put his foot on Becket's neck, thrust his sword into his open skull and scattered his brains on the floor, crying: 'Let us away, knights. This fellow will rise no more!' During the whole ordeal, Grim says the victim did not let out a cry of pain and had never made any attempt to avoid death, expressing the hope 'that in my blood, the church may find liberty and peace'. The assassins left the church immediately, clearing a passage through onlookers with the flats of their swords. Then, after a spot of looting in the archbishop's palace, they rode off. Grim, of course, praised the archbishop's saintly devotion to the Church, but he also paid tribute to his political nous, saying he exhibited 'the wisdom of the serpent' along with 'the simplicity of the dove'. Becket 'presented his body to the killers' to keep the Church safe, and 'because he abandoned the world, the world – wanting to overpower him – unknowingly elevated him'.

Thomas Becket's assassination was one of the most notorious in history. This is how it is depicted on a carved altar in Antwerp.

When Henry heard what had happened, he appeared to be genuinely consumed with remorse. He denied he had issued any order for Becket's death, and locked himself away for three days. Would it have been a different story if the Earl of Essex's mission had got to Canterbury first? Becket might have felt less insulted when confronted by a senior noble, but is it likely that he would have met the king's demands or agreed to be arrested? For Becket, being assassinated proved a great career move. In Canterbury people rushed to dip pieces of cloth in his spilt blood, and by the time Henry re-emerged into the world, miracles were already being attributed to it. Outrage at the murder surged through the whole of Christendom, and the king had to drop his plan to bring erring clerics under the jurisdiction of secular courts. He also had to perform public acts of penance, including allowing himself to be publicly flogged by bishops and monks (though some historians suggest the flagellation was more symbolic than painful), while Becket was canonized and his shrine became one of the most popular pilgrimage destinations in Europe. The killers appear to have received no reward from Henry. Plenty of people wanted to string them up, and the king advised them to flee to Scotland, but they had to get out of there too in fear of their lives. Then Henry handed them over to the pope, who banished them to a life of penance in the Holy Land. De Tracy was said to have died in agony from a horrible disease in southern Italy before he ever got there, 'his flesh decaying while he was yet alive, so that he could not refrain from tearing it off with his own hands', while he prayed 'incessantly' to St Thomas. FitzUrse and Morville were dead within five years of the murder, but le Breton may have managed to retire peacefully to Jersey. Ranulf de Broc was not punished and appears to have died around 1179. History does not record the fate of Hugh of Horsea. As for Henry, his prestige was badly damaged, and, though he ruled for another nineteen years, he had to spend much of that time facing down rebellions by his own sons, often spurred on by their mother.

While blood was staining the floors of churches, theologians continued to debate the rights and wrongs of assassination. Thomas Becket's clerk, John of Salisbury, whose biography of his former boss helped establish his credentials as a saint, argued tyrannicide was justified, saying a good king should be the guardian of his people's well-being. When a ruler fails in this duty, it is up to those he rules to correct or, if necessary, slay him. The tyrant's power is based only on force, and, as the Bible says, those who take the sword shall perish with the sword (Matthew 26:52). Perhaps the greatest of all medieval theologians, St Thomas Aquinas, took a similar view, saying a ruler who broke the law of man or God could be resisted even to the point of regicide, though he strongly favoured non-violent means of resistance where possible, and he also suggested that opposition to tyranny should be left to institutions within the state rather than individuals. John the Fearless was the patron of the Franciscan theologian Jean Petit, so it is perhaps no surprise that Petit defended the assassination of the Duke of Orleans in 1407 on the grounds that he was a tyrant, maintaining that it was 'lawful for any subject . . . to kill or cause to be killed a traitor and disloyal tyrant'. But eight years later, at the Council of Constance, the Roman Catholic Church forbade tyrannicide, while Dante put that iconic tyrant-slayer Brutus in the last circle of hell along with Satan and Judas Iscariot.

A Smothering in Burma and the Youngest Assassins

Stabbing remained overwhelmingly the favourite method of assassination in this era, but one murder in which it was not used happened in Burma in 1167. Taking a leaf out of Caligula's book (if it is true that he finished off his father-by-adoption, Tiberius, by putting a pillow over his face), the future King Narathu of Burma smothered his father King Alaungsithu. The 81-year-old ruler was seriously ill and had fallen into unconsciousness, so Narathu had him taken to his favourite temple. Then suddenly the old man revived and demanded to know why he had been removed from his palace. When Narathu heard the news, he raced to the temple and ended his father's life with the help of a blanket. Narathu's brother suspected foul play, but before he could expose it, Narathu had him poisoned. Following his crimes, the new king lasted even less time as ruler than Caligula. After he had one of his wives put to death for showing him insufficient respect, her father sent assassins to stab him to death in 1170.

The youngest assassin in the Age of Chivalry was the great Genghis Khan, who killed his half-brother when he was only fourteen. In those days, he was just plain Temujin. The name Genghis Khan, meaning 'universal ruler', would be given to him later. Temujin came up the hard way. His father, a minor Mongol chieftain, was poisoned when Temujin was nine, and along with his mother, brothers and sisters, he was left to survive as best he could. That meant killing whatever prey they were able to find, but often they went hungry. The story goes that one day in the late 1170s he and three of his brothers were fishing and caught a 'bright minnow'. Temujin's elder half-brother Bekter grabbed it for himself. The previous day he had done the same with a lark they had shot. So Temujin and another brother stalked Bekter and found him sitting on a hill. Temujin crept up behind him, fired an arrow and shot him dead. The future emperor may have had another motive apart from hunger. Some have suggested Bekter was beginning to flex his muscles as the alpha male in the little group, and Temujin decided he needed to remove a dangerous rival. Many assassins come to a sticky end, but Genghis Khan ended up conquering and ruling an empire that extended from Beijing to the Caspian Sea.

Another teenage assassin was Duke John of Swabia. In 1306 he was due to take the throne of Bohemia, but John's uncle, Albert I of Habsburg, installed his own son instead. Two years later, the young man assembled a group of plotters and attacked Albert as he crossed a river at Windisch in what is now Switzerland, delivering the fatal blow himself with an axe. As Albert's sons sought vengeance, John fled and was never heard of again.

DURING THE AGE OF CHIVALRY we have forty assassinations with enough information for analysis; 23 took place in Europe, including five in what is now the United Kingdom, twelve in the Middle East and five in East Asia. Eighteen of the victims were rulers, including nine kings and three emperors. Among the others were five significant religious figures, a low-born rebel and a prince's mistress (the only female victim). In 37 of the assassinations, we know the identity of the killer or killers. Twelve involved a lone assassin, including on three occasions a Hashishin. In another five cases the Hashishin worked in groups. We have only one clear instance of hired killers being used – the bunch of ruffians who murdered the Duke of Orleans – while it apparently became more common for royalty to do their own dirty work, with six kings or kings-to-be taking part in killings, and five princes participating in

Genghis Khan.

the assassination of the Mongol emperor Gegeen Khan in 1323.
Actively participating became more common for royalty than
commissioning killings, which happened in only five cases, two
of them involving the same sultan. In our sample from this era,
assassination appears to be an exclusively male preserve, with
no women involved in the forty cases, either as killers or
commissioners. There also seemed to be a decline in murder
by close associates, with just two trusted servants wielding the
blade. In contrast with the assassinations of the Roman Empire,
on only one occasion were the murderers the victim's own soldiers.
There was also a fall in the number of assassins from within the
family, with just one son and a half-brother involved as killers, plus
two nephews as instigators. This perhaps reflected the fact that
dynastic ambition was less common as a motive, playing a part
in just nine cases, compared with sixteen where other political
objectives were the spur. Resentment at a perceived injustice was
important in eight killings, while revenge was significant in six and

fear in six, whether that was fear of being punished, of being made to face a formidable enemy, or of loss of aristocratic privileges. Religion was a factor in five assassinations.

Of the thirty cases where we know the method, in all but five it was stabbing. Of the others, an axe was used in two, while smothering, strangling and hanging each claimed one victim. In 33 assassinations we know the fate of the assassin or instigator. In twelve they were killed or executed virtually immediately, while in another six they met a violent death within five years. In two instances they were banished. In seven they may have escaped punishment, while in three they were rewarded, and Henry II of Castile in Spain, who murdered his own half-brother in 1369, succeeded him as king. Four victims became saints, while a couple of others had more temporal rewards, with the Medici, for example, consolidating their rule in Florence after Giuliano's murder.

As to broader consequences, on at least twenty occasions there was serious instability. For example, the three kings who followed the murdered Sverker I of Sweden all met violent deaths, but in sixteen of the twenty cases there had also been instability before the assassination. In at least five instances, the disorder ended with success for the assassin, as in the troubles that followed Robert the Bruce's assassination of his rival for the crown of Scotland in 1306. He had to fight a series of wars with the English, but emerged as the ruler of an independent Scotland. On the other hand, the murder of Duke John of Burgundy had disastrous consequences for its perpetrator, the dauphin, as John's successor made a deal with France's English enemies, helping Henry V of England take the throne of France. Twice assassinations in the Age of Chivalry led to serious reprisals, notably when the murder of Count Raymond of Tripoli in 1152 brought an indiscriminate massacre of Muslims. But on three occasions, the assassination perhaps led to calmer times, as the murder of Wat Tyler, for example, may have hastened the end of the Peasants' Revolt. Overall, in 29 cases where the assassination had a fairly clear outcome, perhaps ten could be said to have failed – having a result the assassins would not have welcomed – while about fourteen could be put down as a success, with five others partially successful.

As we noted, breach of faith was an important factor in many murders in the Age of Chivalry. Five involved breaking a promise to the victim, and one a betrayal of hospitality, while no fewer than ten happened in holy places – seven in churches, two in mosques and one in a temple. One victim was killed saying mass in the open air, another was in a religious procession, while King Sverker was on his way to church on Christmas Day. An eloquent comment on the lack of reverence for holy places is the story of Pedro de Arbués, a senior figure in the Spanish Inquisition, who was wearing chain mail and a helmet when he was assassinated in Zaragoza Cathedral. Perhaps even more revealing is the fact that the pope and an archbishop were involved in the plot to kill Giuliano de' Medici during mass in Florence Cathedral.

4

THE WARS OF RELIGION

Tradition has it that on 31 October 1517, Martin Luther nailed his 95 theses to a church door at Wittenberg in Germany and launched the Protestant Reformation. Many modern historians doubt whether the document was ever posted in this way and argue that, in any case, Luther's criticisms of the Church at this point were questioning rather than condemnatory, but the effect was the same. The Christians of Western Europe split into Catholics and Protestants, and for two and a half centuries the continent would be riven by religious divisions and wars. We have already seen how religious disagreements motivated assassins in Islamic countries. Now that same force would spread through Christendom as Catholics denounced Protestants as heretics, and vice versa.

New Theories on the Ethics
of Assassination and How to Avoid It

The idea that a ruler had a 'social contract' with those he ruled and that this limited his powers had first been put forward by ancient Greek philosophers, but it gained new traction during the Wars of Religion. At the end of the sixteenth century, the Spanish Jesuit Juan de Mariana would argue that if a monarch was a heretic, he violated his contract and could therefore be removed, so any subject had the right to kill him. The Protestant bishop of Winchester John Ponet would not have agreed with Mariana on much, but he took a similar line in his book *A Short Treatise on Political Power* (1556), arguing that a ruler who abused his position should be treated as a common criminal and killed if necessary, though he and Mariana would no doubt have had opposite views on which specific rulers qualified for assassination. Ponet fled England when Queen 'Bloody' Mary started burning Protestants. Almost a century later the great poet John Milton, writing shortly after the execution of King Charles I, quoted the classics and the Bible to justify tyrannicide, citing Seneca's words that there was 'No sacrifice to God more acceptable than an unjust and wicked King', and pointing out that tyrant-killing had been 'not unusual' among the Jews in biblical times.

Around the time Luther was working on his theses, Niccolò Machiavelli was composing his masterpiece of cynical statecraft, *The Prince* (1532). Often regarded as the founder of modern political science, the Italian was less concerned about the rights and wrongs of assassination than with offering handy hints to rulers on how to avoid falling victim to it. His main recommendation was straightforward, but perhaps easier said than done. The ruler should avoid being hated or despised, because if he remains popular a conspirator will believe that killing him will enrage the people, and 'he will not have the courage' to go through with it. Taking the property or the women of his subjects will make a ruler hated, while 'if he is considered changeable, foolish, weak, mean, and uncertain', he will be despised. If a ruler does have to upset some people, he should make sure they are among the weak rather than the powerful. Machiavelli added that the ruler should get his henchmen to do the dirty work and ensure he is seen doing only the things that look good: 'princes ought to leave affairs which may upset some people to the management of others, and keep those which will make people happy in their own hands.'

Reassuringly for those in charge, he notes: 'there have been many conspiracies, but few have been successful.' A 'highly respected' ruler 'can only be attacked with difficulty'. On the other hand, Machiavelli, who was a boy in Florence when Giuliano de' Medici was murdered in the cathedral, notes that a ruler has no real defence against an assassin with 'resolved courage' who is not afraid to die, though he notes that such killers are 'very rare'. He pointed to France as one of 'the best ordered and governed kingdoms', where the king had a good chance of maintaining the affection of his people, but Machiavelli's rational mind did not anticipate the religious fanaticism that would poison France and other countries, making killers who were not afraid to die much less rare than they had been.

The French Wars of Religion

The French Wars of Religion are normally considered to have begun in 1562 when supporters of the leading Roman Catholic family, the Guises, massacred a congregation of Protestants, or as they tended to be known in France, Huguenots. The conflict would last for 36 years. Gaspard de Coligny, Admiral of France, emerged as the Huguenots' leader, demanding religious toleration, while the Catholic Guises pressed for the suppression of 'heresy', with the monarch often caught in the middle. The summer of 1572 saw one of the many attempts to find peace. A marriage was arranged between the leading Protestant Henry of Navarre and King Charles IX's sister, the Catholic Marguerite de Valois. The flower of the Huguenot nobility came to Paris, a Catholic stronghold, for the wedding on 18 August. Four days after the ceremony, Coligny was walking back from a meeting of the king's council at the Louvre when a shot rang out. Fortunately he had just bent down to adjust his shoe, otherwise he might well have been killed. As it was, the bullet broke his left arm and tore off the index finger of his right hand. Friends who were with him rushed into the house from which the shot had been fired and, by an open window, found, literally, a smoking gun. (In Frederick Forsyth's classic novel of assassination, *The Day of the Jackal* (1971), President de Gaulle cheats the bullet meant to kill him because he leans forward unexpectedly.)

The would-be assassin, who escaped, was thought to be Charles de Louviers, seigneur de Maurevert, a small-time noble and adventurer, but for whom was he working? It looked pretty damning for the Guises. Maurevert had once been their servant, and three years earlier he had murdered one of Coligny's lieutenants. The house from which the shot came had been rented by a former tutor of the family, and Maurevert had been taken there by another man who worked for them. But there were other suspects. The Spanish ambassador believed he detected the hand of the king's mother, Catherine de' Medici. She had ruled as regent when Charles was a boy and still had a powerful influence over the 22-year-old young man. Now she was worried that Coligny was starting to gain his ear. Whoever was behind the attack, Henry of Navarre and other friends of Coligny went to see Charles IX to demand justice, making it quite clear that if they did not get it, they were prepared to take the law into their own hands. Charles promised to find and punish the assailant, but his court was fearful about what the Huguenots might do next, and Charles appears to have decided on a pre-emptive strike.

Before dawn on 24 August, the Duc de Guise led a squad of soldiers to Coligny's residence. They killed the soldiers guarding the admiral, ran him through with a sword and threw his dead body out of the window into the street where it fell at Guise's feet. It was then dragged through the city and hung upside down from a gibbet. All over Paris, the Huguenot nobles who had been invited to the wedding were murdered alongside their soldiers, though Henry of Navarre was spared on condition he converted to Catholicism, and the Catholic mob joined in for good measure, targeting ordinary Huguenot citizens and shopkeepers. In provincial towns too, Protestants were slaughtered, sometimes by the authorities, sometimes by mobs. In what became known as the St Bartholomew's Day Massacre, it is estimated that about 3,000 died in Paris alone, with tens of thousands across the country. Charles

The assassination of the French Protestant hero Gaspard de Coligny, in a 19th-century edition of *Foxe's Book of Martyrs*.

IX seems to have sent out an order to stop the killings after a couple of days, though he did take responsibility for the deaths of Coligny and his lieutenants, declaring he had 'to defend the good and exterminate the wicked'. It is said that he remained haunted by the massacre. His health deteriorated and he died less than two years later of tuberculosis. After the killings, a group of Calvinist Protestant thinkers emerged and were dubbed the 'Monarchomachs', a term of abuse derived from the Greek, meaning 'someone who fights against the monarch'. They began to advance a similar theory to Mariana, maintaining that if a ruler broke his contract with the people, resistance was justified.

The massacre did not end the Wars of Religion – far from it – and assassination continued to be an important tactic. Charles IX's successor, his brother Henry III, tried fighting, making concessions to the Huguenots and then withdrawing them, all to no avail. Henry appears to have been involved in organizing the St Bartholomew's Day Massacre, but the Catholic Holy League, led by the Duc de Guise, thought he was weak, and tried to depose him. In 1588 Paris rose against the king and he was forced to flee. Henry then set up the murder of Guise and, on Christmas Eve, of his brother Louis, a cardinal, and sought the help of Henry of Navarre to lay siege to Paris. On 1 August 1589 a Dominican lay brother named Jacques Clément made his way to the king's headquarters. A fanatical supporter of the Catholic League, he had managed to get hold of letters for Henry. Once admitted to the royal presence, he said he had an important, confidential message

Paul Delaroche, *The Assassination of the Duke of Guise*, 1834, oil on canvas.

to deliver. When the king's attendants withdrew, Clément stabbed Henry with a dagger he had hidden in his cloak. The attendants rushed in and killed the assailant, but the king died the next day. What was it Machiavelli had said about assassins who do not care about their own survival? Clément was praised by the pope, and there were even suggestions he should be canonized.

Before he died, Henry had named Henry of Navarre as his successor, and he now took the throne as King Henry IV. He was a Protestant once more, his conversion of 1572 having lasted only a couple of years. Henry was no religious fanatic. He was a notorious womanizer, and fathered at least eleven illegitimate children with a series of mistresses. Now to cement his hold over France's capital city, on the advice of one of his paramours, he embraced Catholicism again, commenting: 'Paris is well worth a mass.' He became very popular and was known as 'Good King Henry'. He brought an end to the Wars of Religion and to Spanish interference in France on the side of the Catholic League. He sorted out the chaotic royal finances, revived the economy and the fortunes of ordinary French people, and embarked on a formidable programme of public works, laying the foundations for France to become Europe's dominant power.

The assassination of Henry III of France by Jacques Clément, according to a 16th-century engraving.

The assassination of Henry IV, according to a 17th-century engraving.

But all that was neither here nor there as far as the extremists were concerned, and by some estimates Henry faced up to twenty assassination plots. Seventeenth-century Paris was the biggest city in Europe, and its narrow streets were notorious for traffic jams. On 14 May 1610 the king was on his way to see his finance minister with three courtiers when his coach juddered to a stop in the Les Halles district. Suddenly a tall figure with flaming red hair leapt from the crowd into the carriage, stabbing Henry three times. The king died shortly afterwards. The assassin made no attempt to escape or resist as the crowd seized him, and the police had to save him from being lynched. François Ravaillac, a fanatical 32-year-old Catholic from Angoulême, a small Catholic enclave surrounded by Protestants, had been born in poverty, and his father had abandoned his mother. Now scraping a living working as a scribe or a valet, Ravaillac had tried and failed to join the Jesuits. He was prey to visions and was nursing the idea that Henry was going to make war on the pope. At his trial, Ravaillac said he had kept trying to get an audience with the king to tell him he needed to make all Protestants re-join the Catholic Church, but that the king's guards had turned him away. He said Henry was a tyrant and God wanted him removed. Many people believed the assassin must be part of some wider conspiracy, but, even under torture, he maintained he had acted alone, though he may have received financial help from a Catholic noble who was involved in a number of plots against the king. Ravaillac suffered a brutal execution, being ripped apart by horses. His relatives were sent into exile and forbidden to use their surname ever again, while the French loudly lamented Henry's death, with women tearing their hair in 'an orgy of weeping and wailing' according to a contemporary, and a lot of people started blaming Juan de Mariana for at the very least creating the atmosphere that led to the assassination. The Jesuit had argued that Henry's Protestantism made him ineligible for the throne, meaning he was a tyrant who ruled unlawfully. Mariana continued to live peacefully in Spain, but in France, his book *De rege et regis institutione* was publicly burned, and in 1615 the pope reiterated the Church's prohibition of tyrannicide. Henry's death meant his eight-year-old son became King Louis XIII, and there was terrible foreboding that France might collapse again into anarchy. In fact, Louis was king for 33 years and handed on the crown to his son, Louis XIV, the Sun King, who would reign for more than seventy years, and put an end to the religious toleration that Henry IV had won for Protestants.

Gunpowder Makes an Appearance

The era of the Wars of Religion not only brought new motives for assassination, it also brought new technologies, and one, gunpowder, featured in the murder of the husband of Mary, Queen of Scots, in 1567. Mary described her cousin Lord Darnley as the 'lustiest and best proportioned man' she had ever seen. Certainly, he was tall, over six feet, which would have been a good deal more striking in the sixteenth century than it is now. Mary had been queen of Scotland since she was a few days old, but from the age

Lord Darnley, an 18th-century print from an earlier portrait.

of five she had spent her time at the French court preparing for her marriage to the future King Francis II, whom she wed when she was fifteen. Two years later, Francis was dead from a brain tumour, and in 1561 Mary left her adopted country, then on the verge of the Wars of Religion, to take power in her native land, which was also a snake pit of vindictive religious politics. Mary was Catholic, while Scotland was officially Protestant, and the hell-fire preacher John Knox regularly denounced her from his pulpit as a heretic, a jezebel and a foreigner. For the first couple of years, though, she took advice from the leading Protestant lord, her half-brother the Earl of Moray, even though in 1559 he had deposed her mother, the Catholic Mary of Guise, who had been acting as regent for her daughter. Then in 1565 Mary married Darnley in a Catholic ceremony and started packing her council of advisers with Catholics. Moray and other Protestant lords rose in revolt and were driven across the border into Protestant England.

Unfortunately, whatever upside Darnley offered in the realm of good looks was more than outweighed by the downside of his character. His only interests were hunting, drinking and sex with women other than Mary, enabling him to perform the considerable feat of uniting the Protestant and Catholic factions against him. He was also jealous and gullible, and the Protestants managed to make him believe, almost certainly wrongly, that the queen was having an affair with her Italian secretary, David Rizzio. In March 1566 Darnley and a group of Protestant nobles burst into a small supper party Mary was giving for Rizzio and other friends, dragged him from the table and stabbed him more than fifty times before the queen's horrified eyes. Within a couple of days, Mary, who was pregnant with Darnley's child, feigned a reconciliation with her husband, but in fact she never forgave him. On the night Rizzio was killed, the assassins had another target at the dinner table, the Earl of Bothwell, but he managed to escape through a window. Bothwell was also a handsome fellow, though rather a rough diamond. He was officially a Protestant, but he had won Mary's confidence by trying to defend the interests of her mother and by helping defeat Moray's revolt. The result was that he became one of her closest friends and advisers. Following Rizzio's murder, he persuaded the queen to allow Moray and the other exiled Protestant lords back home while they decided what to do about Darnley. They considered two solutions: divorce or assassination. The problem with divorce was that in June 1566 Mary had given birth to a son, and she did not want any doubts raised about his legitimacy. So assassination it was.

In early 1567 Darnley was recovering from smallpox, and Mary took him to Edinburgh to nurse him. In the early hours of 9 February she was away attending a wedding masque when a huge explosion reduced the house where he was staying to rubble. Someone had planted two barrels of gunpowder under Darnley's room. But the blast did not kill or injure the queen's husband. When his body and that of his valet in their nightclothes were found in the grounds, it was clear they had been strangled. Had the blast been meant to kill him, and had he escaped, only to run into the arms of assassins? Had he been tipped off by friends or by people working with the assassins? Or were there rival groups of assassins at work? The exact explanation might be unclear, but fingers of suspicion started pointing in one direction – towards Mary and Bothwell. In response, the earl abducted her, and, according to Mary, raped her so that she was compelled to take him as her husband. Not everyone was convinced, believing the pair were already in an adulterous relationship before Darnley's death, and that the rape story was just an attempt by Mary to mitigate the opprobrium the marriage could be expected to attract. The couple were united in a Protestant ceremony, but that was not enough to placate the Protestant lords who rose in revolt, made Mary give up her throne and imposed Moray as regent for her infant son, King James vi of Scotland (later King James i of England). Bothwell escaped to Denmark, but died in prison there in 1578. Mary ended up a prisoner of Queen Elizabeth i in England, where, because of her claim to the throne as a great-granddaughter of Henry vii, she became a dangerous focus for Catholic opposition. She was executed in 1587 after getting involved in a plot against Elizabeth. It is still not clear who killed Darnley. Three of Bothwell's henchmen were arrested. At least one was tortured and all three were executed. The earl himself was tried and acquitted, but some say the trial was rigged. In 2015 an investigation by the Royal Society of Edinburgh using modern techniques concluded that Mary was not involved in Darnley's murder. It also said there was evidence that the queen's husband may have been murdered somewhere else and the body dragged to where it was found.

The Hour of the Gun

The most important new assassination technology of the era was the gun. As we saw, it failed in the attempt on Gaspard de Coligny's

James Hamilton about to assassinate the Earl of Moray at Linlithgow:
a 19th-century view.

life in 1572, but by then it had already been used successfully. In
1566 a Japanese warlord, Mimura Iechika, was shot dead at a meeting. Two brothers, acting on the orders of a rival, used a
short-barrelled musket on Iechika, who had made many enemies
by shifting his allegiance between different clans. Even earlier, in
1536, there was the mysterious case of an English member of parliament named Robert Pakington. A Protestant sympathizer, a
stern critic of what he saw as the greed of the clergy, and a successful merchant, he had connections with Henry VIII's chief minister,
Thomas Cromwell, who was then masterminding England's break
with Rome. On 13 November 1536 Pakington was shot dead while
crossing London's Cheapside on his way to mass. No one was ever
apprehended for the killing, even though the authorities offered a
'great reward', so we do not know whether it was a political or
ideological assassination, or whether other motives were in play.
In England, too, this was a turbulent time. A Catholic rebellion
that became known as the Pilgrimage of Grace had begun, and a
fellow MP claimed Pakington had been killed by, or on the orders
of, the clergy, but there is no conclusive evidence.

If we discount the case of Pakington, the first known assassination by firearm in Europe came in 1570 in Scotland. After her abdication, Mary, Queen of Scots, had tried to make a comeback, but the Earl of Moray, acting as regent for her son, had won a final victory over her at Langside in 1568. Among those fighting on her side that day was James Hamilton, the nephew of the Archbishop of St Andrews. On 23 January 1570, as Moray was riding through Linlithgow, Hamilton waited for him in a house owned by the archbishop, armed with a carbine supplied by the Abbot of Arbroath. The operation had been well planned. There was a mattress on the floor of the room where he hid to muffle the sound of his footsteps and black curtains at the window to conceal his shadow. Where Maurevert failed, he succeeded, fatally wounding Moray with a bullet of tempered steel shot from the window. According to a contemporary account, Hamilton then escaped through the back garden onto a 'very good' waiting horse. Moray's men pursued him, but he outran them, at one point plunging a dagger into his mount's hindquarters to make it leap a wide pond. The earl had been hit in the abdomen and he died the same day, making this one of the first assassinations successfully carried out at a distance. While Hamilton escaped, his uncle the archbishop was captured, tried and executed in double-quick time for his involvement in this assassination and also, allegedly, the murder of Darnley. There are suggestions that private resentment over what he saw as Moray's mistreatment of his family may have played a part in motivating James Hamilton. Anyway, he escaped to France, where it seems he was approached to help in Coligny's assassination, but declined indignantly, 'asserting that he had avenged his own just quarrel, but he would neither for pence nor prayer avenge that of another man'. He was, however, involved in failed Spanish plots to kill William, Prince of Orange, often known as William the Silent, the Protestant leader of the Netherlands' struggle for independence against Catholic Spain, and was imprisoned for a time.

William the Silent

There was a whole series of plots against William, thanks partly to a considerable price put on his head by King Philip II of Spain. Some involved exotic ideas such as secreting poison in a dish of eels, of which William was said to be especially fond, or planting explosives under his seat in church. A Dominican friar was one of two conspirators executed in 1582; another would-be killer met the same fate in Antwerp in 1583 and yet another at Flushing the following year. By then, a fanatical Burgundian Catholic named Balthasar Gérard had been nurturing the wish to kill the prince for at least seven years. He had received encouragement from a Jesuit, a Franciscan friar and the Duke of Parma, who was Philip II's man in the Netherlands and a redoubtable general. But Parma was unwilling to advance any money to help progress Gérard's scheme. Having been bitten several times, he was now shy about gambling any more on supposed assassins who promised much, but failed to deliver.

Gérard was not easily discouraged. He wormed his way into William's confidence in July 1584, posing as a devout Calvinist whose father had been executed during the French Wars of Religion. The prince gave him what Parma refused, money, and Gérard used it to buy a couple of pistols. On 10 July he went back to William's house at Delft, asking for a passport so he could return home. The prince's wife, who was Gaspard de Coligny's daughter, was suspicious, but William asked his secretary to prepare the passport while he and his family had lunch. In his monumental history of *The Rise of the Dutch Republic,* J. L. Motley describes the 27-year-old Gérard as short, 'meagre . . . and altogether a man of no account – quite insignificant'. Everyone thought him 'inoffensive, but quite incapable of any important business'. Now he hid beneath the stairs just outside William's dining room and waited. After an hour and a half the family emerged, with the prince leading the way. He had barely stepped on the stairs when Gérard leapt out and shot him three times in the chest from just a couple of feet away. One bullet went straight through the prince. William fell to the ground, crying: 'My God, have pity on my soul!' and died a few moments later. The assassin ran out through the back into a narrow alley. He was planning to jump from the town's ramparts, swim the moat and leap onto a waiting horse to make his escape. Soon halberdiers were in pursuit, and when Gérard fell over a rubbish heap they grabbed him. The killer made no further attempt to get away and spoke proudly of what he had done.

Taken before magistrates, he declared he was like David slaying Goliath. After that he was subjected to 'excruciating tortures' but suffered them so bravely that even his tormentors were impressed. He remained utterly unrepentant, and studiedly avoided implicating Parma. The execution arranged for the killer was equally unpleasant, involving, among other things, having his flesh torn from his bones with red-hot pincers, and being quartered and

A 17th-century depiction of the assassination of William the Silent.

disembowelled alive. Even Motley, who tended to see the Dutch rebels simply as the goodies and the Spanish as the baddies, admitted the assassin bore all this 'with astonishing fortitude'. Parma rewarded Gérard's mother and father with enough land to raise them to the aristocracy. The Spaniards saw William the Silent as the inspiration for and the brains behind the Netherlands' revolt, believing that his death would bring it to an end. In fact, though Parma reconquered the Southern Netherlands, modern-day Belgium, in 1588, the northern provinces, what today we call the Netherlands, carried on the fight and their independence was finally recognized in 1648. Belgium did not become a country until 1830.

A Honey Trap in Italy

Religion may have provided a new motive, or pretext, for assassination, but older ones still operated. In Protestant England, Italy was often portrayed as a land of endlessly inventive and, well, Machiavellian villainy. So in Webster's rather lurid tragedy *The Duchess of Malfi* (1613), a would-be assassin conceals a pistol in his codpiece. Almost as racy was the real-life assassination of Alessandro de' Medici, half-brother of Catherine de' Medici, mother of the murdered French king Henry III, who fell victim to what we might now call a honey trap. Alessandro was known as 'the Moor'. His mother was an African slave, and his father was Lorenzo de' Medici, the Duke of Urbino, though some historians now argue he was sired by Lorenzo's cousin Giulio, who went on to become Pope Clement VII. When Alessandro was 22, Emperor Charles V installed him as Florence's first duke after a siege of eleven months, bringing to an end the Florentine Republic that had endured for four hundred years. In 1536 the duke married Charles V's illegitimate daughter Margaret, but within a few months he also took a fancy to a beautiful and virtuous married woman named Caterina de' Ginori. Lorenzino de' Medici, a distant cousin of Alessandro, and his pimp according to his critics, promised the duke she could be seduced, and on 5 January 1537 he brought news that Caterina's husband was far away in Naples. He offered Alessandro the use of his apartment and told him to go and wait there until he brought the lady.

Alessandro was dressed up to the nines, but missing from his outfit was the doublet lined with fine chain mail that he normally wore as protection against stabbing. Once inside Lorenzino's apartment, the duke took off his sword and lay down for a nap, anticipating the delights to come. Lorenzino found Alessandro sleeping, quietly moved his sword out of harm's way, and then crept out of the apartment to make contact with his accomplice, a man named Scoronconcolo, who owed him a favour. Without disclosing Alessandro's identity, he told his companion that sleeping in his apartment was an enemy who had cheated him. They managed to go in without rousing the duke, who woke up only when Lorenzino plunged his sword into his stomach. Alessandro tried to make it to the door using a stool as a shield, but Scoronconcolo slashed his cheek with a knife. Lorenzino dragged their prey down, but Alessandro bit his thumb so hard that for a moment he fainted. Then Scoronconcolo stabbed the duke in the throat and it was all over. They left his body under a canopy on the bed, and Lorenzino fled to Venice.

Lorenzino maintained that he assassinated Alessandro in order to foment an uprising that would restore the Florentine Republic. In fact, no such revolt happened, and Alessandro's relative, Cosimo, became the new duke. Others suggest different motives: that Lorenzino resented Alessandro's failure to help him in a legal dispute, that he was acting on behalf of other enemies of the duke (there were plenty of them) or simply that he was envious of his kinsman. One thing that is certain is that he himself fell victim to a hired killer in Venice in 1548, on the orders of Cosimo or perhaps of Charles v.

Killing a Conquistador

Martin Luther King warned that 'violence begets violence', and just as Lorenzino had found, assassination often begets assassination. So it proved with the man who killed the great conquistador Francisco Pizarro. If you rise from poverty, go halfway across the world with a handful of men and conquer a great empire in an unknown land, you are probably going to have to upset a few people along the way, and that had certainly been Pizarro's experience. Early on in his career, he stitched up his erstwhile comrade Vasco Núñez de Balboa, with whom he had discovered the Pacific Ocean, handing him over to a rival who had him executed. Next he fell out with another of his fellow adventurers, Diego Almagro. In 1538 Pizarro's brother Hernando had Almagro executed after they had defeated him in battle.

We can be fairly certain Pizarro had not read *The Prince*. He was illiterate, and he certainly did not seem to follow Machiavelli's prudent advice. While Pizarro worked on his new capital of Lima, he seemed blissfully unaware of the hornets' nest he and his brother had kicked by killing Almagro. He could have tried to win over some of his old comrade's supporters, but as the great historian of the conquest of Peru William H. Prescott wrote, he 'had not the magnanimity' to do it. Hernando suggested that he should at least ensure his enemies were scattered around his territory and not allowed to gather in one place, but Francisco rejected his advice, refusing to 'stoop to precautionary measures'. He let Almagro's son stay in Lima, and Almagro's old adherents became the son's followers. At the same time, Pizarro denied the young man money, and deprived him of the governorship of New Toledo that his father had left him. Pizarro was warned that as Almagro's men got more and more hard up, they were becoming more and more resentful, and he saw signs of it himself as they refused to doff their hats to him in the street. On one occasion, three ropes were found hanging from the public gallows with the names of Pizarro and two of his henchmen attached. Still the conquistador travelled around as freely as ever, and his supporters antagonized the Almagristas even more by ostentatiously flaunting their finery in front of them.

By mid-1541 Almagro's followers had had enough. They decided they would kill Pizarro on 26 June. The plan was to meet in their late leader's house, where his son now lived, in the great square next to the cathedral, and then fall upon the conquistador as he emerged from mass. It is hard to believe that Almagro's son did not know about the plot, but he does not appear to have played a leading role. That fell to his main adviser, Juan de Harrada, often known simply as 'Rada'. One of the conspirators had an attack of guilty conscience and told all to his confessor, who ignored any nonsense about the seal of the confessional, and quickly passed the word on to Pizarro. But the old warrior kept calm and carried on, making no attempt to arrest the plotters, though he did agree not to go to mass on the appointed day, pleading illness.

Come 26 June, Rada's group of about twenty were gobsmacked when they realized Pizarro was not coming to church. Did this mean they were discovered? Some wanted to call it off and disband, in the hope that Pizarro had not been aware of what they were planning, while others said they should strike their enemy in his house. In the end, the issue was forced by one of their number who threw open the door and ran into the street, saying he would proclaim their plan to the world if they did not join him. The time for hesitation was now surely through, and they all poured out, shouting; 'Death to the tyrant!' Plenty of Lima's inhabitants saw what was happening, but none rushed to Pizarro's aid. His house also stood on the square. To reach it, you had to go through two courtyards. The first had a great gate that could have been defended against a much larger force than Rada had assembled, but it had been left unguarded.

Still crying: 'Death to the tyrant!' the Almagristas penetrated into the second where they encountered a couple of servants. They struck one of them down, while the other ran off shouting for help.

The assassination of Pizarro, in a French engraving from the late 19th century.

Pizarro was dining with perhaps twenty friends who had come to inquire about his health. Some now escaped into the garden. As the conquistador ordered a trusted soldier, Francisco de Chaves, to bar the door, he and his half-brother, Don Martinez de Alcantara, started putting on their armour, hoping the guests who had fled would return with help. Unfortunately, Chaves did not bar the door, and tried instead to reason with the insurgents. The conversation proved short. They ran him through and flung his corpse downstairs. A number of Pizarro's attendants now tried to hold up the would-be assassins but met the same fate. Alcantara saw what was happening and rushed to confront Rada's men with a couple of Pizarro's pages, while their boss still struggled with his armour. In a desperate fight, two of Rada's men were killed, while Alcantara and the pages were wounded repeatedly. Though in his mid-sixties, the conquistador now threw himself on his attackers like a tiger as Alcantara fell. He killed two of them, and because the passageway was narrow, he and his pages, like Horatio on the bridge, were able to hold up the bigger force for a while, but eventually both pages were laid low. Another assailant was run through, but not before he had wounded Pizarro in the throat, and the end came when the conquistador could not extract his sword from his opponent's torso. As the conqueror of the Inca Empire fell to the ground, others plunged their swords into him. With his finger, he drew a cross in the blood now covering the floor, and then the *coup de grâce* was administered. The plotters rushed into the street, brandishing their bloodied weapons and shouting: 'The tyrant is dead!' Pizarro was hastily buried with minimum formality in an obscure corner of the cathedral, his men were removed from office and young Almagro was installed as the new governor of Peru. But just fifteen months later he was executed after being defeated in battle by the new governor sent out by the Spanish crown. Another dozen of the Almagristas who had taken part in Pizarro's assassination were killed in the battle or executed afterwards.

Assassination Starts to Go International

As the world got bigger for Europeans thanks to the exploits of Pizarro and other conquistadors and explorers, so the arm of the assassin grew longer, with political murder going international. Cambridge University's first professor of history was a Dutch

Calvinist named Isaac Dorislaus. He was head-hunted at the age of 32 in 1627 and quickly stirred up controversy. Lecturing on the origins of royal authority in ancient Rome, he quoted the removal of Lucius Tarquinius Superbus to demonstrate that a king who oppresses his people should be deposed. The Master of Peterhouse considered his lectures to be full of 'dangerous' ideas and King Charles I, who was starting to experience the difficulties with Parliament that would lead to civil war, banned him from delivering any further talks. By 1649, the king had lost the Civil War and was on trial for his life. (Although the English Civil War is generally portrayed as a political conflict between king and parliament, it had a strong religious dimension, with radical non-conformist Protestant 'Puritans' generally found on the parliamentary side and High Church Anglicans and Roman Catholics supporting the king.) Dorislaus, who was also a lawyer, was appointed one of the counsel for the prosecution. There was even a rumour that he was one of the masked executioners who beheaded Charles on 30 January 1649. In the spring that followed, the Dutchman was due to become a librarian, but before taking up the position he agreed to undertake a diplomatic mission to The Hague on behalf of Oliver Cromwell, who held him in high regard. Working with Parliament's ambassador, Walter Strickland, he was charged with negotiating an alliance with the Dutch Republic.

It was an assassination waiting to happen. Charles I's son, who would go on to become Charles II, was in The Hague and the city was crawling with exiled Royalists. News that one of the regicides was coming sent them into a fury. The great Scottish Royalist general, the Marquess of Montrose, channelled the anger, putting together a hand-picked team from the flower of Cavalierdom north of the border who had followed him into exile – men like Sir John Spottiswood and Colonel Walter Whitford, the son of a bishop. On 29 April Dorislaus took lodgings at the White Swan Inn. The plotters bragged noisily about the scalp they were going to claim and the news reached Strickland. The ambassador tried to persuade

Dorislaus to move into his house where it would be easier to protect him, but, with an insouciance worthy of Pizarro, the only concession the Dutchman would make to security concerns was to cancel a journey across the city to see Strickland. On 1 May the plotters made a failed attempt on Dorislaus's life, but still the envoy remained unmoved.

The next day, so Dorislaus would not have to travel, Strickland arranged to go and see him at the White Swan. After their meeting, the ambassador went home, while the Dutchman sat down to his supper. A group of about a dozen armed men entered the inn. They had done their homework and knew which room the regicide was in. Blowing out the lights in the corridor they ran along with swords and pistols drawn, while serving staff shouted: 'Murder!' Two servants leant against the door inside Dorislaus's room to try to hold it against the assassins, while the envoy searched for another way out. Finding none, he appeared to resign himself to his fate, the servants saying: 'he returned to his chair, and folding his arms, leant upon it, with his face towards the door.'

The killers burst in to find their prey sitting calmly, looking them in the eye. As they held the unarmed servants at sword and gun point, Whitford slashed his sword across Dorislaus's head, then ran him through. The other conspirators plunged their weapons into the dying body, and ran off, shouting: 'Thus dies one of the king's judges.' Whitford escaped across the border into the Spanish Netherlands with the help of the Portuguese ambassador, who was in on the plot, and survived to live on royal pensions. Spottiswood was less fortunate, dying at the hands of the executioner after a failed attempt to raise Scotland for Charles II, while Montrose too was executed after Charles abandoned him. Parliament buried Dorislaus in Westminster Abbey, but after the restoration of Charles II, he was demoted to nearby St Margaret's.

A Japanese Assassination Revives Chivalric Ideals

While many in Europe must have been horrified at the prevalence of assassination, in Japan there was a murder that is now sometimes described as the country's national legend. We saw how in fifteenth-century Japan, there were worries that chivalric ideals were dying, but a killing at the beginning of the eighteenth century seemed to exemplify *bushido*, the code of honour of the samurai, Japan's hereditary military caste. In Edo (now Tokyo) in 1701, Kira Yoshinaka, a high shogunate official, was instructing two visiting lords, Asano Naganori and Kamei Sama, in etiquette. It was customary for such lords to bring gifts for their teacher, but Kira felt those brought by Asano and Kamei were rather beneath his dignity, so he started being rude to them. Asano bit his tongue, while Kamei was furious and began planning to kill Kira. At this point, Kamei's

Oishi Yoshio, leader of the 47 samurai, from an embossed colour woodblock print by Ogata Gekko, 1897.

people discreetly handed over a bribe to the official. This secured better treatment for him, but Kira, perhaps incensed that his other pupil had not also paid a bribe, started behaving even worse towards Asano, saying he was a country bumpkin devoid of manners. Asano flew into a fury and rushed at Kira with a dagger, stabbing him in the face before guards dragged him off. Attacking a shogun official in this way was a grave offence and Asano was made to commit *harakiri* by the traditional method of disembowelment.

When the three hundred samurai who followed Asano learned what had happened, they were enraged, and 47 of them banded together in accordance with the *bushido* code to avenge his death by killing Kira. The official, though, had been expecting just such a development, and ensured that he was always well guarded. To lull him into a false sense of security, the 47 split up, with their leader Oishi Yoshio divorcing his wife and apparently going to the dogs with a life of whoring and drinking. Others posed as merchants or workmen to gain admittance to Kira's house and learn its layout. By 1703 Kira's guard had slipped and Oishi's team was ready. On a cold, snowy December morning, they attacked, killing at least sixteen of the official's men before they cornered him. The assailants invited him to do the decent thing and commit *harakiri*, but he refused so Oishi decapitated him. Then the 47 took his head to Asano's grave, said prayers and gave themselves up to the shogun. At first, they were sentenced to death, but after the shogun received petitions from people admiring their chivalry, Oishi's men were allowed to commit *harakiri* and die honourably. Just one of the group, Oishi's son, was pardoned because of his youth. The story of the 47 has featured in plays, opera and more than half a dozen films.

Assassination as Official Policy

The unusual thing about assassination in the Turkish Ottoman Empire is that it had official sanction. Sultan Mehmed II, the conqueror of Constantinople in 1453, declared that if 'any of my sons ascend the throne, it shall be acceptable for him to kill his brothers for the common benefit of the people.' He said most Muslim scholars had approved this approach. It might sound brutal but you could see his point. The idea was to ensure peace by eliminating any possible rival to the throne. At the beginning of the fifteenth century, a contest for the crown between four princes had resulted in a decade-long civil war, and about a hundred years later, the Syrian Hanbali scholar Karmi would give intellectual approval to the killing of brothers and half-brothers on the grounds that it was the lesser of two evils: it was permissible to kill a few to save the lives of many more. Mehmed had not set down any clear rule of succession; the luckiest or most resourceful would rise to the top, and, of course, the ruling sultan might give a helping hand to the son he favoured. The fratricide rule was not universally applied, but it did result in the deaths of eighty members of the royal family over 150 years. When Mehmed III became sultan in 1595, he had nineteen of his brothers strangled with silk handkerchiefs, even though some were still infants. (Strangulation was a favourite method because Turkish tradition prohibited shedding the blood of members of the royal family.) This mass assassination caused such an outcry that Mehmed's son, Ahmed I, ended the practice. Some have argued that this precipitated the decline of the empire, because the earlier survival-of-the-fittest approach had on the whole resulted in the most able candidate taking the throne. Instead, the succession began to pass to the sultan's eldest surviving brother. This had the benefit of reducing the risk that a child would succeed to the throne, but it had a major drawback. From Ahmed I's time, instead of being killed off, other members of the royal family were kept virtual prisoners in Istanbul's Topkapi Palace, entertained only by barren concubines and macramé. If any then had to be summoned to serve as sultan, they would be singularly ill-prepared for the task.

The Thirty Years War

The most devastating of all the wars of religion, and the first pan-European conflict, was the Thirty Years War, which laid waste to central Europe between 1618 and 1648, fought as it was over the vast lands that were then called the Holy Roman Empire. Dismissed by Voltaire as 'neither holy, nor Roman, nor an empire', it was a collection of hundreds of largely independent territories, spread over what is now Germany, but also including Austria, Belgium and the Czech Republic as well as parts of other countries such as France, Switzerland and Poland. The emperor had some authority over them all, but the individual territories guarded their rights jealously. What began as a battle between Catholics and Protestants finally morphed into a struggle for supremacy between Catholic Spain and Catholic France, with the French taking the side of the Protestants as a way of keeping Spain in check. By the time the war ended, around 8 million had perished from the fighting, famine or disease.

Albrecht von Wallenstein was the greatest general on the Roman Catholic side. Raised as a Protestant in Bohemia in what is now the Czech Republic, in his early thirties he converted to Catholicism. There is a story that this was because he credited the Virgin Mary with saving his life when he fell out of a window, but he may have been motivated by the fact that it was virtually impossible for a Protestant to get a top job in Bohemia. Either way, once he did convert, his confessor helped him marry a rich elderly widow, who died after five years, leaving him a wealthy man.

By the time the Thirty Years War began, Wallenstein was already an experienced commander, and he used his wealth to raise a cavalry regiment that distinguished itself in the service of the Catholic Holy Roman Emperor, Ferdinand II. Soon the general had his own army of more than 20,000, and by 1625, he was the commander of all imperial forces. Like many commanders in the conflict, he ran his military operations as a business, coining the phrase: 'war feeds itself', and a series of stunning victories saw him become

Watercolour from c. 1840 envisaging the assassination of Albrecht von Wallenstein.

even richer, as the emperor made him ruler of some of the territories he conquered. From the end of the 1620s, Wallenstein seemed to get a bit carried away, holding talks with Protestant princes about establishing a great trading company with himself at the centre. By then he had made plenty of enemies and the empire's myriad small rulers considered an imperial army a threat to their independence, so, in 1630, they persuaded Ferdinand to sack him. At this point, the great Protestant champion, King Gustavus Adolphus of Sweden, 'the Lion of the North', entered the fray. Determined to wreak revenge on the emperor, Wallenstein began intriguing with him, but the king was wary. Then Gustavus defeated the imperial army under its new general in a major battle, and in 1632 the emperor had to go cap-in-hand to Wallenstein, restore him to the imperial command and once again hand over territories to him.

When the two great commanders finally faced each other, Gustavus Adolphus was killed, but Wallenstein lost the battle, and then off his own bat started peace negotiations with Sweden and other enemies of the emperor. The Bohemian was a devotee of astrology and believed the stars were assuring him his generals were completely loyal. In fact, a number of them, as well as his astrologer, had denounced him to Ferdinand. In January 1634 he launched a revolt as the emperor sacked him again and ordered his capture dead or alive. With his soldiers slipping away, in February Wallenstein moved his much-diminished force to what is now the Czech town of Cheb, hoping to link up with the Swedes. Among his officers were two Irish mercenaries, Walter Devereux and Walter Butler. Butler commanded Wallenstein's bodyguard, a squadron of dragoons. He organized the murder of the commander's main supporters while they were having dinner. Then Devereux burst in on Wallenstein while he was asleep. The commander begged for quarter, but the Irishman ran him through with his halberd. The emperor rewarded Butler and Devereux, but Butler died of the plague before the year was out and Devereux did not survive the war, which raged for another fourteen years and ended with the emperor's power diminished as the individual states increased their authority.

The Thirty Years War also saw what must have been the most bizarre assassination of the wars of religion – that of Jörg Jenatsch in Chur, the oldest town in Switzerland, in 1639. The capital of the Grisons, it was strategically important because of its Alpine passes. Most of the population had embraced Protestantism, but the Catholic bishop still held his cathedral and his citadel overlooking the town. This was a recipe for trouble. One night in 1621 in the early years of the war, Jenatsch, a Protestant pastor, led a band of men to the castle of Pompeius Planta, a nobleman who led the Catholic faction in the area. The story goes that Planta tried to hide up a chimney, but his presence was given away by his dog. The assassins then laid about him, with Jenatsch himself perhaps applying the death blow with an axe. After the killing, he left the clergy and devoted himself to soldiering.

Jörg Jenatsch, a
contemporary
portrait.

With the help of a French army, he and his followers expelled
Spain's Austrian allies from the Grisons. The French stayed to help
defend the area, but as they grew more and more overbearing,
Jenatsch converted to Catholicism in 1635, and made a secret deal
with the Austrians to expel them. The end result was that the
Grisons was cleared of all foreign troops, and Jenatsch was confirmed as one of the most significant Swiss figures of the war. In
1639, during Chur's Carnival, he hosted a party for his officers.
During the festivities, a group in fancy dress turned up and surrounded him. It all looked like a bit of fun, until one dressed as a
bear hacked Jenatsch to death with an axe – some say the same
weapon he had used to kill Planta eighteen years before. The killer's
identity was never discovered. Was it a Protestant, angry at Jenatsch's
defection, or Pompeius Planta's son taking revenge? We will probably never know.

The Second Choice Victim

If Jenatsch's was the strangest assassination of the era, that of Archbishop James Sharp of St Andrews was perhaps the unluckiest. In Scotland, even before the English Civil War broke out, the Presbyterian Covenanters had taken up arms to resist Charles i's efforts to impose bishops north of the border, and their struggle continued long after the Restoration of his son in 1660. On 3 May 1679 a couple of local lairds, a weaver and half a dozen tenant farmers gathered on Magus Moor, near St Andrews, to try to kill the sheriff-substitute of Fife, a leading persecutor of Covenanters, whom they were expecting to come by. There was no sign of him, but just as it looked as though they had been wasting their time, they were tipped off that Archbishop Sharp's coach was approaching. Sharp had played an important role in restoring Charles ii to the throne, the subsequent imposition of bishops on the Church in Scotland, and the suppression of Presbyterianism. He had become a leading hate-figure for the Covenanters, and in 1668 a would-be assassin had shot at him in the High Street in Edinburgh.

Archbishop Sharp being assassinated in front of his daughter in 1679, as envisaged by an artist 150 years later.

To the plotters, it must have seemed a shame to let their efforts go to waste, so the approach of Sharp looked like a literal godsend, and they exclaimed: 'God hath delivered him into our hands!' And to some at least, not attacking the archbishop would have seemed a repudiation of the Lord's will. Their leader, who had a private quarrel with Sharp, scrupulously declined to take part, but the rest went to it with gusto, their enthusiasm undiminished by the presence in the coach of the archbishop's daughter. The carriage tried to shake them off, but the assassins pursued it for half a mile, firing their pistols. One managed to get ahead of it and struck the horses on their heads with his sword. Another fought the driver and seized the reins. Yet another wounded Sharp with his gun and halted the coach. According to one account, the assassins were worried the archbishop might be invulnerable to bullets, and so they compelled him to get down and set about him furiously with their swords until he lay dead. A few hours after the assassination, one of the killers was shot and wounded by soldiers who came to arrest him, and he died soon after. Another was mortally wounded a month later at the Battle of Bothwell Bridge, in which the Covenanters were defeated by government forces. Four others were executed over the next four years. Another was captured, but his fate after that is unknown. The other two appear to have escaped. The aftermath of the assassination features in Sir Walter Scott's historical novel *Old Mortality* (1816).

AS WE SAW, the Ottoman Empire's attitude to assassination was something of a special case, so I omitted its eighty murders of members of the royal family from the analysis of assassinations during the era of the Wars of Religion. That left 23 to examine. First, the victims: ten were rulers, including six kings and a regent, and there was one queen's husband. Six others were important politicians, while two were senior religious figures, two were generals and three were rebels or former rebels. There were no women. Two of the victims fought fiercely, with both Pizarro and a Persian Shah, Nader, said to have dispatched a number of their assailants. As for location, fifteen happened in Europe, with five in France and four in what is now the UK, including three in Scotland. There were seven in Asia and one in South America.

Although up to three kings, an emperor and possibly a queen (if Mary, Queen of Scots, was involved in Darnley's murder) were behind assassinations, none of them actually did the dirty work themselves. Indeed, on only four out of the 23 occasions did the instigators take part in the killing. As in the Age of Chivalry, assassination remained an overwhelmingly male activity, with Mary, Queen of Scots, the only female suspect in the sample as killer or commissioner. Seven of the killers from this era were lone assassins, but perhaps only two of these were operating without the support of other conspirators. Murder in the family continued its decline. There were no killers among close family members, while among the instigators there was a son and possibly a nephew and a wife. As in the Age of Chivalry, treachery by bodyguards was rare, happening in only two cases. Four or five assassinations, a similar proportion to the Age of Chivalry, involved breach of faith. The Duc de Guise had been enticed to a meeting, William the Silent's murderer had wormed his way into his victim's confidence, while Alessandro de' Medici fell to a honey trap. Fake news as a means of justifying assassination made an appearance, with the killing in 1617 of Louis XIII of France's minister, Concino Concini, justified on the probably spurious grounds that he was resisting arrest. After his death his wife was executed on trumped-up charges of sorcery. In almost half of all cases, eleven, the killers were soldiers or supporters of an enemy. Perhaps not surprisingly, during the Wars of Religion, among the killers or instigators were an archbishop, an abbot, a pastor and a lay brother, but in contrast with the Age of Chivalry, churches and holy places were not favoured venues for assassination, though Cardinal Guise was slain on Christmas Eve.

Religion emerged as the main motive, at work in up to seven of the assassinations. Anger or resentment was the next most significant, seen in up to five, with revenge the main mover in three, and fear in another three. Just two or three were spurred by dynastic ambition, while three had some other political aim. In one case, material reward was probably the key factor, while there were doubts about the sanity of two assassins. Stabbing remained the favourite method, used in thirteen of the nineteen where we know the means. Guns made their first appearance, being employed in six cases including two where the victim was also stabbed, and then there was the mysterious involvement of explosives in the assassination of Lord Darnley. In spite of the appearance of these new technologies, we know of only one assassination, that of the Earl of Moray, where we can be certain the victim was killed at a distance. The only assassination that involved significant collateral damage was that of Kira Yoshinaka by the 47 leaderless samurai, who had to kill at least sixteen other people before reaching their victim.

As to the fate of the assassins, of the 22 cases where we know what happened, in one they were killed immediately, while in another eight, some or all were executed within a year. In four more cases, at least some of those responsible met a violent end within five years. They say that what goes around comes around, but sometimes it takes a while. So, it was sixteen years before the duc de Guise, instigator of Gaspard de Coligny's murder, was himself assassinated, while fate took eighteen years to catch up with Jörg Jenatsch. In at least three cases, the killers escaped punishment altogether, and in another, some of the assassins went unpunished, while one of the 47 leaderless samurai was pardoned. At least two assassins were rewarded, as was the family of William the Silent's murderer. The 47 leaderless samurai became legendary figures in Japan, while the man who killed the unpopular royal favourite, the Duke of Buckingham, in 1628 became a hero in England, and the pope considered canonizing the murderer of the French king Henry

III. At least eight of the assassinations were followed by disorder and instability, but there had already been instability before the killings, and in the case of Henry IV of France, the assassination generated less disorder than might have been expected. Following Nader Shah's murder in 1747, his empire fell apart, while in spite of the murder of Alessandro de' Medici, his family's regime endured for another two centuries. Of the sixteen assassinations with motives and outcomes clear enough to make a judgement, half a dozen might be seen as clearly successful with five others partially successful. One was a distinct failure, and four more of a failure than a success.

5

THE AGE OF REVOLUTION

The year 1789: the French Revolution. One of the most memorable dates in history. Much of the century or so that followed would be dominated by revolutions and wars of national liberation. But while the king of France still had another three decades to sit securely on his throne, a people in the Philippines on the other side of the world tried to light the torch of liberty. The Seven Years War, which raged from 1756 to 1763, is sometimes dubbed the 'First World War', as the struggle between a British-led coalition on one side and France and Spain and their allies on the other spread across five continents. Among the Ilokano people on the biggest Philippine island, Luzon, there was discontent about high taxes, monopolies and forced labour imposed by the Spanish colonial authorities. So when the British launched an attack in September 1762, a humble courier named Diego Silang decided Spain's difficulty might represent the Ilokano's opportunity. He raised a force and drove the Spanish out of his home city of Vigan, hoping to establish an independent Ilokano state, though he also recognized King George III of England as his sovereign. The British gave him presents and titles, but promised military help never arrived.

Silang still managed to defy the Spanish civil authorities, but the Catholic Church showed it was made of sterner stuff. As the rebel imposed financial levies on priests, the Bishop of Vigan proclaimed himself the new ruler of the province, then excommunicated

Silang and ordered his followers to desert him. When that did not work, on 28 May 1763 he tried assassination, persuading two of the rebel's friends to go round to his house and shoot him in the back. Silang died in the arms of his wife, Gabriela, who took over as leader of the revolt, earning the title 'the Philippines' Joan of Arc', but after four months she was captured and executed along with her remaining followers.

The French Revolution

Twenty-six years later, the French monarchy was overthrown, and assassination would be used both for and against the revolution. On the very day the Bastille was stormed, 14 July 1789, it reared its ugly head. Jacques de Flesselles, then in his sixties, was provost of merchants in Paris, one of the most important officials in the city. The authorities faced threats from left and right, with extreme revolutionary mobs roaming the streets threatening the homes of the rich, while fears that a royal army might storm the city were also rife. So a group of prosperous bourgeois appointed itself as the municipal government, and set up a Permanent Committee at the Hôtel de Ville to oversee the defence of the French capital, with Flesselles presiding. The committee decided to create a citizens' militia, but when thousands appeared outside the Hôtel on 13 July demanding weapons, Flesselles seemed distinctly unenthusiastic. Perhaps he thought these were the wrong kind of citizens. Anyway, he managed to rustle up just three muskets, and suggested they try their luck at a Carthusian monastery and a local gun factory, but this proved a wild goose chase. The citizenry now marked Flesselles down as an 'enemy of the people', who had deliberately obstructed their attempt to arm themselves. The next morning a huge crowd showed up at Les Invalides, and with the garrison aiding and abetting rather than resisting, they were able to equip themselves with 30,000 muskets. Then what they needed was gunpowder, which they secured through the iconic storming of the

Bastille, during which more than eighty of the assailants were killed. When the governor surrendered, he was murdered by the mob. Soon afterwards, Flesselles showed his face on the steps of the Hôtel de Ville, and was killed by a pistol shot. No one knows who fired it. Then he was decapitated, and his head was paraded around Paris on a pike.

But as in the Philippines, so in France, the most famous assassination was not by, but of, a revolutionary. One of the most incendiary firebrands of this combustible era was Jean-Paul Marat. As a young man, he had studied medicine and become an expert on diseases of the eye. He practised as a doctor in London and the Netherlands, but fell into debt, and there was a story that he was caught trying to steal medals from a museum. On his return to France, he managed to carve out a niche as a fashionable physician, his writing paper adorned with a fake coat of arms. Working in the household of Louis xvi's brother, the Comte d'Artois, he acquired as patroness a marquise whom he appeared to cure of tuberculosis, though Marat's reputation suffered when it was discovered that his patent treatment was actually just chalk and water. The proto-revolutionary wrote scientific papers on a number of subjects, but challenged the accepted orthodoxy of Isaac Newton's theories, and, to his great resentment, he was never admitted to the prestigious Academy of Sciences.

Half-Sardinian, Marat was dark and intense, 'with a cadaverous complexion', according to John Moore, an English doctor who observed him in Paris. The revolutionary claimed to work 21 hours a day and sleep for just two. He seemed unable to keep his body still, and when he was reading his mouth twitched convulsively. On top of that, he had a disfiguring skin disease which meant he gave out a horrible smell, while, according to a contemporary, 'open sores, often running, pitted his terrible countenance'. Some said he contracted it after hiding in the sewers during one of his many run-ins with the authorities over his extremism. He wore ostentatiously grubby clothes – this was a time when any touch of elegance might imply counter-revolutionary sympathies – with a dirty red bandana soaked in vinegar on his head to soothe the constant irritation from his skin.

Marat was 46 when the Revolution broke out, and it was the making of him, bringing, as he put it, 'the hope of seeing humanity avenged and myself installed in the place which I deserved'. He started a newspaper, the vitriolic *L'Ami du peuple*, which fulminated against all and sundry, seeing treachery and betrayal everywhere, and declaring: 'In order to ensure public tranquillity, 200,000 heads must be cut off.' He delivered blood-curdling warnings against the dangers of moderation: 'Let your opponents triumph for an instant and torrents of blood will flow. They'll cut your throats without mercy, they'll slit the bellies of your wives, and in order to forever extinguish your love of liberty, their bloody hands will reach into your children's entrails and rip their hearts out.' Marat was elected to the Convention, France's first republican assembly, where he joined the Montagnard faction of far-left Jacobins. Dr Moore recorded that he seemed 'always to contemplate the Assembly . . . with eyes of menace or contempt. He speaks in a hollow, croaking voice, with affected solemnity.' He was so extreme 'that even the party which he wishes to support seem to be ashamed of him, and he is shunned and apparently detested by everyone else'. Whenever he entered the Convention, he was 'avoided on all sides'. As he sat down, those nearby would get up and move away. If he should touch a fellow member, they would recoil 'as from the touch of a noxious reptile' and shout: 'Don't touch me!' For Marat, it was all water off a duck's back. He considered that having a wide circle of enemies proved he was on the right track.

Besides, outside the Convention, it was a completely different story. Marat was the darling of the crowd. In April 1793, taking advantage of the absence of a number of Jacobins in the provinces, the more moderate Girondins had him arrested. In court, the sansculottes cheered him wildly. Then, when he was acquitted, they carried him shoulder high into the Convention, brandishing weapons and proclaiming their willingness to fight to defend him. With the tables turned, over the next few weeks more than twenty Girondins were executed. Marat read out the names of the condemned with relish. A number of others fled to Normandy where they plotted against the revolutionary, who they said was destroying liberty and creating a dictatorship. One of those who fell under their spell was a 24-year-old woman named Charlotte Corday, who came from a noble family that had fallen on hard times. Tall and strong, she had been educated at a convent, but then studied Plutarch and the classics, as well as the great Enlightenment writers such as Rousseau and Voltaire.

Having promised to help the exiled Girondins in some unspecified way, on 11 July 1793 Corday arrived in Paris. Women had played an unusually prominent role in the Revolution, for example, during the March on Versailles in October 1789 when thousands descended on the royal palace demanding cheaper bread and forcing the king and queen to return to Paris. Now Corday formed a

Charlotte Corday: an engraving based on a painting by the 19th-century American artist Alonzo Chappel.

plan to assassinate Marat in the Convention, but by this time the summer heat was too much for the revolutionary's tormented skin, and he spent his days lying at home in a medicinal bath from which he continued to conduct business and write his newspaper, so Corday decided to kill him there. Early on the morning of 13 July, she bought a kitchen knife which she hid in her bodice and set off to Marat's house, but the sister of the revolutionary's mistress turned her away saying he was too ill to see her. So she wrote him a letter, declaring: 'I come from Caen. Your love of country must make you wish to know the plots that are hatching there.' After it had been delivered, she put on her best clothes and set off again. This time the cook tried to turn her away, but when Corday remonstrated, Marat's mistress came to the door. She repeated that the revolutionary was too ill. Could she come back in a few days?

Marat heard the commotion, and asked who it was. On being told it was the woman who had sent the letter about Caen, he insisted they let her in. In addition to the knife hidden in her bodice, Corday had pinned in her dress her baptismal certificate and an 'Address to the French People' explaining her motives. She found Marat immersed in a copper slipper bath, with a damp turban on his head. Across the top of the bath lay a board covered with documents and letters. Corday reeled off a list of eighteen Girondin deputies she said were working against the Jacobins. Marat wrote down their names, saying: 'They shall soon all be guillotined.' Corday immediately took out her knife and stabbed him in the chest, severing a main artery and puncturing his lung. Marat shouted for help and his distraught mistress ran in and put her hand over the wound, trying to stop the blood. In a few moments, he was dead. Corday had probably landed an amateur's lucky strike. (When, at her trial, the prosecutor remarked on the skill with which she had struck, Corday was horrified, exclaiming: 'Good heavens! He takes me for an assassin!')

Her mission accomplished, the young woman calmly walked off, but one of Marat's colleagues on *L'Ami du peuple* hit her with a chair and flung her to the ground. Her response was: 'The deed is done. The monster is dead.' Soon the authorities arrived, and Corday was taken to prison. One journalist was astounded at her composure: she went off 'as though she were going to a ball'. Four days later she was put on trial. When the prosecutor asked what she had hoped to gain by killing Marat, she replied: 'Peace for my country.' But did she believe by killing him, she had killed 'all the Marats'? 'This one dead – the others perhaps will be afraid,' she said. Then she reproached the metropolitan elite: 'It is only in Paris that people have been hypnotized by the man. In the provinces he has always been regarded as a monster.' Declaring she had been a republican since before the Revolution, she invoked Chanakya's defence of assassination: 'I killed one man to save a hundred thousand; a villain to save innocents; a savage wild beast to give repose to my country.' She was executed the next day, impressing friend and foe by her calm courage, and comparing herself to Brutus. This must have been especially annoying for the revolutionary authorities who had adorned France's town halls and public spaces with busts of the Roman assassin as the embodiment of republican virtue. On her last journey, she made polite conversation with the executioner. When the guillotine came into view, he stood up to hide it from her, but she asked him to sit down, saying she was 'curious' to see it. After her head was cut off, the assistant executioner held it up and slapped her face, arousing so much anger in the crowd that he was sent to gaol for a while. The Jacobins insisted Corday could not have been a virgin and that her deed must have been directed by a man sharing her bed, even though she had always maintained she acted alone. They ordered a post-mortem examination, perhaps hoping the result might dent growing public sympathy for the assassin. If there was going to be a martyr from this episode, the revolutionaries wanted to make sure it was Marat. Unfortunately for them the answer came back that Corday's virtue was intact.

As it turned out, the firebrand was almost certainly more useful to the Revolution dead than alive, more effective as a murdered

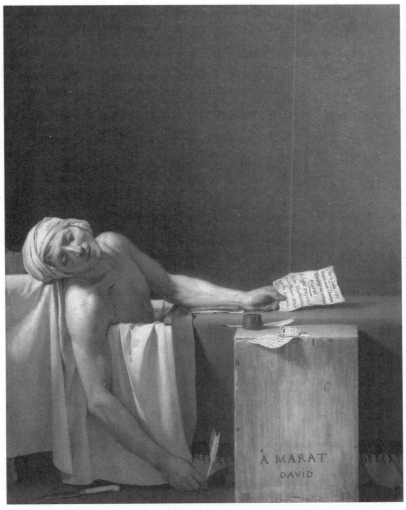

Jacques-Louis David, *The Death of Marat*, 1793, oil on canvas.

martyr than as a living intransigent fanatic. One contemporary said Charlotte Corday had 'killed a man and created a god'. Having de-Christianized France, the revolutionaries needed replacements for traditional saints. Marat's body was displayed for as long as the summer heat would allow. Then he was given a hero's funeral. Poems were written about him. His bust popped up everywhere, sometimes replacing images of Christ or the Madonna. His ashes were given a place of honour in the Pantheon. Streets, squares and even towns were named after him. The painter David depicted him as a martyr, turning the scene of his death in a bath into a masterpiece, and some of Marat's pet schemes, such as introducing the death penalty for hoarders of food, were enacted. Corday too would become a martyr, featuring in paintings, plays and poetry, but her deed failed to end the Revolution's Reign of Terror during which 17,000 were executed, and which went on for another long year.

A Revolutionary King

Not all revolutionaries came from the wrong side of the tracks. Some were monarchs – described in Europe as 'enlightened despots' – who wanted to modernize their countries, often putting themselves at loggerheads with those doing nicely out of the status quo: rulers such as Catherine the Great of Russia, Frederick the Great of Prussia, Josef II of Austria and Gustav III of Sweden. Gustav became king at the age of 25 in 1771 and within a year he had introduced a new constitution that reduced the power of parliament and increased his own. He used it to bring in a slate of reforms – banning torture of suspects, freeing the press, introducing religious toleration, promoting free trade and economic development. A cultured man, he wrote plays, contributed to an opera, built an opera house and founded the Swedish Academy, but the nobility were unhappy about his newfangled ideas. So, like many rulers faced with troubles at home, Gustav tried to create a diversion by fomenting war abroad. The Turkish Ottoman Empire attacked Russia in 1787, and the Swedish king sought to take advantage by declaring war on the Russians the following year, but a group of more than a hundred army officers went behind his back and wrote to Catherine the Great calling for peace negotiations. They also demanded Gustav's abdication. Even when he offered a full pardon if they would withdraw the documents, they would not back down, and Gustav faced more trouble when he had to fight off an invasion from Denmark.

The king had one of the officers executed and he imprisoned many more. Then, in 1789, he appealed to the three lower estates of the realm – the clergy, burghers and peasants – and they stripped the nobility of their powers and privileges, turning the king into an absolute monarch. By now Gustav's opponents were calling him a 'tyrant', and a group of disgruntled nobles led by an old general, Carl Fredrik Pechlin, devised a plan. At midnight on 16 March 1792 Gustav was due to attend a masked ball in the very Royal Opera House in Stockholm that he himself had commissioned. Shortly beforehand, he was having dinner with friends when he received an anonymous letter pleading with him to postpone the ball until 'more positive' times, because there were people who 'only breathe hatred and revenge' and wished to murder him. 'Bandits,' it continued, 'do not like lanterns; there is nothing more serviceable for an assassination than darkness and disguise.' It was actually written by a colonel in the Life Guards, but Gustav had got used to receiving threats and he decided to ignore it.

When he arrived at the ball, the king was immediately surrounded by men in black masks, and a young aristocratic captain,

Jacob Johan Anckarström being flogged after assassinating the Swedish king Gustav III.

Jacob Johan Anckarström, moved in behind him and shot him in the back. (Earlier, Anckarström had been accused of defaming the king's name, but the case against him was suspended for lack of evidence.) Immediately, the doors were sealed and no one was allowed to leave. The police found the captain's pistol, and he was arrested and charged. It had been loaded with broken shot, making the wound especially painful as Gustav languished for thirteen days, finally giving up the ghost on 29 March. He made a deathbed plea for clemency for his assassin, but to no avail. Anckarström was flogged publicly for three days, then executed. The king's assassination inspired Verdi's opera *The Masked Ball*. Gustav's son took the throne as King Gustav IV and ruled for seventeen years. He continued his father's side-lining of the aristocracy, but a series of military disasters during the Napoleonic Wars led to him being deposed by liberal elements in the army and the government.

Assassination of Modernizers in Asia

In Japan, too, revolution was top-down. In 1868 a coup d'état finally ended centuries of military dictatorship by the shoguns and brought the restoration of imperial rule under the emperor Meiji. In its final years, the shogunate had been humiliated by Western powers, who bombarded Japanese ports and dictated treaties. The emperor's advisers promptly launched a programme of modernization so the country could close the gap with the West, but the traditionalists were not going to take this lying down. The decade following the coup saw four significant rebellions and eight assassinations. Yokoi Shonan was the son of a samurai and had worked for the shogun government before being put under house arrest because of his demands for change. He wanted economic reform, the opening of the country to foreign trade, and the establishment of a modern Western-style military. The restored imperial regime appointed him a senior state counsellor. At about two in the afternoon on 15 February 1869, Yokoi, now aged 59, was on his way home in a litter from official business at the Imperial Palace in Kyoto when suddenly his conveyance was confronted by half a dozen samurai armed to the teeth. Yokoi got out and drew his short sword, but he had been ill, and his assailants made short work of him, shooting him, cutting off his head and then fleeing. Four of the six were arrested. They garnered a lot of sympathy by denouncing Yokoi as a traitor conspiring with foreigners, and they were not executed until November 1870.

Less than eight months after the attack on Yokoi, 64-year-old Ōmura Masujirō, regarded as the 'father of the modern Japanese army', was also assassinated in Kyoto. He was a samurai himself and had been an important adviser to the shogun government, specializing in military policy. After the imperial restoration, he became senior vice-minister of the Army-Navy Ministry and bought ships and rifles from the West. He wanted to replace the old system of military service based on hereditary soldiers by one of universal conscription. Other reforms included banning anyone other than the official military and the uniformed police from carrying swords. Many samurai, already feeling under attack as the central government increased its powers, saw this as another assault on their ancient privileges, and Ōmura was well aware that there were plenty of people who would like to kill him. While he was looking for premises for a new school to train non-commissioned officers, he was warned that some suspicious characters had been following him. On the night of 9 October 1869 he and his colleagues were relaxing in an inn on a street called Kiyamachi Dori that was famous for its cherry blossom and also boasted the residencies of two important feudal lords from the old regime. Five years earlier a reformist politician had been murdered on this very street. All at once, a band of eight men burst into the inn. During a fearful struggle, Ōmura was wounded several times, and narrowly escaped with his life by hiding in a bathtub full of dirty water. The worst injury was to his leg, and obstinately refused to heal. Eventually he was taken to see an eminent Western surgeon in

Osaka, who wanted to amputate the limb immediately, but for a person of Ōmura's rank this required the government's permission. It prevaricated and the minister died on 7 December. His assailants were sentenced to death, then reprieved, then finally executed a year after the attack. Ōmura's death did not stop the reform programme, and in 1873 military service was made compulsory for most men.

Among the other leading figures assassinated during this turbulent decade was Home Minister Ōkubo Toshimichi, considered to be the most powerful man in Japan, who was killed in 1878 by another group of disgruntled samurai – offended by his policy of prioritizing internal reform at the expense of their plan to conquer Korea. After that, the pace of assassinations slackened, but 1889 saw another important modernizer fall victim, the minister of education, Mori Arinori. He developed a new centralized system, from primary school to university, and even advocated adopting the Western alphabet. Mori was murdered by an ultra-traditionalist who claimed he had shown insufficient respect at an important Shinto shrine.

Reformers also became targets for assassins in other Eastern countries. Like Japan, Burma found itself under threat from the West in the persons of the British in India, and for the Burmese too, the obvious solution seemed to be: if you can't beat them, join them. As King Pagan's army suffered heavy losses, and Rangoon and other cities fell in the Second Anglo-Burmese War of 1852–3, he was overthrown by his two half-brothers, Mindon and Kanaung. Mindon became king, and Kanaung his right-hand man and designated heir. On taking the throne, Mindon quickly negotiated a ceasefire, while he launched a comprehensive modernization programme, giving Kanaung responsibility for new technologies and reforming the military. Under the prince's direction, factories started making rifles and ammunition to replace antiquated muskets. He bought artillery and steam ships from Europe, and reorganized the army, sending some officers to the

West for training. He also helped Mindon remove trade barriers
and reform administration, taxation, the police and the penal code.

While they were young, Mindon's sons put up with having
Kanaung named as their father's heir, but as they got older they
found this more irksome, particularly when the king got their uncle
to discipline them if they stepped out of line. On 2 August 1866
two of the princes tried to mount a palace coup. Kanaung was chairing a top-level meeting on fiscal policy when they burst in, swords
drawn. They killed six top officials as well as their uncle, decapi-
tating him and parading his head. It was the prelude to a full-scale
rebellion, which saw the assassination of three other princes, but
Mindon was able to defeat it, and the two rebel princes fled the
country. The king also had to fight off a rebellion by Kanaung's
son, but none of this derailed the modernization project, and in
1873 Mindon introduced measures to establish a free press.

Ōkubo Toshimichi,
painted after his
death.

Latin America

Revolution also coursed through Latin America, as former colonies threw off the yolk of European rule, and then often fought each other over the boundaries of the new countries created, while at the same time struggling to develop their economies. Here assassination became endemic. Argentina, Bolivia, the Dominican Republic, Ecuador, Guatemala, Paraguay, Peru and Uruguay all lost presidents or former presidents – Uruguay on three occasions. Bolivia's Pedro Blanco Soto lasted just a week in 1829. Taking office on Christmas Day, he was dead by New Year's Day. In at least three cases, the assassinated president had himself taken power by force. Half a dozen of the victims faced serious domestic discontent. Three were killed after their countries got into economic difficulties, another after losing territory in a war, and yet another after a tyrannical campaign of imprisonment, banishment and murder against those who opposed him.

President Gabriel García Moreno of Ecuador was also tough on opposition. A devout Catholic, he seized power in 1860 after the country had suffered fifteen years of disorder. He handed a lot of power to the Church, putting it in control of education, for example. This antagonized liberals, and he faced a number of rebellions. On the other hand, he was also an active reformer, centralizing government, reducing corruption and strengthening the economy, and before he became president, he had written in support of tyrannicide. After early morning mass in Quito on 6 August 1875, President Moreno ran into Captain Faustino Rayo and had quite a long chat with him. Rayo, who had left Colombia after finding himself on the losing side in a civil war, had fought bravely in Moreno's army, and the pair had been on good terms until relations soured when the Jesuits complained that Rayo had been exploiting the native population. On this August morning, their encounter seemed amicable, but in fact Rayo was involved in a plot. A few hours later, as the president was climbing the steps of government headquarters with his aide-de-camp, the captain and a group of young men with liberal sympathies fell in quietly behind them. The first sign that anything was amiss came when the president's hat flew off as Rayo landed a glancing blow with a machete. The other conspirators fired guns, but managed to inflict only grazes. An official coming out of the building to post a letter tried to grab Rayo's arm, but the captain was too strong, and after a short struggle, he continued the attack. His second blow broke Moreno's arm just as the president was trying to open his jacket to reach his pistol. The aide, by now also wounded, shouted for help and three guards ran from the nearby artillery barracks to investigate. Rayo roared a familiar refrain: 'Die, tyrant, die!' Moreno replied: 'God never dies,' then fell about three metres to the plaza below, landing outside a tavern.

Women ran from nearby shops to help, but as one cradled the president in her arms, Rayo burst through the crowd and landed two fatal blows to his head. The other conspirators fired more shots, but these were as wayward as their first efforts. Then Rayo tried to make his escape, but he was grabbed by a lieutenant and two non-commissioned officers. As they were marching him away, someone in the throng shouted: 'Kill the assassin!' and another soldier stepped forward and blew Rayo's brains out. Then the mob took his body to the cemetery, mutilated it and left the remains for the vultures to feed on. The killing of Rayo before he could be questioned helped spawn a host of conspiracy theories, just as the murder of Lee Harvey Oswald would ninety years later. Who shouted: 'Kill the assassin'? Was it an order from an army officer or just a cry of anger from the crowd? There were stories that the assassin's pockets were stuffed with large sums of money, that the Freemasons were behind the murder, or Germany's 'iron chancellor' Otto von Bismarck, whom Moreno's supporters considered anti-Catholic, or maybe both. The conspirators denied it all. Certainly, they were, like Moreno, devout Catholics. Nor did they seem to have much money. One had to pledge his father's credit

The assassination of President Gabriel García Moreno of Ecuador, according to *Les Mystères de la franc-maçonnerie* (1886). There were claims that Freemasons were behind his murder.

to buy a revolver. An associate of Rayo's was executed for the murder, though he almost certainly had nothing to do with it. Of the three gunmen who helped the killer, one was executed, another fled to Peru, while the third lay low for many years and was never brought to justice. For Ecuador, Moreno's assassination was followed by another long period of disorder.

The Balkans – National Heroes Assassinated

During the Age of Revolution, the Balkans were a kind of European version of Latin America, as countries such as Greece, Romania, Serbia and Albania fought for and won their freedom from the Ottoman Empire. In the wake of the commotion came the assassinations of a motley collection of notables – a president, a prime minister, a former prime minister, princes, rebels and revolutionaries, men of the left and of the right. Nor did being a national hero provide immunity. Ioannis Kapodistrias, Greece's first head of state after it won independence, was murdered on the steps of a church on 9 October 1831 by relatives of warlord Petrobey Mavromichalis, whom he had had arrested. Mavromichalis was also a hero of the rebellion against the Turks, but he resented the reforms Kapodistrias introduced to try to modernize the country. Stefan Nikolov Stambolov, who served for seven years as Bulgaria's prime minister, was dubbed the 'Bulgarian Bismarck'. He had fought as a guerrilla against the Ottoman Empire and then moved into politics, becoming regarded as one of the founders of modern Bulgaria, though his despotic rule angered plenty of people, and he resigned as prime minister in 1894. On 15 July 1895 three assassins halted his carriage, in which he was travelling with his bodyguard, and brutally stabbed him to death.

Assassination of a Man of Ideas

While the assassins were busy, so were the theoreticians, but the Age of Revolution saw perhaps the first assassination of one of their number. Not Marat. Though he was a propagandist for extreme ideas, he was murdered because of his deeds. The German August von Kotzebue, on the other hand, although he had done some work as an agent for the tsar of Russia, was killed because of his writings. His plays included a drama about the assassinated conquistador Francisco Pizarro, but the works that would cost him his life were his regular fierce attacks on those demanding political liberty. By 1819 what we now call Germany was still made up of more than thirty smaller independent states, though that was far fewer than the hundreds that constituted the Holy Roman Empire at the time of the Thirty Years War. Napoleon had turned much of it into a French satellite, but at Leipzig in 1813 he had suffered a decisive defeat. Many Germans hoped that driving out the French would bring liberty, but the leading Central European statesman of the time, Count Metternich from the Austrian Empire, was determined to resist such dangerous notions. One of those who volunteered to fight Napoleon in the campaign that saw his final defeat at Waterloo in 1815 was a nineteen-year-old German theology student named Karl Ludwig Sand. On his return, he joined one of the secret student societies that were springing up across Germany.

The nineteenth-century French novelist Alexandre Dumas is best known for books such as *The Three Musketeers* and *The Count of Monte Cristo*, but he also compiled an eight-volume history of *Celebrated Crimes*, which included a full account of the one committed by Karl Ludwig Sand. Dumas noted that young men like Sand had fought Napoleon 'in the name of liberty, but soon perceived they had been used as tools to establish European despotism'. By the autumn of 1817 Sand was incensed by Kotzebue's 'venomous insults' against the cause of liberalism, noting in his diary: 'By what a fury that man is possessed against . . . all who love Germany!' By May of the following year, he was confiding that he was 'amazed there is none among us found courageous enough to drive a knife into the breast of Kotzebue', because 'a man is nothing in comparison with a nation; he is a unity compared with millions.' The last entry in his diary comes on New Year's Eve 1818, when he commits himself to killing 'the wretch, the traitor, the seducer of youth, the infamous Kotzebue'.

By this time, the theology student had become an assiduous attender of anatomy classes, exhibiting particular interest in the heart. One day, when a friend entered his room, Sand leapt on him, hit him lightly on the forehead, and then, as the friend put up his hands to protect himself, struck him hard on the chest, remarking: 'when you want to kill a man, that is the way to do it; you threaten the face, he puts up his hands, and while he does so you thrust a dagger into his heart.' His friend just laughed. By the spring of 1819 Sand's friends noted he was exhibiting unusual 'serenity'. Without telling them, on 23 March he went to Kotzebue's home in Mannheim. When he first called, he was told the writer was out walking in the park. After failing to find him, Sand went back to the house, but was sent away again because Kotzebue was having breakfast. On the third attempt at five in the afternoon, the student at last came face to face with his quarry. Using the gambit he had practised on his friend, Sand stabbed him in the heart. According to Dumas, 'Kotzebue gave one cry, staggered, and fell back into an armchair: he was dead.' As he cried out, the writer's six-year-old daughter came running into the room, and threw herself on her dead father. Sand was so overcome with remorse that he plunged his dagger into his own chest. Wounded though he was, he managed to stagger into the street, where he encountered a routine patrol of soldiers. As he saw them, he stabbed himself again and fell unconscious.

Sand was taken to hospital, where for three months he hovered between life and death. There was no doubt about his guilt. The university authorities had raided his flat and found a letter in which he railed against Kotzebue as 'a real talking machine emitting all sorts of detestable speech and pernicious advice. His voice is skilful in removing from us all anger and bitterness against the most unjust measures, and is just such as kings require to put us to sleep again in that old hazy slumber which is the death of nations.' Bemoaning the fact that no one else would take responsibility for removing Kotzebue, Sand decided that though he himself was 'not born for murder', he must do the deed, adding: 'I was to pass gently through this life as a preacher of the gospel . . . But would that suffice to avert the danger that threatens Germany?'

By May 1820 the student, though still weak, had recovered enough to be prepared for execution. During all the time he was planning and carrying out the assassination, his religious faith had never wavered, and in his final letter to his parents, he wrote: 'God comes to my help, and gives me courage and firmness.' He met his end bravely, expressing 'contempt . . . for everything fragile and earthly' when 'weighed against the fulfilment of an idea'. The authorities were afraid of disorder, so they moved Sand's beheading from eleven to five in the morning, and drafted in an extra 1,500 soldiers. They were helped by cold, rainy weather, but even so, 'all Mannheim' – perhaps 20,000 people – turned out, throwing flowers at the coach carrying the assassin on his last journey. Sand had promised not to make a speech from the scaffold, but in a low voice that could be heard only by those around him, he intoned: 'I take God to witness that I die for the freedom of Germany.' As the sword fell on his neck, 'notwithstanding the efforts of the soldiers, their line was broken through; men and women rushed upon the scaffold, the blood was wiped up to the last drop with handkerchiefs; the chair upon which Sand had sat was broken and divided into pieces, and those who could not obtain one, cut fragments of bloodstained wood from the scaffold itself.' In spite of this outpouring, far from advancing the cause of liberty, if anything Kotzebue's assassination set it back. Metternich persuaded the German princes to clamp down on universities, introducing censorship, outlawing student societies and blacklisting teachers, writers and students suspected of holding liberal views.

A Trio of American Presidents

As we saw, during the sixteenth and seventeenth centuries, religion was the leading oxygen for assassination, and as politics started to replace it, a new theory was advanced. It was an Italian duke whose family was down on its luck, Carlo Pisacane, who declared: 'The propaganda of the idea is a chimera. Ideas result from deeds, not the other way around.' He argued you needed violence to generate publicity for a cause. Pamphlets, posters and meetings on their own were not enough. Pisacane died fighting for Italian reunification in 1857. He led a small rebellion in Calabria that was defeated when the local peasantry sided with the authorities to suppress it. Pisacane was reluctant to order his men to fire on the peasants, so instead they tried to escape. He was wounded and later died of his injuries.

While the idea of the 'propaganda of the deed' was crystallizing in Europe, the United States experienced one of the most notorious assassinations in history, but it was committed by a right-wing reactionary rather than a revolutionary. In mid-April 1865 it looked as though the American Civil War was finally coming to an end. Robert E. Lee, the South's great general, had just surrendered, though other Confederate armies were still in the field, and some would not give up for another couple of months. Unsurprisingly, the victorious Unionist president, Abraham Lincoln, was much hated in the slave-owning states, and those who wanted to portray him as a tyrant had plenty of ammunition. Although he was first elected on just 40 per cent of the vote, he had widened presidential powers to an unprecedented degree, suspending habeas corpus and introducing martial law, for example, though his supporters could claim he had exercised his power cautiously and had held a presidential election in 1864 in spite of the war. On 14 April 1865, Good Friday, a well-known 26-year-old actor named John Wilkes Booth went to Ford's Theatre in Washington, DC, to pick up his mail. He was not appearing in the current production, *Our American Cousin*, though he had often performed at Ford's. Now he heard that President Lincoln and his wife, along with the Union army commander, General Ulysses S. Grant, were due to attend that night's performance.

Booth's father had been something of a star of the London stage, before abandoning his wife and family and heading off to America with his new love, who then gave birth to John Wilkes Booth (named after the great English radical John Wilkes). It was not a happy home, with Booth Sr prone to fits of depression and other mental illness, and his son ran away at seventeen and went on the stage himself. His two brothers also became actors, making the Booths America's most famous theatrical family. John grew into a drinker, a ladies' man and a white supremacist. He did not fight in the Civil War, but he did approach the Confederate secret service with a plan to kidnap Lincoln early in 1865. It came at a time when problems with his voice were damaging his theatrical career and when some of his investments had gone sour. The plot failed because Lincoln did not appear where the conspirators were expecting him.

On 11 April Lincoln had hinted in a speech that more black people might be allowed to vote. Booth was incensed. 'That is the last speech he will ever make,' he exclaimed, and came up with a scheme for the assassination of the entire Union leadership: Lincoln, Vice-President Andrew Johnson and Secretary of State William Henry Seward. His chosen accomplices were David Herold, a 23-year-old pharmacist, a 29-year-old German immigrant named George Artzerodt and a former Confederate soldier, Lewis Paine, who had been wounded at Gettysburg and had lost two brothers in the war. He was given the task of killing Seward while Artzerodt dealt with Johnson and Booth murdered Lincoln. Herold was to help the assassins escape. Vice-President Johnson was a southerner and a former slave-owner who had changed sides. During the afternoon of 14 April, Booth delivered a note to his house, saying: 'Don't wish to disturb you. Are you at home?' Was this an attempt to discover the vice-president's whereabouts or was there collusion of some kind between the two men?

That was not the only thing Booth did. He knew Ford's like the back of his hand, so at some point he popped in and drilled a peep hole in the wall of Lincoln's box. He also handed a letter to a fellow actor, John Matthews, asking him to deliver it to a newspaper editor. Matthews forgot. Booth then performed another important

John Wilkes Booth,
c. 1862.

task – downing a whisky or two in the bar next to the theatre – and got rather maudlin when he saw a group of Confederate prisoners, declaiming: 'Great God! I have no longer a country!'

Lincoln knew very well he was a target. The previous summer, a sniper had hit his hat as he rode back home from the White House. Early on in his presidency he had received some bad press for what was seen as his timidity in pulling out of a stop in Baltimore after threats to his life, and from then on he usually resisted pleas to take fewer risks. For example, he visited the Confederate capital of Richmond just hours after it fell. Now on Good Friday 1865, Mrs Lincoln played the opposite role to Julius Caesar's wife. Calpurnia had tried to persuade her husband not to attend the senate, but Mrs Lincoln urged hers to go to the play even though he was tired. Knowing Grant had already cried off, Lincoln gave in to her pleas.

The president's regular bodyguard was Ward Hill Lamon, known for sleeping outside his boss's door at the White House armed to the teeth, but Lincoln had sent him on a job to Richmond. So his protection that night fell to John F. Parker. Parker was an interesting choice for presidential bodyguard. He had been hauled up before the police authorities for being drunk on duty and for sleeping on duty. At the interval, he popped into the saloon next door for a little refreshment. He may even have been imbibing there at the same time that Booth took another drink, a brandy, as part of his final preparations. The actor slipped back into the theatre, then took a route below the stage. When he approached the president's box, which the Lincolns were sharing with a couple of friends, there was no sign of Parker at his post in the passage-way outside it. Was he still in the saloon, or had he gone to watch the play? Either way, when Booth approached, the only person stationed outside the president's box was his messenger, Charlie Forbes. After Booth gave him a card or note, Forbes let him in. Unusually for assassins, the actor was already quite a famous figure, and Lincoln may well have seen him perform.

Booth had apparently chosen a moment in the play which he knew would provoke loud laughter, and before either Lincoln, his wife or their friends had spotted his presence, he shot the president in the head with his pistol. Many of the audience probably did not hear the bang, or perhaps thought it was part of the action. As Mrs Lincoln shouted 'Murder!' one of the president's friends tried to grab Booth, but the assassin stabbed him in the arm, and then leapt down about twelve feet to the stage, shouting 'Sic semper tyrannis!' – so always to tyrants – the words Brutus was supposed to have uttered as he stabbed Julius Caesar, and the motto of the state of Virginia. As he landed, the actor broke his ankle, but managed to hobble out of the theatre, find his waiting horse and ride off into the night with Herold, as a Unionist colonel set off in pursuit. The authorities threw a security cordon around the u.s. capital, but Booth got away. Lincoln died just before half past

John Wilkes Booth about to shoot President Abraham Lincoln at Ford's Theatre, Washington, DC, based on a glass slide made within ten years of the event.

seven the next morning, but the rest of the assassination plot did not go so smoothly. Paine got into Seward's house, where the secretary of state was ill in bed, and stabbed him, but Seward would survive, while Artzerodt slunk off home without attempting an attack on Johnson.

He and Paine were quickly arrested, but as Booth and Herold disappeared, a $50,000 reward was put on the assassin's head with a price of $25,000 on his assistant's. The pair were helped by a number of Confederate sympathizers, but a black assistant ferryman reported having seen the fugitives even though his boss said they had not. Twelve days after the murder, the fugitives were tracked down to a barn in Virginia where they were hiding disguised as Confederate soldiers. Herold gave himself up, but Booth refused, and when Unionist soldiers set fire to the barn, he came out armed with a rifle and a pistol. He was shot in the neck, and died a few hours later. After Lincoln's murder, Booth's actor friend John Matthews suddenly remembered the letter the assassin had given

him, and opened it. He saw to his horror that it was a justification
of Booth's deed. He promptly destroyed it, but later recollected
that the actor had written: 'Many, I know – the vulgar herd – will
blame me for what I am about to do, but posterity, I am sure, will
justify me.' Booth had quoted the example of Brutus, saying
Lincoln was the embodiment of tyranny and that he had inflicted
intolerable suffering on the South. But when he was on the run,
Booth began to feel sorry for himself, recording that he was 'hunted
like a dog . . . for doing what Brutus was honoured for, what made
[William] Tell a hero'. (As well as shooting an apple placed on his
son's head, Tell is also supposed to have used his crossbow to kill
an oppressive governor, inspiring the people of medieval Switzerland
to rise up against Austrian rule, though some historians question
whether he really existed.)

At their trial, before a military tribunal, Paine argued the assassination was a legitimate act of war as there were still Confederate
armies in the field. But he, Herold, Atzerodt and a woman named
Mary Surratt, who had helped the conspirators, were convicted
and hanged on 7 July. The prosecution for its part claimed Booth
was part of some great Confederate conspiracy, but Johnson and
other leading Unionists rejected the idea. Before Booth and his
accomplices struck, Seward had been warned about the dangers of
assassination, but took the view that it was 'not an American practice or habit, and one so vicious and desperate cannot be engrafted
into our political system'. It was the product of oppression or a
tactic used in palace intrigues. Now Seward seemed to be proved
wrong, and the arrival of assassination in America horrified the
leading black social reformer Frederick Douglass: 'We had heard
of it among the monarchs of Europe, where men were goaded to
desperation by tyranny', but Americans never dreamed it would
take root 'in this land of free ballots'. This was a popular view, and
some Americans consoled themselves for the aberration by putting
it down to the exceptional and, it was to be hoped, not-to-be-
repeated circumstances of the Civil War. Those who appeared

before the military tribunal were, figuratively at least, not the only ones to go on trial. Southern newspapers were condemned for urging that Lincoln should be killed, with the *Richmond Dispatch* opining: 'to slay a tyrant is no more assassination than war is murder. Who speaks of Brutus as an assassin?' Lincoln was the first U.S. president to be murdered, but over the next century another three would fall victim to assassination, and in the cases of presidents McKinley in 1901 and Kennedy in 1963 the press would again be castigated for its intemperate tone. Newspapers played another important role after Lincoln's assassination, though – rapid communication. Thanks to the telegraph and the penny press, on 15 April 1865 most American cities woke up to the news that their president had been shot, and on the day of Jesus's crucifixion of all days. If you wanted to see Lincoln as a martyr . . . Up to 7 million people watched his coffin pass on its journey from Washington to the family home at Springfield, Illinois.

Benjamin Disraeli told the British parliament that heinous deeds such as Lincoln's assassination have 'never changed the history of the world'. The killings of Julius Caesar, Henry IV and William the Silent could not 'stop the inevitable destiny' of their countries. But Lincoln's killing did seem to have some serious consequences, making the South look treacherous and souring the mood in the North, so that Lincoln's plan to reintegrate the Confederate states 'with malice toward none' was scuppered. Did it also help to inspire a campaign of violence against those trying to advance the cause of black liberation? Booth meanwhile was celebrated in a poem, 'Our Brutus', and there were plenty of people who believed he was really still at large and that accounts of his death were fake news. At the same time, the commander of the troops who had tracked him down became a celebrity on the lecture circuit. Perhaps the most surprising aspect of the whole affair is that John Parker was not sacked as one of the president's bodyguards even though Lincoln's grieving widow flew into a fury when he was assigned to protect her. How could he be 'on guard in the White

House after helping to murder the president?' she shouted. He lasted for three more years until he was fired for once again falling asleep on duty.

The second u.s. president to be assassinated was James Garfield. Garfield had risen to become one of the youngest generals in the Unionist Army during the Civil War, and was then chosen as the Republican party's compromise candidate for the presidency in 1880 when there was a three-way split between better-known contenders, including former president Ulysses S. Grant. Garfield won the popular vote in the presidential election by fewer than 2,000 votes, but that was enough to see him inaugurated in March 1881. Like Abraham Lincoln, he had made the journey from log cabin to White House. His father had died when he was two, and the young Garfield had grown up in rural poverty in Ohio. A pious Christian and passionately anti-slavery, he was generally regarded as a good man, though the Republican Party's so-called Stalwart faction was annoyed that he had beaten their man Grant, and the Stalwart press wrote some vitriolic attacks on him.

Four months after he became president, on 2 July 1881, Garfield set off for a holiday with his wife, who had been his childhood sweetheart and who had just recovered from an illness that nearly killed her. As they waited for the train at Washington's Baltimore and Potomac Railroad station, also prowling around in a rather shady manner was 39-year-old Charles Guiteau. He had dabbled around on the fringes of Garfield's presidential campaign, demanded to be made a consul in Europe as his reward, then condemned the president as 'ungrateful' when the appointment was not forthcoming. Mental illness ran in Guiteau's family, with a number of his aunts and uncles ending their days in asylums. His mother had died when he was seven, and he was brought up by his father who was a 'Perfectionist', believing sin and death were illusions. Charles joined the cult, perhaps attracted by the free love they practised, but when he found he could not get on with other members, he left to live a life of debauchery.

His ambitions were grand, and included being president, but in reality he worked as an itinerant preacher and a debt collector, though he tended to do a moonlight flit whenever his own rent was due. He would deliver long speeches to empty halls, and often claimed to be friends with Garfield, once giving his name as a reference to a landlady. Then on 18 May 1881, apparently God told him he had to kill the president to prevent a new Civil War, so he borrowed some money, bought a pistol and started practising with it, while at the same time composing a long justification of his actions. In June he found out Garfield was going on a train journey and decided the station would be a good place to kill him, but when he saw the president's poorly wife on her husband's arm, he could not go through with it. The next time Garfield was passing through the station, Guiteau turned up again, but it was a hot day and he found he was not really in the mood for assassination.

On 2 July he went there for a third time, and the man in the ticket office helpfully told him which train the president was taking. Although Guiteau was cutting a suspicious figure, no one took much notice of him when he left two thick wads of paper addressed to the press by a news stand. As for Garfield, he shunned bodyguards, believing that if a president took excessive security precautions it would damage democracy. When Guiteau saw Garfield, he came up behind him and fired from close range. The first shot just winged the president's arm. Then as he fell to the ground, Guiteau shot him again in the groin. The assassin fled from the building, straight into the arms of a policeman. As witnesses came up to identify him as the gunman, he quickly confessed. While the president was being taken to hospital, a rather rambling letter of self-vindication was found in Guiteau's pocket. He described himself as a Stalwart (though if he really was, why had he helped Garfield's campaign?). The president's death was a 'sad necessity' that would unite the Republican Party and the country. 'A human life is of small value,' he maintained. After all, thousands of young men had died in the Civil War. It was no worse for Mrs Garfield to lose her

A satirical San Francisco magazine mocks Charles Guiteau, assassin of President James Garfield, 1882.

husband in this way than from natural causes, and, as a Christian, Garfield would be happier in heaven than on earth.

The medical care received by Garfield was heavily criticized, and after weeks of suffering, he died on 19 September. While Guiteau was in gaol, a soldier and a fellow prisoner each tried to kill him. At his trial, he pleaded not guilty, saying the president's death had resulted from causes other than being shot, that in any case it was only like killing someone in a war, and that God had told him to do it. He managed to babble on in the witness box for a week, and spent much of the proceedings playing the fool – mocking his own counsel, mimicking the judge, lapping up the attention. Guiteau said he was insane on the day of the shooting and would not do the same thing again for a million dollars. In a battle of the doctors, the prosecution found thirteen who said he was sane, while the defence fielded 23 who testified he was mad, but the jury took just an hour to convict him. Guiteau was hanged on 30 June 1882, after reciting a lengthy poem he had written, still believing to the last that he would be reprieved and that a statue would be erected to honour him.

Although James Garfield was the second u.s. president to be assassinated in sixteen years, no additional security precautions were put in place for his successors. The Secret Service had been founded back in 1865, but it played a role in protecting the president only at times that were considered especially dangerous, as, for example, when it got wind of a plot to kill President Cleveland in 1894, but even then the presence of additional guards attracted so much adverse comment in the newspapers that the president himself insisted they were removed. The early part of William McKinley's second term in 1901 was also rather a tense period. America had just fought a war with Spain, while at the same time in Europe, anarchists were assassinating key figures such as the empress of Austria and the king of Italy. So when the president went to the Pan-American Exposition in Buffalo, New York, that September, there was a stepping up of security, though some of the measures were cut back when McKinley's wife declared them wasteful.

Like Garfield, McKinley came from Ohio, and also like Garfield he was generally regarded as a good man who always tried to seek consensus. He was also seen as being on the side of the ordinary worker, though he had been helped to the presidency by the businessman Mark Hanna, regarded by some as a ruthless capitalist. At the exposition his secretary was worried about his safety and twice removed a visit to the Temple of Music from his schedule, considering it too risky, but on 6 September McKinley insisted on going. A line of well-wishers gathered on the steps to greet him. One seemed to have a handkerchief or bandage around his right hand. His name was Leon Czolgosz, a 28-year-old factory worker of Polish descent from Detroit. He had fallen under the spell of a Russian anarchist called Emma Goldman who had come to America in her teens. In 1893 she had been gaoled for 'incendiary speaking' and four years later, she declared that all rulers should be 'removed', though she said this did not apply to McKinley because he was too insignificant. Not always the clearest of theoreticians, in May 1901 she made a speech in Cleveland announcing that she did not support violence, but that those who resorted to it because they could not stand by and witness dreadful wrongs should not be condemned too severely. In the audience was Czolgosz and in the interval he approached her to ask which books he should read. After that, the young man started to mix in American anarchist circles, but he was never really accepted and some thought he seemed so fanatical that he must be a police *agent provocateur*.

On 31 August 1901 Czolgosz, who hunted and was a decent shot, bought a gun and travelled to Buffalo. A few days later, on the morning of 6 September, he thought about trying to shoot McKinley as he took a train from Buffalo to Niagara Falls, but there were too many people around. He went to the Falls himself, but could not get near the president. Finally, in the late afternoon, he found himself standing in line to greet McKinley at the Temple of Music. Perhaps he had second thoughts for a moment because he tried to step away, but a policeman pushed him back into the

The assassination of President William McKinley at the Pan-American Exposition in Buffalo, NY, based on a drawing made shortly afterwards.

McKinley's assassin, Leon F. Czolgosz, appears on the cover of a popular American magazine, 9 September 1901.

queue. As the president reached Czolgosz and offered his hand, the young man pushed it away with his left hand, and shot him twice with his bandaged right – first in the chest, then in the abdomen. (As we saw, the assassin of the Roman Emperor Domitian in AD 96 hid his dagger in bandages around a supposedly injured arm.) Detectives and by-standers pulled Czolgosz to the ground and roughed him up, so his face was bleeding while McKinley pleaded: 'Be easy with him, boys,' and the police managed to take the gunman away before he suffered any more damage. As for the president, his wounds were thought to be serious, but not life-threatening.

The police found Czolgosz calm, saying he had shot McKinley because it was his 'duty'. He also talked about how Goldman had influenced him: 'Her doctrine that all rulers should be exterminated was what set me thinking so that my head nearly split with pain.' From his sick bed, McKinley urged Czolgosz should be treated 'with all fairness' as Goldman and a number of the gunman's associates were rounded up, with police wondering whether they were investigating a major conspiracy. They spent days interrogating Goldman while she offered to nurse McKinley who was 'suffering . . . and merely a human being to me now'. Across America there were blood-thirsty demands to punish Goldman and violent attacks against anarchists. One of the Russian's friends nearly got lynched in Pittsburgh. She was released when police could find no evidence against her, but as with Garfield, the doctors proved unequal to the task of saving McKinley, and on 14 September he died from gangrene.

At his trial Czolgosz admitted the assassination and added: 'No one else told me to do it, and no one paid me to do it.' He was quickly found guilty and sentenced to the electric chair. Just before he died, he said he killed McKinley 'because he was the enemy of the good people. I did it for the . . . working men of all countries!' The sexologist Havelock Ellis studied Czolgosz as part of his work on criminality. He found the killer rather an attractive character, a good man, a 'philanthropic assassin', driven to violence by 'the very excess of his sympathetic sensibilities . . . He execrates the few because he loves the many.' This was a problem that 'most easily arises in young, narrow, and ill-trained minds'. After his death, doctors cut up Czolgosz's brain to examine it. They found nothing abnormal. The year after McKinley's assassination, the Secret Service was given responsibility for protecting the president at all times.

Propaganda of the Deed

It may have been perpetrated by a racist reactionary, but Abraham Lincoln's assassination inspired many revolutionaries, such as a secret nihilist group in Russia known as 'Hell', who planned to assassinate the tsar as a way of fomenting revolution. Although the Italian Carlo Pisacane in the 1850s had advanced the proposition that actions created ideas, the actual phrase 'propaganda of the deed' was not coined until two decades later, by a young French doctor named Paul Brousse, who described it in a pamphlet as 'a mighty means of rousing the popular consciousness'. He argued for the supremacy of actions because ideas could be distorted by the bourgeois press and because even if workers got hold of politically sound pamphlets, they were too tired to read them after a hard day's toil. Inconveniently, Brousse also questioned whether assassination was effective, but by now 'propaganda of the deed' was up and running. It was developed further by the Russian anarchist Peter Kropotkin, a former page to the tsar and the son of a prince, who advocated: 'Permanent revolt by word of mouth, in writing, by the dagger, the rifle, dynamite,' saying a single deed would have more impact than a thousand pamphlets, that one action would bring forth another and soon there would be so many, it would undermine the government. His views got him locked up, but on a personal level he seemed a very gentle soul. George Bernard Shaw considered him 'amiable to the point of saintliness', and Kropotkin was actually ambivalent about violence, stressing the importance of cooperation and fearing assassination might turn into 'a publicity stunt'. Later in life, he criticized 'mindless terror' and admitted revolution would not come through individual acts of violence, though he still defended the assassination of Tsar Alexander II of Russia (see below), for example, as the act of people driven to desperation by the intolerable conditions of their lives.

Kropotkin's fellow anarchist Mikhail Bakunin was also of noble birth, the son of a diplomat. Karl Marx said he was like a bull, and he weighed at least 125 kilograms (20 st). Bakunin saw his job as making the apathetic masses realize that what they really wanted was revolution. Married, but said to be impotent, he declared revolution to be his fiancée, adding he would be 'really happy . . . only when the whole world is engulfed in fire'. In 1848 revolutions swept

Mikhail Bakunin,
c. 1872.

through Europe, and Bakunin headed off to try to foment trouble in Poland, but most of the risings petered out and the anarchist found himself in a Russian prison. That was followed by exile in Siberia, until he escaped in 1861. He believed European society was exhausted and that it needed to be burned down so a new world could emerge: 'The passion for destruction is at the same time a creative passion.' In 1869 he wrote his *Catechism of a Revolutionary*, saying 'utter destruction' was needed to bring the chaos from which this new order could emerge, via the agency of young 'revolution-ists': 'The Revolutionist is a doomed man. He has no private interests, no affairs, sentiments, ties, property, nor even a name of his own. His entire being is devoured by one purpose, one thought, one passion – the revolution . . . he has severed every link with the social order and with the entire civilised world . . . He is its mer-ciless enemy and continues to inhabit it with only one purpose – to destroy it.' The anarchists he inspired were 'young fanatics, believers without gods' who accepted that 'many, very many of them must perish at the hands of the government.' Bakunin sug-gested they should cooperate with other enemies of the state – criminals and robbers. Indeed, at one point, he wrote that brigands were the only true revolutionaries. One of the means he advocated was assassination of representatives of the state, especially intelligent ones. The revolution was to be based on action, not agitation or propaganda. One of the problems about his ideology is that it could be seen by any misfit, loner or psychopath as justification for taking revenge on a society they felt had wronged them.

Bakunin had a young co-author on *Catechism of a Revolutionary*, Sergei Nechaev, who impressed him because he 'feared nothing'. He had been an inoffensive schoolmaster disfigured by acne that he tried to disguise with a beard, until he met a revolutionary student called Orlov. They created their own underground committee of three, devoted to ending the existing social order so as to establish a new world with 'complete freedom of the renewed personality', and Nechaev became all mysterious about his past. By the time he met Bakunin, he was a systematic liar, stage-managing a fake arrest, inventing exciting stories of prison escapes and declaring he was in charge of a great revolutionary organization. His pronouncements were so inflammatory that, as with McKinley's assassin Leon Czolgosz, other agitators thought he must be an *agent provocateur*, and even toyed with the idea of assassinating him. But Bakunin was smitten, seeing Nechaev as a 'pitiless warrior', and perhaps, though he would never admit it, as someone who, unlike him, had trousers as well as mouth. For his part, Nechaev was prone to falling under the spell of father figures. There were even stories that the pair were lovers. But the deception was not just one way. Bakunin boasted of his fictional 'World Revolutionary Alliance', and gave Nechaev a membership card for its 'Russian Section' numbered 2771. In fact, it was the only one ever issued.

Nechaev did manage to commit one assassination – of a fellow member of his little revolutionary cell who had had the temerity to criticize him. Eventually Bakunin turned against his protegé, warning his friends that the young man would lie, intrigue against them and seduce their wives and daughters. In 1873 Nechaev was convicted of murder and sent to Siberia for life. Meanwhile Bakunin kept trying to take control of the International Workingmen's Association, but Karl Marx contemptuously rejected his ideas, believing revolutions were made by the masses and not a few conspirators, and wrecked the organization rather than let his rival prevail. So in 1881 anarchists from Russia, Europe and the USA held their own International Congress in London. They passed a resolution saying 'propaganda of the deed' should be used to speed along the general conflagration that was clearly on the way, though the paradox was that in order for the deed to be effective, knowledge of it had to be spread via conventional printed propaganda. The authorities made the mistake of believing there really was a huge international network, which represented a terrible threat, so that police agents sometimes financed the anarchists in an attempt to infiltrate their ranks.

Another misfit who sang the praises of violence as a means for achieving political ends was the German Johann Most. His mother died of cholera when he was two. Then when he was seven, he picked up an infection that left him horribly disfigured. Like Kropotkin, Bakunin and Nechaev, he was in and out of prison. 'Propaganda of the deed' might be all very well, but Most also understood the importance of the burgeoning mass media, how it would spread news of terrorist deeds rapidly across the world, leading, he hoped, others to imitate them in an 'echo effect'. So he founded his own magazine, *Freedom*, in which he expounded his theories, publishing a poem in praise of dynamite: 'To dynamite that is the force . . . The world gets better day by day.' His enemies were deemed sub-human: pigs, dogs, parasites, scum. He recognized that if you used dynamite, some 'innocents' were bound to get hurt too, but it was up to them to make sure they were not in places where bombs were likely to go off, and anyway governments committed far worse crimes. Most stressed the importance of another revolutionary ingredient – money: to buy explosives and pay bribes, for example. He favoured a twin-track strategy: have a legal or semi-legal organization specializing in propaganda, while others got on with the violence in as much secrecy as possible. He also argued that it was important to play to the strengths of individual revolutionaries, recognizing, for example, that not everyone was cut out for cold-blooded assassination, not even those who might be very brave in the heat of a battle. (The 'Hell' organization took a different view, arguing the assassin should be chosen by drawing lots. Then, like some religious hermit, he should sever all ties with friends and family, avoid marriage and shun even his revolutionary colleagues. On the day of the assassination, he must disfigure his face with chemicals to avoid being recognized. He should carry in his pocket a manifesto explaining his motives, and poison himself once the deed was done.)

As we saw, Karl Ludwig Sand was consumed with remorse when he realized he had broken the heart of his victim's daughter. So were killers motivated by politics more soft-hearted than those we saw in earlier times who were driven by religion? Some would-be assassins during the Age of Revolution said it was easier to be killed than to kill. Timofey Mikhailov exhibited no weakness when he was about to be executed for his part in the plot to assassinate Tsar Alexander II in 1881, but when he had had the opportunity to throw his bomb on the fatal day, he had sloped off home instead. The Italian anarchist Michele Angiolillo, who would murder the Spanish prime minister, Canovas del Castillo, in 1897, failed to shoot him when he got his first opportunity because the politician's family was with him. Eventually Angiolillo gunned down his quarry at a spa where he was staying with his wife. She later slapped the killer's face. He responded: 'Madam, I respect you as a lady, but I regret that you were the wife of that man.' Angiolillo too died bravely when he was executed by garrote. Another Russian revolutionary named Ivan Kalyayev, who was also a poet, set out to throw a bomb at Grand Duke Sergei Alexandrovich, the son of Alexander II and a highly influential figure at the court of Tsar Nicholas II, on 15 February 1905, but, like Angiolillo, he initially backed off when he saw the prospective victim was with his wife

The poet and
revolutionary Ivan
Kalyayev, c. 1903.

and members of his family. Two days later he did kill the Grand
Duke and was hanged. Kalyayev's dilemma was explored in Albert
Camus' play *Les justes* (1949). Some of his fellow revolutionaries
say he was right not to attack the Grand Duke when his children
were there because the creation of a better world should not begin
with children being murdered. A hardliner bitterly disagrees, complaining that the lives of a couple of children are nothing when
compared with the thousands who die every year because of a
political system that needs to be destroyed. Kalyayev maintains
that murder is wrong because all life is sacred, and that he must
pay for his deed with his life, so he refuses to take any steps to seek
a pardon.

Even the fearsome Johann Most mellowed as he got older.
When an assassination attempt was made on Kaiser Wilhelm I in

Berlin in 1878, the revolutionary had praised it as a 'Brutus deed', but in later years, he started saying it was illusory to think the assassination of individual monarchs or politicians would overthrow the system unless there was a general uprising. He was even horsewhipped by Emma Goldman for criticizing an assassination attempt on the ruthless American industrialist Henry Clay Frick, who amassed the famous Frick art collection.

One of the disappointments about tyrannicide down the centuries had been, as Cicero put it 2,000 years ago, how often it seemed to get rid of the tyrant but not of the tyranny, suggesting that an attack on a wider front might be needed. The German radical Karl Heinzen argued tyrannicide was justified but insufficient. There could be no real progress until kings, generals and all the enemies of liberty were removed, so the liquidation of hundreds or even thousands could be justified in the interests of humanity. He liked the idea of weapons of mass destruction – rockets, mines, poison gas that could destroy 'whole cities'. Even those who despised the anarchists, such as Nietzsche, felt that adopting some of their rhetoric made them look rather cool. So he said he wanted to 'assassinate' Europe's Christian heritage, declaring: 'I am not a human being, I am dynamite.' This meant Emma Goldman was able to draw on Nietzsche when she wanted to justify assassinations, maintaining that there was no objective truth, only the perspective favoured by an individual. She argued that an assassin's violence simply mirrors the violence directed against him, and that force and violence are inherent in government. The assassin is motivated by an 'abundance of love', but, noting how the American people mourned President McKinley, she declared, in words eerily reminiscent of those of John Wilkes Booth, that this was all 'too deep for the shallow multitude to comprehend'. Indeed, the people were often a disappointment to the revolutionaries. When Dmitry Karakozov shot at Tsar Alexander II in 1866, and passers-by apprehended him, he shouted: 'Fools, I have done this for you.' For his pains he was hanged. (Incidentally, thirteen years later when he

The assassination of French president Sadi Carnot, from the news magazine *Le Monde illustré*.

was confronted by a student with a revolver in his hand while he was taking a walk, the tsar tried an old-fashioned, but on this occasion successful, response. He ran for it. The student fired a series of shots, but missed each time. This would-be assassin too was caught and hanged.)

Revolutionary ideology often led to targeted assassination being subsumed by indiscriminate murder. Bourgeois or establishment symbols were seen as fair game: banks, stock exchanges, even cafés and music halls. France suffered eleven anarchist attacks in the dozen years from 1882 to 1894. François Claudius Koenigstein, known as Ravachol, gave a new word to the French language, *ravacholiser*, meaning 'to blow up'. He began his career of violence with the murders of two destitute old men, then bombed a Paris apartment building which housed senior judges. Émile Henry made even fewer pretensions to targeting the rich and powerful. In 1894 he bombed a Paris café that served mainly working men, killing one and injuring twenty. In justification, he said: 'There are no innocents.' He was executed, as was Ravachol. The assassin who killed the French president Sadi Carnot in 1894 said he had done it because Carnot would not pardon Henry.

Assassination by Bomb

The explosives so idolized by Most, and used by Ravachol and Henry, were an important development in the technology of assassination. As we saw, they made an appearance back in the sixteenth century in the murder of Lord Darnley, but now they were more available and more effective. In spite of the Russian nobleman's description of his country's political system as 'despotism tempered by assassination', by 1880 only two tsars had actually fallen to an assassin. The one then on the throne, Alexander II, was fundamentally conservative, but he had pushed through the emancipation of the serfs – though not, perhaps, from completely altruistic motives. Some had blamed serfdom for Russia's defeat in the Crimean War, some believed it was a barrier to the development of capitalism and was holding the country back, and others that if they did not emancipate the serfs, the serfs might rise up and emancipate themselves. Nor was the reform all it was cracked up to be. Though they were no longer the property of their masters, freed serfs would have less land, and their freedom was not a gift but something they would have to pay for, perhaps for the rest of their lives. The 'People's Will' revolutionary organization was not impressed, and its 'revolutionary tribunal' sentenced Alexander to death. It also sent an open letter to the tsar saying the state ruled by arbitrary violence and that the group would be murdering government officials to 'strengthen the revolutionary spirit of the people'. The organization's bulletin argued that although assassination was useful for propaganda, it was above all an act of revenge, and that if a dozen pillars of the establishment could be killed at the same time, the government would panic and the masses would wake up. One of its editors reasoned that assassination was less expensive and more cost-effective than a mass uprising, saying that since there was no limit to human inventiveness, it was impossible for rulers to guard against personal attacks. In the guise of modern scientific analysis, the old argument that assassination and terrorism were more humanitarian because they would cost fewer lives than armed conflict was revived, with the rider that even if some innocent people got hurt, it was a price worth paying. Not every member agreed. There was a fierce debate within People's Will over the degree to which it should concentrate on violence, and eventually it split over this question.

People's Will was happy to use traditional assassination methods, stabbing the head of the tsar's secret police in the street in 1878 after condemning him to death over his cruel treatment of prisoners, but along with other revolutionaries, they also embraced the new technology of explosives, not always successfully. At least four members were killed trying to make bombs. Another got a job as a carpenter at the Winter Palace and managed to stash a pile of dynamite, which was far more destructive than earlier explosives, under the dining room floor. On 5 February 1880 he lit a slow-burning fuse and made his escape. The bomb went off at the time he had planned, killing eleven people, but the tsar escaped because the late arrival of the guest of honour meant he was not in the room. The group also made a number of attempts to blow up the tsar's train. On one occasion the detonator failed. On another they destroyed the wrong train. In January 1881 People's Will decided to have another go, renting a shop in St Petersburg on a route taken by the tsar every Sunday on his way to a military roll call, and by the end of February they had constructed a mine they could detonate as he passed. Concerned that the police might be closing in, the revolutionaries decided that if Alexander took an alternative route on 1 March, bypassing their mine, they should instead attack him with small hand-held bombs. This was risky, as they were not sure the bombs would work. Before he set off that day, Alexander signed an important document that would be a first step towards giving Russia a constitution. Then when he went out, he did indeed change his route, steering well clear of the mine. So, Plan B it was. The conspirators managed to catch up with the tsar's party. A woman among them fluttered a handkerchief as a signal, and one of her male colleagues threw a bomb. It exploded under the tsar's armoured carriage, injuring the horses and killing a Cossack outrider. As the coach stopped, Alexander emerged unhurt to try to help the wounded. Then a second conspirator threw a bomb and this one landed right at the monarch's feet, killing the bomber and causing severe injuries to the tsar, who died a few hours later. The new technology had claimed its victim, but only when it was deployed at close quarters like a knife. And one of its downsides was emphasized: collateral damage, as about twenty people in the crowd who had gathered to watch the tsar go past were injured.

Alexander's death raised some interesting questions about the ethics of assassination. Julius Caesar's murder had been justified on the grounds of what he had done by becoming a tyrant, and what the killers feared he planned to do. But the tsar had done good things, even if some would regard them as inadequate:

The explosion that killed Tsar Alexander II.

emancipating the serfs, taking steps towards a constitution. So could he be regarded as a tyrant? On the other hand, might you argue that the lives led by most Russian people were so awful that their ruler could be regarded as a legitimate target just because he was their ruler? That he was being assassinated not because of what he did, but because of who he was? Interestingly, some peasants believed Alexander's murder had been instigated by landlords angry about emancipation. Reporting the event, *The Times* declared philosophically that all forms of government produce assassins. It must certainly have been sobering for anyone in a position of power that one of the world's great emperors had been sent to his grave by a rag-tag group that never numbered more than about fifty operatives, and lasted barely five years. Alexander II was succeeded by his son, Alexander III. Ten days after the assassination, People's Will wrote to the new tsar offering to call off all terrorist action in return for a general amnesty and a constitution providing fairly basic civil liberties. The moderation of these demands led to the group being dubbed 'liberals with bombs', but Alexander III was having none of it. He had six of the conspirators executed, and put an end to all this constitutional reform nonsense. Instead there was a security crackdown. His father became a martyr, with the Church on Spilled Blood being erected on the site of his assassination. Alexander III died peacefully in his bed.

While assassins deployed science to find new ways of killing, scientists and medical men tried to use it to understand the assassins. The highly influential 'criminal anthropologist' Cesare Lombroso, professor of legal medicine and psychiatry in Turin, thought all criminals were victims of 'evolutionary regression' and displayed physical signs of their 'degeneration'. Assassins, he discovered, 'have prominent jaws, widely separated cheek bones, thick, dark hair, scanty beard, and a pallid face'. As for anarchist assassins, 'to have reached this militant stage a tremendous degeneration must have taken place, not merely of the intelligence, but also of the moral sense.'

Ireland: The Phoenix Park Murders

By the time Alexander II was murdered, assassination plots related to British rule in Ireland had been rife for years. Queen Victoria and other members of the royal family were targeted, along with prominent politicians and landlords. The British authorities feared that Irish Nationalists were adopting the tactics of the Russian nihilists. In 1881, the year of Alexander II's assassination, a particularly militant group, the 'Invincibles', began to emerge from the Irish Republican Brotherhood. It aimed to pursue a tactic of 'perpetual action', which some thought very similar to 'propaganda of the deed', and it had a list of British 'tyrants' it wanted to eliminate, including the Chief Secretary for Ireland, W. E. Forster, and the Under-Secretary Thomas Henry Burke. A number of plots against Burke and Forster failed, including one using a letter bomb. Then the political temperature rose even higher, with two women killed at a demonstration in favour of land reform, while assassins trying to murder a landlord in West Meath shot and killed his sister-in-law by mistake. Forster and the viceroy, Earl Cowper, both resigned over what they considered the government's excessively soft approach, and the prime minister, W. E. Gladstone, persuaded a reluctant Lord Frederick Cavendish, a politician from his Liberal Party and the husband of his favourite niece, to take over from Forster.

On 5 May 1882 police fired on a pro-Home Rule demonstration, killing a twelve-year-old boy. The following day Cavendish arrived in Dublin. The Invincibles had been scouting out Phoenix Park, next to the viceroy's residence, as a place where they might waylay and kill Burke. Late that lovely spring afternoon, seven plotters armed with surgical knives gathered in the park. Only one, a man named Joe Smith, knew what the target looked like. But the Under-Secretary did not appear, and as the clock struck seven the would-be assassins were about to give up, when Smith suddenly spotted two men walking together. Excitedly, he told his fellow plotters that Burke was one of them. His comrades then sent him home. The group of Invincibles waited and as the pair passed, they launched their attack. The few witnesses who saw the encounter believed it was drunks or ruffians fighting. As Joe Brady, a stonecutter, stabbed Burke, Cavendish hit him with his umbrella. Enraged, Brady stabbed the new Chief Secretary in the arm. Then the rest joined in, leaving both men dead from multiple stab wounds. Later the gang delivered cards to newspapers saying they had been 'Executed by order of the Irish Invincibles', though, in fact, there had been no plan to kill Cavendish, and the plotters probably did not even know who he was at the time they attacked him. Just like the killing of the landlord's sister-in-law, or the twenty bystanders injured by the bomb that slew the tsar, it was an illustration that assassination is not an exact science. Johann Most's *Freedom* was about the only publication to praise the murders, which led to another police raid on its premises.

After months of painstaking detective work, more than twenty people were eventually arrested over the assassination, including a landlord named James Carey, who, since the killing, had been elected a Dublin City councillor. Carey had actually planned the operation, and was one of four suspects who turned Queen's evidence. Five men were hanged, including Brady, the godfather of Carey's youngest child. Carey had his windows smashed, his tenants refused to pay their rent, and in the summer of 1883, using an assumed name, he fled with his family to South Africa. During the journey he was befriended by an Irish American named Patrick O'Donnell, who discovered his true identity. One night while they were having a drink together, O'Donnell calmly drew his pistol and shot the informer dead in front of his family. In December 1883 he was convicted of murder at the Old Bailey and hanged.

The Empress Elisabeth of Austria-Hungary

By modern standards, some of the victims of this era seem to have exhibited extraordinary carelessness: Abraham Lincoln sitting in his state box at the theatre while his bodyguard went AWOL, Lord Cavendish strolling with a friend in the park. The Spanish prime minister José Canalejas y Méndez was in the habit of walking at the same time every day to the Ministry of the Interior in Madrid. He usually had two detectives with him, but he liked them to keep at least twenty paces away. On 12 November 1912, about fifty yards from the ministry, he stopped to look in a bookshop window. He had been there for a couple of minutes when a 32-year-old anarchist named Manuel Pardinas came up and shot him three times. Canalejas died a few minutes later, but by then the gunman had already shot himself dead.

Carelessness was also a factor in perhaps the most widely condemned assassination of the Age of Revolution, the murder of Empress Elisabeth of Austria-Hungary, then still one of Europe's great empires. The murder was also notable for the ingenious weapon that was used. It was highly unusual for a woman to be assassinated, and Elisabeth exercised virtually no real power; she was simply the wife of the emperor. She was also a revered philanthropist, often visiting the poor and the sick unannounced 'like an angel of mercy', and like Archbishop Sharp she seems to have been a substitute for the assassin's intended victim. But the 'propaganda of the deed' did not always require a specific individual to be killed. It was sufficient that the victim was the symbol of some power or authority. Elisabeth was very beautiful, and famous for the tightness of her corsets and the narrowness of her waist, which she was said to have got down to sixteen inches in her early twenties, and which even when she passed sixty was still less than twenty inches. In her thirties, she refused to sit for any more portraits or photographs, so that nothing would sully her image as a glamorous young woman.

Elisabeth considered the court of her husband, Emperor Franz Josef, far too stuffy and escaped from it whenever she could, so the autumn of 1898 found her supposedly incognito in Geneva. On 10 September, accompanied only by her lady-in-waiting, she

The wasp-waisted
Empress Elisabeth,
from a photograph
taken in the 1870s.

decided to take the steamer across Lake Geneva to Montreux. In the city at the same time was a 25-year-old Italian anarchist, Luigi Lucheni, who had gone there to assassinate the Pretender to the French crown, the Duke of Orleans, but he called off his visit, so Lucheni was relieved when a newspaper revealed that the very smart woman staying in the city under the name 'the Countess of Hohenembs' was actually Empress Elisabeth of Austria. As the empress walked with her lady-in-waiting by the lake, a man lurched into her apparently by accident and she felt a blow above her breast. She fell to the ground, but soon picked herself up, with help from bystanders, and got on the steamer, saying she assumed the assailant was trying to steal her watch. But soon after boarding, Elisabeth collapsed unconscious. Her lady-in-waiting cut the laces of the empress's ferociously tight corset to help her breathe and noticed a tiny bloodstain on her chemise. Lucheni had, in fact, stabbed her in the heart with a sharpened industrial needle file.

The empress was carried back to her hotel, but doctors were unable to save her. Lucheni meanwhile tried to make his escape, but was grabbed by a couple of cabmen, who handed him over to the police. The anarchist made no further attempt to get away, but was reported to be singing as he walked along, and saying: 'I did it.' He told the magistrate he had come to Geneva to assassinate 'another important person', but had been unable to complete the mission, when he learned by accident that the empress was there. Lucheni said: 'if all anarchists did their duty as I have done mine, bourgeois society would soon disappear.' When he was reproached for striking down a woman who exhibited such kindness to the poor, the assassin said: 'it did not matter to me who the sovereign was whom I should kill . . . It was not a woman I struck, but an empress.' Sentenced to life imprisonment, Lucheni lamented that the Swiss canton in which he had committed his crime did not have the death penalty. Twelve years after the murder, he was found hanged in his prison cell.

Rasputin

As we saw, Tsar Alexander III passed away peacefully in his bed, but his son, Nicholas II, was less fortunate. Both he and, more particularly, his wife would fall under the spell of Grigori Yefimovich Rasputin. Born to a peasant family in a Siberian village in 1869, at the age of eighteen Rasputin was caught stealing and sent to a monastery for three months as punishment. Though he has featured as the 'mad monk' in a number of lurid films, he never, in fact, took holy orders. Instead he married a local woman who would bear him four children, but wanderlust soon called him. Claiming the Virgin Mary had appeared to him and told him to become an itinerant pilgrim, he took off to Jerusalem and Greece, living off charity and gaining a reputation as a filthy, unkempt holy man with burning eyes who could heal the sick and predict the future. He devised a novel theology, maintaining that by sleeping with a woman, he

Grigori Yefimovich Rasputin, the 'mad monk'.

could take on her sins and help her find God's grace, and plenty seemed prepared to put the idea to the test. Many Russian courtiers were fans of mysticism and the occult, and in 1903 rumours of Rasputin's powers reached the royal family when he prophesied that within the year, the tsarina would give birth to the male heir she and Nicholas were longing for. Sure enough, in August 1904 the Tsarevich Alexei was born, and Rasputin got an invitation to court.

Alexei was haemophiliac, and Rasputin did seem to be able to stop the uncontrollable bleeding that happened whenever he was cut. Some say it was because he could calm the boy and lower his blood pressure; others that he simply stopped the royal physicians giving Alexei aspirin, which is an anti-coagulant. From then on, for the tsarina he could do no wrong. His fame led hundreds to queue to see him, sometimes waiting for days. Knowing Rasputin had the ear of the tsarina and the tsar, who was widely believed to be under her thumb, some would bring gifts, hoping he would help advance them in the world. Attractive women he would invite for a quiet tête-à-tête in his study. Some modern historians have suggested his lasciviousness was exaggerated, but certainly plenty of stories circulated about his amorous exploits, claiming, for example, that he held orgies with nuns in their convent. The tsar's prime minister presented Nicholas with a dossier, and for a time, he banished Rasputin from court, but the holy man was soon back.

In June 1914, a month before the First World War broke out, a former prostitute stabbed Rasputin in the street in Siberia while he was visiting his wife and children. She appears to have been acting on behalf of a monk with whom he had fallen out. Rasputin was nearly disembowelled and had to have extensive surgery. It destroyed much of his energy, and he became addicted to opium which he took to dull the pain. At first he advised the tsar against getting involved in the war, but once it was under way, he got on board, blessing troops at the front, though the Commander-in-Chief, the tsar's cousin Grand Duke Nicholas, said he would have Rasputin hanged if he saw him. The holy man then prophesied that if the tsar did not take personal command, Russia would lose the war. The tsar duly sacked his relative and took over himself, leaving the tsarina in charge of domestic matters with Rasputin as her main adviser. The holy man bragged at a drunken dinner that he had slept with her, though this was probably untrue. But the tsarina was already an object of suspicion in Russia because of her German origins, and in November 1916, with the war going badly, Vladimir Purishkevich, from the ultra-nationalist Black Hundreds, stood up in the Russian parliament and declared: 'The tsar's ministers have been turned into marionettes, marionettes whose threads have been taken firmly in hand by Rasputin . . . and the tsarina who has remained a German on the Russian throne.'

Next Purishkevich got in a huddle with another of the tsar's cousins, Grand Duke Dmitry Pavlovich, and with Prince Feliks Yusupov who was married to Nicholas's niece. Like Alessandro de Medici's assassin nearly four hundred years before, they decided to use a honey trap, luring Rasputin to Yusupov's home on the night of 29 December with the promise of an assignation with his beautiful wife. In fact, she was far away in the Ukraine, as the conspirators plied the holy man with cakes and wine spiked with cyanide. This had no discernible effect, so Yusupov shot him in the chest and left him to die, while the conspirators went off to Rasputin's apartment, one of them wearing the holy man's coat and hat to make it look as though he had returned home that night. But when the plotters returned to dispose of the body, Rasputin suddenly leapt up and grabbed the prince by the throat. The two accomplices shot him twice more, but still he fought, so they bludgeoned him, wrapped him in a carpet and dumped him in the freezing waters of the River Neva. When his body was found three days later, it was minus the carpet, and some said there were signs Rasputin had managed to free himself. The tsarina had him buried at a royal estate near St Petersburg. The following year, during the Russian Revolution, local peasants dug him up and set fire to his body. The story goes that the dead man suddenly sat bolt upright. (Modern pathologists say tendons contracting in the heat could have caused this.)

Some scholars have cast doubt on the conventional account of his death, with suggestions that he was not poisoned or drowned, but simply killed with a single shot to the head, perhaps delivered by a British agent who was a friend of Yusupov. The British government was supposedly worried that Rasputin was angling for Britain's ally Russia to make a separate peace with Germany. Coming to clear conclusions is difficult because the autopsy report disappeared during Stalin's time, as did most of the people who had witnessed the post-mortem.

Nicholas II was overthrown the year after Rasputin's death, and he, the tsarina and most of their family were killed by the Bolsheviks. The tsar's wife and her four daughters were each found to have a locket holding a picture of Rasputin around their necks. Before he fell, Nicholas had exiled Yusupov and the Grand Duke; the prince to one of his more remote estates, and Dmitry to the

Persian front. It was a great stroke of luck for them because it meant they were among the few Romanovs to escape death after the revolution. Both would die peacefully in exile in France, the Grand Duke having had an affair with Coco Chanel. Because Purishkevich was so popular in 1916, he escaped being punished by the tsar, but he was imprisoned for a time by the Bolsheviks. Then he managed to get away to the south, which was controlled by the anti-Revolutionary White Russians. He died of typhus there in 1920.

Assassinated Revolutionaries

But revolutionaries did not only assassinate members of the ruling class or those serving them. They also murdered each other. V. Volodarsky was the alias of Moisei Markovich Goldstein. (The 'V' did not actually stand for anything.) Born into a poor Jewish family in Ukraine, he was exiled to Archangel for his political activities while he was still a schoolboy. After a general amnesty in 1913, he went to America where he was employed in a sweat-shop and became a trade union activist, and then worked with Trotsky on a socialist magazine. In 1917, as Russia lurched towards the October Revolution, he returned home. One of his colleagues praised his 'outstanding talent as an agitator'. He edited a Bolshevik newspaper and raced tirelessly around workers' meetings. Like Marat, he was ruthless: 'profoundly convinced that if we were to falter in lashing out at the hydra of counter-revolution it would devour not only us but along with us the hopes that October had raised all over the world', as one of his comrades put it. On 20 June 1918 he was shot dead by Grigory Ivanovich Semyonov, a member of the rival Socialist Revolutionary Party, after his car had been halted by a burst tyre while he travelled between meetings of workers in Petrograd. As a revolutionary martyr, Volodarsky was given a magnificent funeral. Two months later, on 30 August, another prominent Bolshevik, Moisei Uritsky, the head of the secret police in Petrograd, was also killed, by another Socialist Revolutionary

Party member, and on the same day Lenin was shot and wounded. These attacks led to the Bolshevik 'Red Terror' in which the secret police shot about 6,000 prisoners and hostages, and locked up 25,000 more. As for Semyonov, after being arrested, he changed sides and provided evidence to the Bolsheviks for a show trial of the Socialist Revolutionary leaders.

While Russia was limbering up for violent regime change, in the early years of the twentieth century, Mexico was another turbulent country of revolution and counter-revolution. It threw up two great heroes: Emiliano Zapata, portrayed on film by Marlon Brando, and Pancho Villa, who was played by Yul Brynner, Telly Savalas and dozens of others. Both Zapata and Villa were assassinated.

Zapata was a mestizo – of mixed race – born in Morelos in southern Mexico in 1879. Thanks to its sugar growing, it was one of the richest regions in the country, but like most of its people, Zapata was poor. Mexico was grotesquely unequal, with a tiny few holding most of the land. The mestizo began dabbling in revolutionary politics in his twenties and got elected head of his village on a promise of land reform. When the authorities dragged their feet, he started reforming by force. Zapata was a great womanizer who took enormous pride in his appearance, with his trademark outfit of silver-buttoned trousers, wide hat and extravagant moustache, which made him instantly recognizable. He joined in the revolution that broke out in 1910, and saw President Diaz deposed after 34 years in power, but he was bitterly disappointed in the new president, Francisco Madero. So, from his power base, Zapata, who had done some military service, led his Liberation Army of the South in pursuit of 'Reform, Freedom, Law and Justice', telling his followers: 'It's better to die on your feet than to live on your knees.' Meanwhile presidents came and went, usually violently. At the height of his power, Zapata commanded about 20,000 men and controlled perhaps a third of the country, financing his operations by threatening to burn crops unless landowners paid him off.

In April 1919 he was fighting another president, Venustiano Carranza, when one of the president's best officers, Jesus Guajardo, managed to convince Zapata he was ready to defect, bringing his soldiers with him. The two men agreed to meet at a hacienda in Morelos, each accompanied by only thirty men. In fact, Guajardo had brought six hundred. He greeted the revolutionary with a guard of honour to inspect. A bugle sounded a welcome, but as the last note died away, the soldiers turned their guns on Zapata and his men at point blank range. Salvador Reyes, Zapata's secretary, who survived the onslaught, wrote: 'Gen. Zapata fell, never to rise again!' Five of his men were also killed. Guajardo was paid handsomely and made a general, while Zapata's body was dragged through the dust by a mule. After his assassination, his army dissolved, but many Mexicans refused to believe he was dead, claiming

Emiliano Zapata in 1911 – always the last word in sartorial elegance.

a lookalike had been killed instead. Much of the land reform he wanted was carried out in the 1930s, and he was immortalized on banknotes and in the names of streets and towns. He was also the inspiration for the left-wing Zapatistas who rose against the Mexican government in the 1990s.

While Zapata prowled the south, Villa's power base was in the north. The two revolutionaries were often wary of each other, and for a time Villa had fought on the side of President Madero against the Zapatistas, though the pair came together to take on President Victoriano Huerta in 1914. Like Zapata, Villa was born into poverty. He claimed that when he was sixteen, he hunted down and killed a landowner's son who had raped his sister. Then he said he stole the man's horse and rode off to hide in the mountains with bandits. In 1902 he was captured and was due to be executed, but a rich man who had been buying stolen mules from him got him reprieved. He was made to join the army, but within a year he had deserted after killing an officer. Villa then got by doing odd jobs and robberies until the revolution of 1910. Persuaded to join the struggle against President Díaz, he quickly proved himself a skilled commander, but while he was helping Madero, he found himself facing execution again, under charges trumped up by one of the president's generals who saw him as a dangerous rival.

Villa, who became known as the Centaur of the North, managed to escape, and from then on he fought a series of presidents as well as American troops, sometimes raiding into u.s. territory. He financed his army through robberies, 'taxing' landowners and printing his own currency. In 1914 he rode into Mexico City to drive out the sitting president, Carranza, who would later return to power and have Zapata assassinated, but this proved to be the high watermark of his power, and in the months that followed he suffered a series of heavy defeats. After his enemies tried to eliminate him through scorched earth tactics and mass killings of his followers, in 1920 he finally agreed to give up fighting,

Pancho Villa, photographed after a successful military operation, Mexico, c. 1911.

accepting President Adolfo de la Huerta's offer of a pension and a 100 square-kilometre (25,000 ac) hacienda.

Yet another president, Alvaro Obregon, then took over. Villa took extensive security precautions and never slept in the same place twice. Like Zapata, he was a womanizer, but he was also a godfather to many children, and took these responsibilities very seriously. He did not realize he had narrowly escaped death on 10 July 1923 while he was on the way to the christening of one of his godchildren. Men with rifles were hiding in buildings at a road junction ready to ambush him, but at the crucial moment hundreds of children came out of a nearby school. They held their fire, and Villa escaped. Ten days later he was back at the same junction. As he passed, a street vendor shouted 'Viva Villa!' It was a signal, and this time seven gunmen opened fire on his car, hitting the revolutionary nine times, killing him instantly. His chauffeur, his secretary and two of his three bodyguards also died. The third was seriously wounded, but managed to escape after killing one of the gunmen. Following the shooting, the assassins left town at a leisurely pace, apparently confident that no one was going to arrest them. But Villa's remaining men managed to track down the six and hand them over to the authorities. Two were given short gaol terms and four others military commissions, suggesting the attack had official approval. A local politician took sole responsibility for giving the orders, and was sentenced to twenty years in prison, but released after three months. As to who was really behind the assassination, historians have tended to blame either President Obregon or the frontrunner for the election due in 1924, who was afraid Villa might stand himself. Or was it revenge on the part of the son of one of his former generals who had switched sides and then been killed by the revolutionary? Whoever it was, Villa was buried with full military honours and thousands of mourners turned out.

Though both assassinated revolutionaries had devoted their lives to fighting Mexican governments, both ended up having their names inscribed on the list of illustrious Mexicans on the walls of the Chamber of Deputies. A contemporary newspaper commented on Zapata's death: 'It is the eternal mistake of all tyrants to believe that their enemies are men, not the ideas that these men embody.'

The Only Assassination of a British Prime Minister

The Age of Revolution also saw the only assassination of a British prime minister, though his death had nothing to do with revolution or great political events. In spite of his unfortunate distinction, his name is little known, but Spencer Perceval became premier in one of the nation's darkest hours. In 1809 Napoleon's armies were running riot in Europe and his trade embargo was throttling Britain's economy, with falling wages, short-time working and businesses closing, while the country's great leader, Pitt the Younger, had died at a tragically early age. Perceval had served under Pitt and other prime ministers, and had become Chancellor of the Exchequer at 44. He was seen by many as mediocre and by some as reactionary, and he was certainly a fierce opponent of Roman Catholic emancipation, but in the *Oxford History of England*, J. Steven Watson wrote: 'His clear head was his greatest asset in politics, along with his courage. Everyone knew him to be both honest and good.' He won admiration and the nickname 'Plucky Perceval' for his determination, against considerable opposition, to find the money for the Peninsular War, enabling the French to be harassed with hit-and-run tactics in Spain and Portugal.

By the spring of 1812 Perceval's policies seemed to have been vindicated. Wellington had cleared Napoleon's troops from Portugal and was well on the way to final victory in Spain, Britain was seizing colonial territories all over the world, and France's trade embargo was beginning to wilt. At about five o' clock in the evening on 11 May 1812, Perceval was walking through the House of Commons lobby when he was approached by a man named John Bellingham. Bellingham was a commercial agent who had been imprisoned for debt, perhaps unjustly, for five years in Russia. He was angry with the British authorities generally, but in particular with the ambassador to Russia, Lord Granville Leveson-Gower, whom he felt had let him down. On his return to England in 1810, he kept petitioning the authorities, becoming a familiar figure to MPs as he constantly tried to lobby them. He even approached Perceval himself, but the prime minister refused to put his plea before parliament.

By May 1812 Bellingham had started practising with a pistol on London's Primrose Hill, and on 11 May he went to the House of Commons to confront Granville, who was also an MP. The former ambassador did not appear, but Perceval did, and Bellingham shot him through the heart at close range. The assassin made no attempt to escape, but instead handed himself over, saying: 'I am the unfortunate man.' In spite of Britain's reviving fortunes, the atmosphere in the country was still febrile, with the Luddites smashing machinery in the East Midlands. A crowd gathered around the coach carrying Bellingham to prison to try to free him, and mobs in Nottinghamshire and Leicestershire celebrated the prime minister's death. A poem appeared comparing Perceval to the tyrant

British Prime Minister Spencer Perceval, assassinated in the House of Commons: engraving made c. 1809–40.

Julius Caesar, and some thought this might be the start of an English revolution. In fact, Bellingham was promptly put on trial. His counsel tried to plead insanity but the motion was refused. The accused told the court that Perceval had denied him justice, 'sheltering himself behind the imagined security of his station, and trampling upon law and right in the belief that no retribution could reach him'. When a prime minister 'sets himself above the laws . . . he does it as his own personal risk'. He hoped his action would 'operate as a warning to all future ministers'. It took the jury only ten minutes to find Bellingham guilty and he was hanged just a week after the killing. Three years later, Britain had won its titanic struggle with Napoleonic France, and soon after the Luddites were crushed. Office had not made Perceval rich. He died virtually penniless, and his family of thirteen children had to be saved from poverty by the charity of Parliament.

I HAVE ANALYSED fifty assassinations from the Age of Revolution, involving 52 victims; 25 were leading politicians, including ten presidents and three prime ministers. Fourteen were royalty, among them four kings, two emperors and two empresses. Three were governors or viceroys, two were military leaders and one the boss of the secret police, while another was a writer and propagandist who opposed liberal reforms. But opponents of the establishment were targeted too; six victims were rebel leaders or revolutionaries. Women victims became more common, but there were still just three among the sample of 52. Nearly half of the assassinations, 24, happened in Europe, and the rest were spread across another four continents, with thirteen in Asia, six in Latin America, five in North America and two in Africa. They happened in 31 countries, with Russia seeing most at seven. Japan suffered six, followed by France with four and the USA with three – all presidents. Three victims tried to fight back, and one Stefan Stambolov, the former prime minister of Bulgaria, managed to shoot one of his assailants in 1895. In four cases, including the American presidents Garfield and McKinley, poor medical care contributed to the victims' deaths.

Twelve of the killers were revolutionaries, two of whom murdered rival revolutionaries, while in Japan, reactionary samurai opposing changes to the established order carried out six murders of politicians between 1860 and 1889 in what to some degree may have been copycat killings. Assassination within the family declined further, with one being carried out by two half-brothers and another by two nephews, while a godfather was behind the murder of a Serbian revolutionary. There was an increase in the proportion of lone assassins to more than a third – at work in eighteen out of fifty killings. Only two women participated in assassinations during the Age of Revolution, and there appears to have been just one instance of *Day of the Jackal*-style hired killers being used – those detailed by a political opponent to murder Antonio José de Sucre y Alcalá, liberator of Ecuador and Peru, in 1830. Among the instigators, there were fewer people in authority than in previous eras, though they included a president, a ruling prince and a bishop, and none of them dirtied their own hands. Two assassinations, those of presidents Abraham Lincoln in 1865 and Gabriel García Moreno of Ecuador in 1875, spawned conspiracy theories.

If we look at motive, at least nineteen assassinations were aimed at advancing revolution or national liberation or stopping the reversal of liberal reforms. On the other hand, fourteen were attempts to hinder revolution or revolutionary extremism, reform, or, in the case of the samurai, Westernization. Half a dozen were prompted by the wish to get rid of a leader seen as unfit or incompetent, while eight were done to achieve other political ends, including one mounted by a foreign power when Japanese assassins killed Queen Min of Korea in 1895 in an attempt to replace her with a more pliant ruler. Another eight were motivated by revenge or resentment, religion was a factor in two cases, while two assassins may have been mentally unbalanced.

There was a big change in method, with guns taking over from stabbing as the favourite, used in 26 of the 44 assassinations where we know the means. They were particularly favoured in Latin America where five out of six assassinations involved a firearm. Stabbing was still the means in seventeen cases, used in conjunction with a gun on a couple of occasions. Bombs were called into action twice, in Russia, while other weapons included a machete, a spear, an axe, a bludgeon, poison, strangling and, in the case of Empress Elisabeth, a customized industrial needle. Guns and bombs meant greater risk of collateral damage, which happened in at least four cases. Twenty bystanders were injured when Tsar Alexander II was assassinated, Grand Duke Sergei Alexandrovich's coachman was blown up, while in 1899 a stray bullet from the assassins of President Ulises Heureaux of the Dominican Republic killed a beggar.

As to the fate of the assassins, four were killed immediately, and one other soon after, four killed themselves, though only one did it immediately at the scene, while three of the killers of Antonio José de Sucre appear to have been poisoned by their comrades to make sure they told no tales. In 25 cases the assassins were executed within a year or so of their crime, while one of the Japanese samurai assassins was executed for other crimes eight years later, and a Chinese instigator who masterminded the murder of the Portuguese governor of Macau in 1849 was put to death by the Chinese authorities only after the Portuguese started a war. Three assassins were exiled and four were imprisoned, one of whom killed himself, while another died in mysterious circumstances. Three were pardoned or given immunity, and two were rewarded. In up to seven cases, no real attempt was made to arrest the killers, while in another five they escaped. A couple of assassins were freed after agreeing to give evidence against their old comrades, but, as we saw, one of these, James Carey, who was involved in the Phoenix Park murders, paid for his informing with his life. Two assassins and one instigator took over the reins of power themselves, but the assassin of President Heureaux had to wait six years before taking office, and he was then assassinated himself twelve years later.

The aftermath of seven of the assassinations was serious instability, but in five of these cases there had already been disorder before the murder. Four led to security crackdowns and another to a full-blown reign of terror, while the assassination of Marat failed to end a reign of terror. In sixteen instances, the assassination did not seriously shake the status quo, with the victim's successor ruling for at least ten years in six cases, including one in which he lasted nearly sixty. After eight assassinations, the regime or policies attacked by the killers survived, notably the Westernization process in Japan, and two attempts to shake colonial regimes in Macau and Malaysia also failed, while in the Philippines in 1763, the assassination of a rebel leader helped end a revolt. In contrast, within two years of the assassination of the French General Jean-Baptiste Kléber in Cairo in 1800, the European power had been expelled from Egypt.

Breaches of faith featured in at least four of the assassinations. General Kléber's killer posed as a beggar and struck as his victim offered alms, while the governor of Macau's assassin attacked as he was handing money to a beggar woman. One victim was killed on the steps of a church, and in the Philippines, Diego Silang had his killing ordered by a man of God, a bishop. One assassin, Vujica Vulićević, who murdered his godson in Serbia in 1817, felt enough remorse to build a church, while the student who killed the right-wing writer August von Kotzebue in Germany in 1819 was so horrified by what he had done that he tried to kill himself. Of the 41 cases where we know enough about the motive of the killer and the aftermath of the assassination to make a judgement, seventeen would appear to have been successful, with ten successful to some degree, while eleven can be put down as clear failures and three more as possible failures.

6

THE MODERN AGE: WORLD WARS AND TERRORISM

Now surely here is one in the eye for Disraeli. Assassinations never changed the course of history? Well, what about the murder of the Archduke Franz Ferdinand, heir to the Habsburg Austro-Hungarian Empire? Everybody knows that caused the First World War!

Archduke Franz Ferdinand

Franz Ferdinand's faults were many. He was bad-tempered, obstinate and a bully, but he loved his wife dearly. He was meant to marry an archduchess, but while he was courting her he fell for one of her ladies-in-waiting, Sophie Chotek. She was a penniless countess, and regarded by the reigning emperor, Franz Josef, as not nearly grand enough to wed the archduke, but Franz Ferdinand stuck to his guns, and in 1900 married they were. The price was that their children would be excluded from the imperial succession, and that Sophie would have to suffer many slights, such as being denied the titles of archduchess and imperial highness and not being allowed to sit next to her husband at official state occasions. All this infuriated Franz Ferdinand, but there was a loophole. He was a field marshal, and inspector-general of the Austro-Hungarian army, and when he was acting in those capacities, his wife could be by his side. So, on Sunday 28 June 1914, their fourteenth wedding anniversary, the archduke took Sophie with him to inspect the army in Bosnia.

Bosnia had been ruled by the Ottoman Empire until 1878, part of the Balkans region that had been a hotbed of assassination during the Age of Revolution. A series of revolts there and in neighbouring Serbia led to the end of centuries of Turkish rule, but, while Serbia got its independence, Bosnia was handed over to Austria-Hungary to the fury of many of its people, especially ethnic Serbs, and within its borders a number of groups formed to try to promote Slavic unity. Pan-Slavism was a major threat to Austria-Hungary's Habsburg rulers, whose subjects included 23 million Slavs, and they grew ever more apprehensive about Serbia's promotion of it. Franz Ferdinand was believed to want to allow more autonomy to the empire's Slavs, but the Serbian government was not overjoyed at this, fearing it might dilute the passion of Slav nationalism, which it was hoping to exploit to expand its borders. Then into this already turbulent scene walked a sinister group known as the Black Hand which aimed to unite all Serbs through terrorism. Heavily influenced by Bakunin and Nechaev's *Catechism of a Revolutionary*, and the 'propaganda of the deed', the group organized a mysterious network of agents, known only by numbers or codenames, and linked only through intermediaries to try to maintain maximum security. One of its founders was the rather dashing Colonel Dragutin Dimitrijević, a leading light in the Serbian intelligence service. With his codename 'Apis' (Bee), he had been busy, if not always successful, in royal assassination projects. In 1903 he organized and was wounded during the brutal murder of King Alexander of Serbia and his queen, whose mutilated bodies were flung from a second-floor window onto a manure heap. (Alexander was thought to be too pro-Austrian and increasingly dictatorial.) This led to Dimitrijević's advancement under the murdered king's successor, but a plot to kill Franz Josef in 1911 failed, so the colonel turned his attention to Franz Ferdinand.

In 1912 an eighteen-year-old Bosnian Serb, Gavrilo Princip, was expelled from his school for taking part in a demonstration against the Austro-Hungarian authorities. A member of the Young Bosnia movement dedicated to ending Austrian rule, he was also said to have threatened with a knuckle-duster boys who were reluctant to attend. Princip was inspired by a martyr, Bogdan Žerajić, a 22-year-old medical student who had tried to shoot the governor of Bosnia in 1910, then shot himself after he missed. Princip said he would spend nights by Žerajić's grave 'thinking about our situation, about our miserable conditions'. Of peasant stock, he had read Bakunin and Kropotkin, but when he went to the Serbian capital, Belgrade, to try to join guerrilla bands fighting the Turks in the Balkan Wars of 1912–13, he was turned down as too weak and sickly. Frustrated, he and a group of friends began to hatch a plot in a Belgrade café. He signed up his roommate Trifko Grabež, aged nineteen and the son of an Orthodox priest. He would be the only one of the conspirators with a criminal record, acquired for hitting a teacher. Another friend of Princip, Nedeljko Čabrinović, was also nineteen and a printer, working with a firm that specialized in anarchist literature. Čabrinović had tuberculosis, but believed he was endowed with superhuman powers. They made contact with the Black Hand – it is not clear who approached whom – and at the end of May 1914 the terrorist group smuggled them into Bosnia. There they joined a four-man cell recruited by 23-year-old Black Hand member Danilo Ilić. The others were Muslim carpenter Muhamed Mehmedbašić, aged 28, who had been involved in at least one failed assassination plot, and two seventeen-year-old schoolboys, Vaso Ćubrilović and Cvjetko Popović.

It may be that their original target was General Oskar Potiorek, the new governor of Bosnia, but that Dimitrijević got them to switch to Franz Ferdinand. (Dimitrijević disliked Serbia's prime minister, and it is possible his main aim in the enterprise was to embarrass his government.) The Black Hand provided a bit of firearms training and supplied the plotters with four pistols, half a dozen bombs and cyanide capsules – it was meant to be a suicide mission. The Serbian government had got wind of the plot and was in a dilemma. There was plenty of sympathy for the Black Hand, but the country was exhausted by the Balkan Wars and the last thing it needed was a dust-up with Austria. On the other hand, too determined an attempt to obstruct the group would upset many Serbs. So the government made a half-hearted, unsuccessful attempt to intercept the conspirators at the border and delivered a half-hearted warning to the Austrian government suggesting Franz Ferdinand should not go to Sarajevo. It was disregarded.

So, the lovely sunny morning of 28 June saw the archduke and his wife being driven in an open-top car to Sarajevo's town hall, along with General Potiorek. The governor was worried about his budget, so he did not request extra police, but made do with what he had. Franz Ferdinand had faced many threats to his life, and took a philosophical view: 'We are all constantly in danger of death. One must simply trust in God.' He asked the driver to go slowly, so the crowds could get a good view of the royal couple. The assassins were stationed at intervals along the route, while Ilić, who may not have been armed, floated between them, making sure all was well. The first to sight Franz Ferdinand was Mehmedbašić, but as the cavalcade of six vehicles came past, a policeman took up a position close to him, and he did nothing. Next was Čabrinović, who threw his bomb, packed with nails, but Franz Ferdinand's driver saw it coming and accelerated. It bounced off the car and exploded in the road, injuring a number of spectators as well as the governor's aide, Lieutenant Colonel Merizzi, and causing a small cut to Sophie's cheek. Čabrinović promptly bit into his cyanide pill, but the poison was past its 'use by' date, so then he leapt into the river, hoping to drown, but the water was too shallow. Vomiting, he was grabbed by the crowd and handed over to the police. Ćubrilović did not fire – he said later it was because he felt sorry for the duchess – and Popović and Grabez lost their nerve and ran off home, just as Mehmedbašić had already done. Princip had heard the explosion and had run towards it. Then Franz Ferdinand's car sped past him before he could shoot. Depressed, he went to a café. The assassination squad had been exposed as a bunch of bungling amateurs, but the archduke was to hand them a second chance.

Philosophical about assassination he might have been, but by the time the motorcade reached the town hall, Franz Ferdinand, perhaps understandably, was in a filthy temper. The mayor, who had himself been in one of the cars, embarked nervously on a welcome speech, only for the archduke to interrupt him, shouting: 'I come here as your guest and you people greet me with bombs!' After a while, Franz Ferdinand recovered his composure, and it was decided to call off a planned visit to the national museum so he could go and see Merizzi in hospital. Some of Franz Ferdinand's staff expressed their concerns, but Potiorek pooh-poohed them, asking: 'What, you really think Sarajevo is full of assassins?' Still, the archduke tried to persuade Sophie to stay out of harm's way, but she insisted on accompanying him. To give extra protection, Count Franz von Harrach, who was in charge of security, stood on the running board of the royal car, but with no Merizzi to coordinate things, there was a mix-up. Potiorek devised a new, supposedly safer route, but neglected to tell Franz Ferdinand's driver. So when the archduke's car took a wrong turning, the governor shouted to its driver to stop, which he did, right outside the café where Princip had taken refuge. Unable to believe his luck, the young man stepped forward, and in a scene reminiscent of the assassination of Henry IV of France while he was caught in a traffic jam in Paris 304 years earlier, he fired twice from less than five yards. Harrach may have been on the running board, but it was the wrong running board, the one furthest from the kerb. The first shot hit Franz Ferdinand in the neck. The second was probably meant for Potiorek, but as the wounded archduke tried to shield his wife, it thudded into Sophie's abdomen. The car sped off, but within a few minutes, the royal couple were both dead.

An Italian newspaper, the *Domenica del Corriere*, delivers the dreadful news of the assassination of Archduke Franz Ferdinand.

Princip swallowed his cyanide, but to no more effect than Čabrinović. He also tried to turn his gun on himself, but the crowd grabbed him and would have lynched him if the police had not intervened and arrested him. The courts of Europe went into mourning, and in Bosnia there were anti-Serb riots. Apprehension spread across the world. In America, the *Christian Science Monitor* agonized: 'What all this will mean no man can tell.' Princip tried to claim he acted alone, but Čabrinović confessed that others had helped with weapons and money. A routine round-up of the usual suspects landed Ilić, who offered to tell all if his life was spared. Soon all the conspirators were arrested apart from Mehmedbašić, who got away to Montenegro. Charges were also brought against nearly twenty others for providing weapons, money or other help. At his trial, Princip was unrepentant: 'I have seen our people being steadily ruined . . . This is why I meant to take my revenge and I regret nothing.' The authorities appeared to have behaved with scrupulous fairness. The five captured conspirators who had actually been armed with guns and bombs were under twenty and therefore not subject to the death penalty. Only Ilić was executed, along with two other men who had provided help. One was Ćubrilović's elder brother. Those who had actually been in place with weapons got gaol terms of up to twenty years. Čabrinović, he of the superhuman powers, Princip and Grabez all died in prison from tuberculosis before the First World War ended. Princip was horrified by the conflict, but did not believe their action had caused it, while Čabrinović was overcome by remorse, saying: 'if I had foreseen what was to happen I should have sat down on the bombs to blow myself to bits.' Dimitrijević was tried and executed in 1917 for his part in a failed assassination plot against another king Alexander, prince regent of Serbia and later king of Yugoslavia, though there is doubt about his guilt. Mehmedbašić died in Sarjevo during the Second World War, while Popović and Vaso Ćubrilović both lived into ripe old age, Ćubrilović having been a minister in Tito's communist government in Yugoslavia.

So, did the assassination of Franz Ferdinand cause the First World War? One view is that the competing alliances into which Europe was divided – Germany and Austria on one side faced by Russia, France and Great Britain on the other – meant war was inevitable. Franz Ferdinand's assassination might have been the spark that set off the conflagration, but if that had not happened, sooner or later there would have been another. Others argue that if anything, animosities seemed to have been easing, with radicals and pacifists dominating the French parliament, and relations between Germany and the UK improving. Then there is a theory that Germany was itching for war, believing that in 1914 its army was at the height of its superiority and that soon France and Russia would catch up, so when Austria approached them for support a week after the assassination, did the Germans see this as a good way to set the ball rolling towards war? (Germany urged its ally to stand firm.) On the other hand, the Kaiser and the German forces chief both went on holiday, and you could argue that the country was well on the way to becoming Europe's top power without a war because of the strength of its industry.

Or was the real cause of the Great War a series of mistakes and poor judgements by politicians following the assassination? Certainly no one seemed in a tearing hurry to use Franz Ferdinand's murder to start hostilities. It was not until 23 July that Austria got round to sending its ultimatum to Serbia. Apparently it had been looking for evidence, which it never found, that the Serbian government was involved in the plot. Though the ultimatum was designed to be humiliating and unacceptable, the Serbs managed to swallow

Did his shot start the First World War? The man who killed the archduke, Gavrilo Princip, in his prison cell, 1914.

almost all of it, but five days later Austria still declared war. Then Serbia's protector, Russia, felt it had to mobilize. Was this meant to be a deterrent rather than the starting pistol for war? We will never know, because soon Germany, France and Britain were all throwing around mobilizations, ultimata and declarations of war, and 37 days after the assassination of Franz Ferdinand the First World War began. Whatever its cause, it did little good to Serbia or Austria-Hungary. Of all the combatants, Serbia lost a higher proportion of its population to violence or disease than any other – 15 per cent – while the great Austro-Hungarian Empire was dismembered.

Peacemakers Look Out!

About 20 million people lost their lives in the First World War, more than half of them civilians, and the twentieth century as a whole has seen human beings die violently in unprecedented numbers; more than 230 million according to one estimate. So perhaps not surprisingly, assassination has proliferated too. It seemed you could be murdered for promoting or opposing virtually any cause: apartheid, abortion, civil rights, gay rights, blasphemy laws, children's rights. You name it. Particularly dangerous was campaigning for peace. One of the anti-war deputies who dominated the French parliament in the months leading up to the First World War was the famous socialist Jean Jaurès. On 31 July 1914, just days before the war engulfed Europe, he was sitting in a café on his way home from the office of his newspaper, *L'Humanité*, where he had been writing another anti-war article, even though it was beginning to look like a futile exercise. A 28-year-old French nationalist named Raoul Villain was incensed by what he saw as Jaurès' lack of patriotism, and had been stalking him for some time. There was mental instability in Villain's family and the young man seemed to find it hard to settle to anything. He had been discharged early from military service, and become involved with a far-right group, though most people he came across commented on his gentleness.

Jean Jaurès' own newspaper carries the story of his assassination,
1 August 1914.

On 30 July, with a revolver in each pocket, he had come within a few yards of Jaurès, but had lost his nerve and done nothing. The next night, he went to the offices of *L'Humanité*, but the deputy was not there. Then close by, Villain spotted his target having a drink in a café, his back towards an open window. Villain watched him for some time before shooting him in the neck. Jaurès died at the café. His assassin tried to run off but was grabbed by one of the deputy's colleagues from *L'Humanité* and handed over to the police. Jaurès' funeral was on 4 August, a day after Germany and France had declared war. Villain never got the chance to demonstrate his 'patriotism' in the conflict. He sat the whole thing out, awaiting trial.

When the case was finally heard in March 1919, France, having just won a titanic struggle at huge cost, was in a patriotic fervour, and Jaurès' killer was acquitted. Releasing Villain, the president of the court praised him for being a good patriot. The left in France was incensed, and organized a series of demonstrations. Meanwhile Villain fell into petty crime, and made a couple of attempts to kill himself. He went abroad, washing up in Ibiza, where he became known as 'the madman of the port'. In 1936, during the Spanish Civil War, he was killed by Republican soldiers, though it is not clear whether they knew who he was.

Michael Collins was a great hero of Ireland's struggle for independence, and he knew a thing or two about assassination. As chief

Michael Collins's funeral, Dublin, 1922.

planner for the Irish Republican Army (IRA), he organized plenty of killings, including the murder of a dozen of Britain's leading intelligence agents on a single day in 1920. The following year, he signed a peace treaty with the British, which divided Ireland into the six counties of Northern Ireland, which today are still part of the United Kingdom, and the 26 which make up the Irish Republic. In addition, Irish MPs were required to swear an oath to 'be faithful' to the king. Collins was not over the moon about the terms, but he believed they were the best Ireland could get at that point, and that the treaty gave his country 'the freedom to achieve freedom'. Still, he had no illusions about how angry it would make some of his IRA comrades. 'This morning,' he wrote, 'I signed my own death warrant.' The treaty did not bring peace but a sword, as pro- and anti-factions fought a vicious civil war. On 22 August 1922 Collins was ambushed in his native County Cork. The assassins, who had learned by accident that he was in the area, waited all day, and, rather like the killers of Lord Frederick Cavendish forty years before, were just about to pack up when his convoy came into view. As they opened fire, one of Collins's close comrades told the driver to 'drive like hell', but Collins ordered him to stop so they could fight it out. The shoot-out lasted half an hour, with Collins trying to defend himself with a rifle, until he was finally hit in the head and killed, probably by a former British army marksman turned Irish rebel. He was the only fatal casualty of the gun battle.

Mahatma Gandhi was a Hindu hero of India's struggle for independence, but also an opponent of violence, and when inter-communal fighting between Hindus and Muslims started tearing the country apart, he battled just as hard for peace. Great Britain's last viceroy, Earl Mountbatten, described him as a 'one-man peace-keeping force'. Although in his late seventies, he would walk barefoot from village to village, visiting nearly fifty in the divided area of East Bengal. His modus operandi was to go first to a Muslim family's hut, and chat with the people there. Then he would stay in the village for a few days, talking and praying, before moving on. And his efforts did have some effect; relations between Hindus and Muslims improved, said one observer, 'perceptibly but insufficiently'. The day after independence in August 1947, Gandhi pitched his tent in Calcutta and announced he would fast until the killing stopped. His prestige was so great that it did subside. Then he moved on to Delhi, preaching non-violence every day, and shaming the city into a communal truce. While he was still trying to halt the troubles, Gandhi was shot dead at point blank range as he walked to evening prayers on 30 January 1948 by a Hindu fanatic newspaper editor, Nathuram Godse. The Mahatma had frequently denounced assassination, describing it on one occasion as a 'Western institution' that had never done any good. Eight men were convicted of involvement in his murder, and Godse and one other were hanged in spite of pleas for mercy from Gandhi's sons. (Godse had been involved in a number of attempted attacks on Gandhi, but as was the Mahatma's wont, he had refused to press charges.) At his trial, Godse accused Gandhi of being 'unfairly favourable towards the Muslims' and said he had brought 'rack and ruin and destruction to millions of Hindus'. More than a million people are estimated to have perished in the great upheaval at the birth of India and Pakistan, either as victims of violence or of diseases contracted on refugee marches.

During the second half of the twentieth century, a total of three winners of the Nobel Peace Prize were assassinated. A veteran of the struggle to free Egypt from British dominance, Anwar Sadat had become president in 1970. In the Yom Kippur War against Israel in 1973, he became the first Arab leader to retake territory from Israel. Then he worked tirelessly for reconciliation, and in 1979 Egypt became the first Arab country to sign a peace treaty with the old enemy, a feat for which Sadat won the Peace Prize along with the Israeli prime minister Menachem Begin. But the initiative was not universally welcomed inside Egypt, and economic problems were also making Sadat unpopular. On 6 October

1981, as he attended a military parade in Cairo to celebrate the eighth anniversary of the Yom Kippur War, a group of Muslim extremists led by a lieutenant in the Egyptian army leapt from a truck and opened fire, killing Sadat and eleven other dignitaries. Security forces managed to slay two of the assailants and overpower the others. Five were later executed. Fourteen years later, it was the turn of an Israeli winner of the Nobel Peace Prize. A leading player in shaping the country's forces for their victory in the Six-Day War of 1967, Yitzhak Rabin had been Israel's military chief of staff before becoming prime minister. He won the prize in 1994 for his peace negotiations with the Palestinian leader Yasser Arafat, who shared it. Rabin also signed a peace treaty with Jordan. The following year, he was shot dead by a right-wing extremist at a peace rally. The peace that Sadat made with Israel has held, while,

President Sadat of Egypt at Camp David, USA, where he made peace with Israel, 1978.

following Rabin's death, Israel and the Palestinians have fought a series of wars, and peace between them remains elusive.

Collins, Ghandi, Sadat and Rabin were national heroes as well as peacemakers, but being a hero is no protection against assassination even if you are not a peacemaker. Mujibur Rahman, the father of Bangladesh, was the country's first prime minister and first president. In 1971, with Indian help in a vicious civil war, the country had won independence from Pakistan, but self-rule did not mean life became a bed of roses. There was conflict with groups who wanted it to remain part of Pakistan, and severe economic problems: inflation, shortages, even famine. At the beginning of 1975 Mujibur Rahman imposed one-party rule, and seven months later disaffected junior army officers invaded his residence, killing him and members of his family and personal staff. There are reports that he ignored warnings about the attack from the Indian intelligence services, saying: 'These are my own children and they will not harm me.' One of his daughters survived because she was away in Germany, and went on to become Bangladesh's prime minister 21 years later. Her father's murder was followed by years of instability, with another president assassinated by army officers in 1981, and the country's politics remained bitterly polarized. Five army officers were executed for their part in Rahman's death in 2010, and a sixth in 2020.

Assassination by Extremists of Left and Right

A wide range of political factions used assassination – anarchists, fascists, communists, Nazis, Sunni and Shia extremists, the Red Brigades, the Red Army Faction, along with nationalists such as the IRA, the Basque separatist group ETA and the the Sri Lankan Tamil Tigers. A Heidelberg statistician calculated that between 1919 and the murder of Foreign Minister Walter Rathenau in 1922, Germany suffered 376 political murders, of which 354 were committed by the right. He also concluded that the courts were far

The assassin of Trotsky, Ramón Mercader, during his trial in Mexico, 1940.

more lenient towards right-wing than left-wing killers. Rathenau, incidentally, was probably the first victim of a drive-by assassination. A group of right-wing ultra-nationalists knew that on his way to the office in Berlin his car had to slow down at a double bend. They followed him in their own vehicle, then drew alongside and opened fire before speeding off. The French Fascist group the CSAR, also known as La Cagoule, committed a number of assassinations in the 1930s and early 1940s. But, as the Heidelberg statistician noted, the left were assassins as well as victims. Anarchists gunned down Spain's prime minister Eduardo Dato Iradier in the street in Madrid in 1921, and sometimes the left murdered each other. Leon Trotsky had been a hero of the Russian Revolution until he fell out with Stalin and had to flee to Mexico, where he was killed with an ice-pick by a Spanish communist, Ramón Mercader, in 1940. Although Trotsky was ill, he fought gamely and managed to bite his assailant's hand. Mercader was sent to gaol for twenty years. On his release, he was named a Hero of the Soviet Union, and spent his last eighteen years in Cuba. The Nazis too were sometimes perpetrators and sometimes victims. In the early 1930s Austria's Chancellor Engelbert Dollfuss was a fascist dictator and an anti-Semite, but he wanted to keep his country out of the clutches of Hitler next door in Germany. In 1934, with the Führer's approval, Austrian Nazis tried to mount a coup. They had no problem getting into the Chancellery, partly because the guards had no ammunition in their rifles. As Dollfuss tried to get away, he was shot dead by the Austrian Nazi leader, Otto Planetta. The coup failed, but four years later Hitler annexed Austria. In 1942 one of the leading Nazi architects of the Holocaust, Reinhard Heydrich, was assassinated in Czechoslovakia (see below).

The end of the Second World War did not bring an end to assassination by political extremists. In 1950 the chairman of the Belgian Communist Party, Julien Lahaut, was shot dead at his front door by two men believed to be Royalists. In Italy in the 1970s and '80s the Marxist Red Brigades murdered nearly fifty people, including politicians, police officers and soldiers. Around the same time, the radical left-wing Red Army Faction, also known as the Baader-Meinhof Group, was doing the same kind of thing in Germany. In Spain right-wing terrorists were assassinating lawyers who specialized in defending workers' rights, while in the twenty-first century Sunni and Shia death squads roamed Iraq.

In the Name of National Liberation

As for nationalist groups, between 1969 and 1994, the Provisional IRA killed about 1,800 people including soldiers, policemen and politicians, while in London in 1975, they gunned down the editor of the *Guinness Book of Records*, Ross McWhirter, outside his home after he had offered a £50,000 reward for information that might lead to the conviction of IRA bombers in London. But their most famous victim was probably Earl Mountbatten of Burma, a great-grandson

Earl Mountbatten
in the uniform of an
Admiral of the Fleet.

of Queen Victoria, the uncle of Prince Philip and the godfather
and mentor of Prince Charles. He had had a distinguished military
career, though not one without serious blemishes, and had ended
the Second World War as Supreme Allied Commander in Southeast
Asia. Then, as India's last viceroy, he had been in charge of ending
British rule in India, the process that turned into a bloody feud
between Hindus and Muslims.

Mountbatten often took holidays at his house in Mullaghmore,
a little village in the Republic of Ireland, a dozen miles from the
border with Northern Ireland. The area was a notorious IRA stronghold, and the Irish police had warned the earl he might be in
danger, but Mountbatten, rather like assassinated Bangladeshi president Mujibur Rahman, trusted to what he thought was his
popularity with local people. On 27 August 1979, then aged 79,
Mountbatten was planning to go out with his family in his boat,
Shadow v. The night before, IRA man Thomas McMahon crept
aboard the unguarded craft and planted a 22-kilogram (50 lb)
radio-controlled bomb. The next day when the Mountbatten party

was out sailing about 500 m (550 yd) from shore, the IRA detonated the bomb remotely, blowing the boat to bits and throwing the occupants into the water. Local fishermen rushed to the rescue, and managed to pull Mountbatten out, but he died before they could get him ashore. His fifteen-year-old grandson Nicholas was also killed, along with his sister-in-law, the 83-year-old Dowager Lady Brabourne, and a fifteen-year-old boathand. Nicholas's twin brother was injured but survived, as did his mother and father. The IRA admitted causing the explosion, saying it was to bring 'to the attention of the English people the continuing occupation of our country'.

Coincidentally, two hours before the explosion, Irish police had arrested McMahon, because they suspected he was driving a stolen car. After forensics experts found flecks of paint from the boat and traces of nitroglycerine on his clothes, he was tried and sentenced to life imprisonment. No one else involved in the attack was ever arrested, and McMahon was released in 1998 under the Good Friday Agreement. On the same day they assassinated Mountbatten, the IRA killed eighteen British soldiers in Northern Ireland in what became known as the Warrenpoint ambush – the deadliest single attack on the British army in the whole of 'The Troubles'.

On the other side of Northern Ireland's religious and political divide, in 1999 Loyalist terrorists used a car bomb to murder solicitor Rosemary Nelson, who had represented many Republican clients. In Spain, assassination was deployed by ETA. In 1973, for example, they used a remote-controlled bomb to blow up a car carrying Prime Minister Luis Carrero Blanco, the man earmarked by the country's dictator, President Franco, to take over from him. The assassins fooled people into thinking it was a gas explosion, and in the confusion they managed to escape into France. In 1991 a woman suicide bomber from the Tamil Tigers murdered former Indian prime minister Rajiv Gandhi while he was campaigning in Tamil Nadu. (Rajiv was the son of Indira Gandhi, who was herself assassinated.) They were angry that four years earlier India had helped the Sri Lankan government against the Tigers.

National liberation of a different kind came into play in apartheid South Africa. The struggle was not to expel an entity seen as a foreign oppressor, but one firmly entrenched within the country – the white supremacist regime. Hendrik Verwoerd was one of the leading architects of apartheid. As South Africa's minister for native affairs in the 1950s, he passed a whole series of laws designed to segregate the races, like the Prohibition of Mixed Marriages Act and the Group Areas Act, which determined which races could live where. He carried on the work after he became prime minister in 1958. Two years later at Sharpeville, police opened fire on a crowd protesting against apartheid laws, killing 69 people – mainly women and children. From then on South Africa began to be ostracized, with the United Nations condemning apartheid, and countries including the UK and the USA imposing arms embargoes.

A couple of weeks after Sharpeville, a farmer from Natal named David Pratt shot Verwoerd in the cheek and the ear from point blank range while he was opening an exhibition, but surgeons managed to save his life. Pratt was found to be 'mentally disordered and epileptic', and was sentenced to be detained indefinitely. He hanged himself in Bloemfontein Mental Hospital in 1961. Five years later, Verwoerd was attacked in South Africa's parliamentary chamber by a uniformed messenger, Dimitri Tsafendas, a mixed-race immigrant from Mozambique, then a Portuguese colony, who was working as a temp. He managed to stab the prime minister four times in the neck and chest before he was disarmed by other members of parliament who also tried to resuscitate the victim, but Verwoerd was dead on arrival at hospital. Tsafendas told police he had killed the prime minister because he was 'so disgusted' by apartheid. He also claimed he had a giant tapeworm in his body that spoke to him on a regular basis. At his trial, like Pratt, he was found to be insane. He spent the rest of life in psychiatric hospitals, dying in 1999 aged 81. A quarter of a million white mourners attended Verwoerd's funeral, and hospitals, roads and other public places were named after him, though most were renamed after the collapse of apartheid in 1994.

In 2018 it was suggested that, far from being insane, Tsafendas was a political assassin of perfectly sound mind. A lengthy dossier to the South African Justice Ministry compiled by eminent legal figures said the Portuguese security services had files on Tsafendas, whom they believed to be an agitator for independence, but that they had concealed this from the South Africans. The report claimed that six years before the killing, Tsafendas had told British anti-apartheid campaigners he was willing to do 'anything' to bring down the South African regime, and that before his successful assassination, he had planned to shoot Verwoerd at a public event but was foiled when the prime minister failed to turn up. They also said that doctors who examined him shortly after the killing had found him to be 'composed', to be showing no signs of mental illness, and that he never mentioned the tapeworm. The report added that it was only after Tsafendas had been subjected to psychological torture that the insanity plea was cooked up and that the South African government grabbed it with both hands so they did not have to admit that a politically motivated killer had been allowed to infiltrate parliament. The report alleges that Tsafendas went along with the story because he was afraid the authorities were going to kill him and make it look like suicide.

Globalized Assassination

In unstable parts of the world, such as the Middle East, much of Latin America and Africa, assassination became almost commonplace. Since 1960 more than sixty leading politicians have been murdered in Africa, and more than forty in Latin America. In the ten years following the British and American invasion of Iraq in 2003, there were at least 24 assassinations of significant figures, including politicians, trade unionists, soldiers and religious leaders, but there was another major development. Just like business, assassination was globalized. As we saw, back in 1649, while he was on an errand for Oliver Cromwell, Isaac Dorislaus was murdered by Royalist agents at The Hague, though they had not travelled there to kill him. They already happened to be in the Dutch city in exile. In the modern age the arm of the assassin got longer, with more and more victims, like Trotsky, meeting their end away from their own country. In 1929 Julio Antonio Mella, the founder of Cuba's first Communist Party, had been murdered, like Trotsky, in Mexico City while he was plotting the overthrow of Cuba's president, General Machado. It is not clear whether he was killed by Machado's agents or by communist rivals. General Carlos Prats was the head of the Chilean army during Salvador Allende's ill-fated socialist regime. After General Pinochet had overthrown the government in 1973, Prats received a number of death threats, and took refuge in Argentina, where he campaigned for the restoration of democracy in Chile. On 30 September 1974 he and his wife were blown up by a car bomb in Buenos Aires. In 2000 an Argentinian court sentenced former Chilean secret service agent Enrique Arancibia to life imprisonment for their murder, but Argentina's attempt to have General Pinochet extradited to face trial fell on deaf ears. After seven years, Arancibia was released on parole. Then in 2011 he was found stabbed to death in his Buenos Aires apartment. Five years after Prats' murder, the president of Nicaragua, Anastasio Somoza, fled to Paraguay when Sandinista guerillas brought down his government. The following year, in spite of tight security, Somoza was killed by a bazooka fired at his armour-plated car by a team of Sandinistas, who had slipped into the country under the leadership of Argentinian revolutionary Enrique Gorriarán Merlo.

Globalized assassination also featured in the bitter, tangled tale of revenge and assassination involving Turks and Armenians fought out over more than a century. Confucius is supposed to have said: 'Before you embark on a journey of revenge, dig two graves.' In fact, many, many graves were needed for this bloody enmity. The Armenians were a Christian minority in the Ottoman Empire. Around the end of the nineteenth century, after years of enduring violence and being treated as second-class citizens, they began agitating for autonomy. Alarmed, Sultan Abdülhamid II started stirring up their Kurdish neighbours against them. In 1894, Kurdish tribesmen teamed up with Turkish troops and killed many thousands. Two years later, Armenian militants seized the Ottoman Bank in Istanbul, and in the mayhem that followed up to 10,000 were killed by Turkish mobs, apparently organized by government troops, but things got even worse when the First World War began. Turkey chose Germany's side, while Russia joined with Great Britain and France. The Russians had also persecuted their own Armenian minority, but as hostilities began the tsar started to woo the Armenians in Turkey and they hoped a Russian victory might mean independence. By then, the Young Turks had effectively taken over from the sultan in Istanbul and they worried the Armenians might become an enemy fifth column. After Turkey suffered a humiliating defeat, in which some of its Armenians fought on the Russian side, the government's propaganda machine flew into action. The result was that more than 50,000 Armenians were murdered in Van province, 17,000 at Trebizond and thousands more in other places. Then there were mass deportations to desert concentration camps with rape and murder along the way. Even though Turkey was Germany's ally, a senior German diplomat said the Turks were 'trying to exterminate the Armenian race' in their country. According to some estimates, 600,000 Armenians were massacred, with another 400,000 dying from the hardships and brutalities of the deportations.

Talaat Pasha was Turkey's interior minister at the time of the massacres. As his country stumbled to defeat in 1918, he had fled in a German submarine and taken refuge in Berlin. Also in the German capital was a young Armenian named Soghomon Tehlirian whose mother and brother had been killed by the Turks. He met other Armenians in exile who told him about 'Operation Nemesis', their plan to assassinate those responsible for the mass murders. One day he recognized Talaat in the street, and began to stalk him. On 15 March 1921, as the former minister was taking the air, Tehlirian came up behind him and shot him in the back of the head. The assassin was almost lynched by bystanders, but at his trial, defence witnesses told the story of the massacres, and his counsel said he was the 'avenger of his people'. It took the jury just an hour to find him not guilty. That December the Turkish Grand Vizier at the time of the deportations was shot dead in Rome. In April 1922 two organizers of the massacres were murdered in Berlin, and just for good measure there were murders of Azeris who had been involved in killing Armenians in Baku. 'Who remembers the Armenians?' was Hitler's scornful question to any who doubted whether he would get away with invading Poland, but actually the Armenian memory proved to be long indeed. In October 1975 three Armenian gunmen stormed the Turkish embassy in Vienna and killed the ambassador. Two days later Turkey's envoy in France was gunned down in his car, while in 1977 Armenian extremists fatally wounded the ambassador to the Vatican.

But the assassinations were not all on one side, and nor did they end with the twentieth century. Hrant Dink was an Armenian newspaper editor who wrote about the massacres in 2005, an activity which resulted in him being arrested for 'insulting Turkishness'.

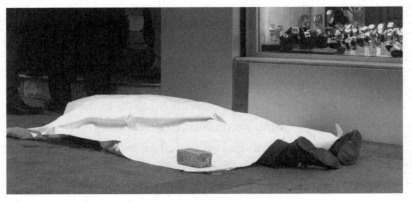

The body of Hrant Dink, who was shot on an Istanbul street, 2007.

In broad daylight on 19 January 2007 he was shot dead by a young man outside his office on a busy Istanbul street. In 2011 Ogün Samast, who was seventeen at the time of the shooting, was sent to prison for 22 years for the killing, while an ultra-nationalist agitator was given a life sentence for inciting him, but Dink's family claimed the Turkish authorities were involved. In 2016, 34 people went on trial, including a police chief and heads of police intelligence, but the fact that a number of them were then alleged to be involved with an attempted coup against President Erdoğan made some believe the charges were politically motivated. Three years later, a former police informer was sentenced to 99 years in prison for his involvement in Dink's killing and other terrorist acts, while four other defendants received short sentences of less than two years.

The Bloody Hand of the State

Extra-territorial assassination tends to be more expensive, so it helps to have governments involved, just as Stalin's probably commissioned the killing of Trotsky, and the modern age has seen governments participating more and more. By the early 1930s Stalin's regime was already heavily bloodstained. As his Five-Year Plan to revolutionize Russian industry ran into trouble, he mounted the first of his show trials, and by the end of 1933, he had already purged more than 1,000 officers from the Red Army and kicked more than a million people out of the Communist Party. While millions were dying from famine in the Ukraine because of his botched 'collectivization' of agriculture, he dispatched 'shock brigades' to seize what little food the peasants had, and sentenced 5,000 to death for supposedly hiding produce.

St Petersburg's world-famous Kirov Ballet is named after Sergei Kirov, Stalin's right-hand man, who was assassinated in the city (then called Leningrad) in December 1934. The Soviet leader made him a national hero and named all manner of things after

A Soviet stamp from 1956 commemorates Sergei Kirov, mysteriously assassinated in 1934.

him besides the ballet. Kirov had been shot in the neck at party headquarters. Instead of leaving the murder investigation to the secret police, Stalin descended on the city with an entourage of subordinates. Within two days of the killing, they had arrested Leonid Nikolaev, who had recently been fired from the Institute of Party History. The authorities said the masterminds were two of Stalin's disgraced former colleagues, but there were a number of discrepancies in the official report. It had the murder taking place in the wrong room. In addition to the fatal bullet fired from point blank range into Kirov's neck, there was another unexplained one lodged in the ceiling, and, most ominously, Kirov's bodyguard died in a mysterious 'car accident' before he could be questioned. All this led to suspicion that Stalin himself had ordered the killing because he saw Kirov as a dangerous rival. Nikolaev was tried in secret and shot. Three people who dared to question the official version of Kirov's murder were also executed. No definitive evidence has ever emerged that Stalin was responsible, though nor has any that he was not, and certainly he used the killing to inaugurate a ferocious reign of terror. In future, those accused of 'planning or carrying out terrorist acts' would have no right to defence counsel and no right of appeal. Of 1,225 delegates to the 1934 Party congress, more than 1,100 were arrested within a year, with most of them dying during interrogation or in the slave labour camps of Siberia, while of 139 members and candidates to the central committee, 98 were arrested or shot.

Of the millions killed by Stalin, assassination accounted for only a tiny fraction, but there was a cynicism and an insolent carelessness about his methods that is particularly chilling. Solomon Mikhoels was an eminent Jewish actor and artistic director of the State Yiddish Theatre. In 1939 he was named a People's Artist of the USSR and awarded the Order of Lenin. Then during the war, he became a member of the Jewish Anti-Fascist Committee, drumming up support for the Soviet Union across the world. But after Russia's victory, Stalin grew ever more paranoid, and Jews became a favourite target. Many members of the Anti-Fascist Committee were tried for treason, but the Soviet leader feared Mikhoels was too popular for him to go down this route. So instead he had the actor murdered by the secret police in 1948. To try to make it look like an accident, his body was then put on a road and run over by a truck. Mikhoels was given a state funeral, and, in an echo of Kirov, the State Yiddish Theatre was named after him, though Stalin shut it down within a year as his persecution of Jews continued.

Plenty of other governments killed systematically. During the three decades following the Iranian Revolution of 1979, the regime was involved in more than 160 assassinations in nineteen countries, according to the Iran Human Rights Documentation Centre. In July 1989 three representatives from a banned Kurdish party agreed to meet a delegation from the Iranian government in an apartment in Vienna. The Iranians claimed that unknown gunmen burst in and shot the Kurds dead. One of the Iranians was also wounded, and, from their injuries, it appeared that one of the Kurds had tried to fight back. Each of them had been finished off by a shot to the head. The police managed to question the wounded Iranian and one of his colleagues. The third had disappeared. The investigators bought the story about the mystery assailants, and the two Iranians were allowed to go back home, but after further inquiries a warrant was issued for their arrest. It was too late, the birds had flown, and the wounded man was promoted to a senior position in Iranian Intelligence.

The long arm of the Iranian state was also demonstrated by the murder of the country's former prime minister Shahpur Bakhtiar in 1991. The shah had appointed him in 1979 in the hope of stopping Islamic fundamentalists from taking over the country, but Bakhtiar sent him into exile. With the shah gone, the new prime minister tried to implement some moderate reforms, but once Ayatollah Khomeini returned from his own exile in France, his days were numbered, and he had to go into hiding before taking refuge himself in France where he had studied and for whose army he had fought in the Second World War. There he set up an Iranian resistance movement. After surviving at least two assassination attempts, he was stabbed to death with his assistant at his home in a Paris suburb. A French court sent two Iranians to gaol, one of them for life. The prosecutor said the crime was organized from 'within the heart of the Islamic Republic of Iran'. The one imprisoned for life was released after sixteen years and returned to a hero's welcome in Tehran. The French government denied that it was part of a deal to secure the release of a French academic the Iranians had detained.

Although Iran has regular elections, many do not regard it as a true democracy because of the power wielded by unelected clerics, and few would consider Stalin's regime democratic. But democratic countries also use assassination. Take Israel, often pointed to as the only free country in the Middle East, as, for example, by the Economist Intelligence Unit in 2016. Assassination played an important part in the creation of the country, and it has remained a crucial tactic ever since. During the Second World War, a Swedish diplomat named Folke Bernadotte saved about 11,000 Jews, negotiating their release from German concentration camps, but three years later that counted for nothing with the extreme Jewish nationalist Stern Gang. In 1948 Bernadotte went to the Holy Land as a UN mediator trying to bring an end to fighting between Jews and Arabs. As we have seen, extremists often consider peacemakers the most dangerous enemies. On 18 September the diplomat was being driven through an area of West Jerusalem newly occupied by Jewish forces in a convoy accompanied by an Israeli army captain, when an Israeli army jeep swerved in front blocking the road. As three armed men in Israeli Defence Force uniforms approached, the passengers started digging out their papers. Then one of the group ran to the car in which Bernadotte was travelling, poked a sub-machine gun through the open rear window and shot the Swede six times. A French colonel and decorated war hero who was with him as chief UN observer was also hit. The Israeli captain rushed them to hospital but they were both pronounced dead on arrival.

Thirty years after the attack, members of the Stern Gang, whose leadership included future Israeli prime minister Yitzhak Shamir, admitted responsibility. The day before his murder, Bernadotte had proposed that Jerusalem, still argued over by Jews and Palestinians seventy years later, should be put under international supervision. Although the assassination was condemned in much of the Israeli press and the country's first prime minister, David Ben-Gurion, used it to justify a crackdown on the Stern Gang, the police investigation that followed was, at best, amateurish, and no one was ever brought to justice. Even sixty years after Bernadotte's death, a former broadcaster on the Stern Gang's clandestine radio station was prepared to defend the murder, saying that without it Israel would never have been able to take Jerusalem.

According to one estimate, during the first seventy years of its existence, Israel was involved in at least 2,700 assassination plots. Its secret service, Mossad, has become one of the most resourceful, and most feared, assassination bureaux. Scientists became an important target as the country tried to maintain its monopoly on nuclear weapons in the Middle East. Six Iranian scientists were said to have been murdered by Iranian opposition groups working for Mossad. Yahya al-Meshad, an Egyptian nuclear scientist working for Iraq, who was bludgeoned to death in a Paris hotel room in 1980, was also thought to be a Mossad victim, but a more celebrated scalp was Gerald Bull. The 61-year-old Canadian was regarded as the world's leading expert on gun-barrel ballistics. His dream was to launch satellites from a huge artillery piece, and it was only when governments lost interest in this project that he got involved with weapons. It is said that Israel had tried to hire him on a number of occasions, but that Bull was not a fan of the Jewish State. So instead he had decided to sell his services to Saddam Hussein, to help him with three super-guns designed to be able to hit Israel with shells spiked with nuclear, chemical or biological materials. On 20 March 1990, as Bull answered the door of his home in a smart district of Brussels, he was shot five times in the head by a three-man team of Mossad assassins, who were on a flight out of the country an hour later. Almost immediately Israeli sources got to work spreading the fake news that Bull had been killed by the Iraqis because he was planning to renege on their deal.

Mossad is said to have a strict code of conduct. Politicians, 'however extreme', should not be targeted, and every assassination must be literally signed off by the prime minister. There is an actual 'licence to kill'. The agency uses a whole variety of methods as well as shooting – bombs, strangulation, electric shock, poison. The operation is meticulous and methodical. Agents are highly trained and victims thoroughly researched, earlier assassination operations are rigorously analysed for lessons, and the agency has an army of sympathizers and helpers such as doctors, bankers and people who can help with more mundane needs like transport or accommodation. Mossad's practice is not to comment on its operations. Some believe this vow of silence makes it even more feared. The audacity of one of its assassinations in 2010 was captured in chilling detail on closed-circuit television in a Dubai hotel. The target was Mahmoud al-Mabhouh, an arms supplier for Hamas. The Dubai authorities later said they were seeking no fewer than 26 people in connection with the killing. The CCTV caught rather podgy men in tennis gear, a woman in a business suit, a man in a cap. They had flown in from a variety of European airports using fake passports. Mabhouh was killed in his hotel room with a paralysing drug. The UK government expressed fury when it was revealed that six of the forged passports used the stolen identities of British citizens, and Mossad's top official at the Israeli embassy in London was expelled. Of course, Israelis have also been victims of assassination. In 2001 the far-right-wing tourism minister, Rehavam Ze'evi, who had called for the expulsion of all Arabs and Palestinians from Israel, was shot dead in a Jerusalem hotel by a Palestinian gunman. This assassination fell into a depressing pattern of tit-for-tat. The Popular Front for the Liberation of Palestine (PFLP) said Ze'evi had been killed in retaliation for the death of PFLP leader Mustafa Zibri in an Israeli rocket attack, and Israel said he in turn had been killed for organizing a series of car bombings.

The United States has also been prepared to assassinate its enemies, but the practice has been subjected to a far more open debate than has been seen in Israel. In 1975 President Gerald Ford let slip that the CIA had been involved in murder plots, and the Senate set up the Church Committee to investigate its activities. Ford tried to get the committee not to go public about the U.S.'s involvement in assassination on the grounds that it would damage the country's reputation and endanger lives. Some in the intelligence community thought this danger was underlined when the CIA station chief in Athens was murdered within months of the committee being set up. But members rejected this plea: 'We believe that the public is entitled to know what instrumentalities of their Government have done.' It argued that, far from being damaged by the revelation of 'embarrassing' material, the United States' reputation would be improved because other countries would respect its honesty.

So a whole series of weird stories emerged. The agency had been involved in plots to kill, among others, Fidel and Raul Castro, Che Guevara, the Chinese communist leader Zhou Enlai, Patrice Lumumba, the African nationalist who helped win independence for the Congo and became its first prime minister, and Rafael Trujillo, right-wing dictator of the Dominican Republic, to whose own penchant for political assassination the Americans had been happy for a long time to turn a blind eye. The intended victims were mainly bogeymen from the left, thought to be too close to the Soviet Union, and even Trujillo had been selected because of fears that he had become so extreme he might provoke a left-wing takeover. Added spice came from the exotic means considered for the killings: poisoned toothpaste for Lumumba or an exploding seashell to eliminate Fidel Castro while he was snorkelling. Most of the agency's plots failed, and in Lumumba's case, the committee concluded that although the u.s. had planned to kill him it was not directly involved in his murder by secessionists in 1961. With Trujillo in the same year, it decided the usa had supplied weapons to his enemies, but that there was not enough evidence to connect it directly to his murder. The investigation revealed that the cia's preferred *modus operandi* was to contract out killings to local assassins. The committee concluded that: 'short of war, assassination is incompatible with American principles, international order, and morality. It should be rejected as a tool of foreign policy.'

The can was carried by two cia bosses, William Colby and James Schlesinger, who lost their jobs. But the question that arose was: how much did u.s. presidents know about what the cia was up to? The agency had a policy of operating 'in such a way that if discovered, the role of the United States could be plausibly denied'. This meant relations between the cia and the government 'were often convoluted and imprecise'. President Eisenhower had said in a meeting that he would like to see both Trujillo and Fidel Castro 'sawed off'. There was also evidence that he had called for 'strong action' to 'remove' Lumumba. The committee acknowledged it was not able to establish a 'clear' picture, and that 'it is difficult to be certain at what levels assassination activity was known and authorized,' adding: 'This situation creates the disturbing prospect that Government officials might have undertaken the assassination plots without it having been uncontrovertibly clear that there was explicit authorization from the Presidents. It is also possible that there might have been a successful "plausible denial" in which Presidential authorization was issued but is now obscured.' Either way, in the committee's opinion, the buck had to stop at the White House: 'Whether or not the respective Presidents knew of or authorized the plots, as chief executive officer of the United States, each must bear the ultimate responsibility for the activities of his subordinates.' In 1976 President Ford issued an executive order that: 'No employee of the United States Government shall engage in, or conspire to engage in, political assassination,' a prohibition that was repeated by Ronald Reagan in 1981.

But the effect was diluted as assassinations were rebadged as 'targeted killings', and the term became much used after the 9/11 terrorist attacks. It is an interesting choice of words as the Church Committee's definition of assassination was the 'coldblooded, targeted, intentional killing of an individual foreign leader'. Some felt it was very difficult to spot the difference. Anwar al-Awlaki was an American citizen and al-Qaeda leader linked by the intelligence services to a series of terrorist plots against America who was felled by a U.S. drone in Yemen in 2011. As to whether this amounted to 'assassination', the U.S. Attorney General, Eric Holder, said he rejected 'the use of that loaded term', but that did not end the argument about state-sponsored killing. The Obama administration had put Awlaki on a hit list, and at his father's request, the American Civil Liberties Union and the Center for Constitutional Rights had taken the U.S. government to court to try to stop him being targeted. The judge threw the case out, with some misgivings, on the grounds that the U.S. constitution reserved decisions such as these for politicians. In May 2011 Awlaki survived a missile strike that killed two al-Qaeda operatives, but four months later he was killed. Altogether President Obama is estimated to have ordered more than 540 drone strikes, killing nearly 3,800 people.

Holder wrote in 2013 that Obama had been as open about America's policy of targeted killing as was possible without endangering national security, and that he was determined that all operations would be 'consistent with our laws and values'. In addition to Awlaki, who had been 'specifically targeted', he said three other u.s. citizens had been killed, though they had not been specifically targeted. It was 'an unfortunate but undeniable fact' that a 'small number' of u.s. citizens abroad had 'decided to commit violent attacks against their own country'. Holder argued it was permissible to kill an American citizen who posed 'an imminent threat of violent attack against the United States' and whom it was not possible to capture. A former u.s. judge, Abraham Sofaer, also argued that 'targeted killings' could be justified on the grounds of self-defence, saying this was different from assassination, which was 'widely defined as murder'. When the Church Committee condemned assassination, the targets were political leaders seen as acting strategically against the u.s.'s interests, not terrorists who might be planning attacks. Sofaer wrote: 'u.s. officials may not kill people merely because their policies are seen as detrimental to our interests, and properly so. But killings in self-defense are no more "assassinations" in international affairs than they are murders when undertaken by our police forces against domestic killers,' though he warned that targeted killings might do more harm than good by stirring up anger, particularly if they went wrong. The American Civil Liberties Union, however, remained deeply disturbed about targeting people 'far from any battlefield, without a legal determination of guilt'. This risked turning 'the whole world into a battlefield. If the u.s. starts sending drones after its suspected enemies all over the world, there's nothing to stop other countries from doing the same.'

Osama bin Laden

The killing of Osama bin Laden ten years after the 9/11 attacks was one of President Obama's greatest triumphs. Bin Laden was the world's most notorious terrorist and the FBI's most wanted man. Born in Riyadh, Saudi Arabia, he was the seventeenth of 52 children fathered by the owner of the country's biggest construction company. He married the first of his five wives at seventeen, and went on to sire 26 children himself. During a privileged upbringing, he took a degree in civil engineering, but while he was a student he fell under the influence of a radical scholar, Abdullah Azzam, who believed all Muslims should rise up in a holy war to create a single Islamic state. After the Soviets invaded Afghanistan in 1979, bin Laden travelled to Pakistan with Azzam, and, close to the Afghan border, they set up an operation to channel money and support to the mujahideen who were fighting the Russians. They also recruited volunteers from across the globe to join the insurgency. When the Soviets withdrew in 1989, bin Laden went back to Saudi Arabia to concentrate on a new organization he had founded, al-Qaeda, 'the base', which was going to concentrate on symbolic acts of terrorism. The Saudi authorities expelled him in 1992, and four years later he was back in Afghanistan, declaring war on the u.s.: 'the evils of the Middle East arose from America's attempt to take over the region and from its support for Israel. Saudi Arabia has been turned into an American colony.'

Al-Qaeda bankrolled a whole series of terrorist attacks against Western interests, such as the murder of 62 tourists at Luxor in Egypt in 1997. Co-ordinated bombings at the u.s. embassies in Kenya and Tanzania the following year resulted in more than 220 deaths, and then came 9/11 – the hijacking of four aircraft in 2001 by terrorists who flew them into New York's World Trade Center twin towers and the Pentagon in Washington, killing nearly 3,000. While the Americans searched for bin Laden, he would issue video and audio taunts, and the terrorist atrocities continued: more than

200 killed by bombs in Bali in 2002; 191 on a Spanish commuter train in 2004, as well as numerous bombings in u.s.-occupied Afghanistan and Iraq. Finally, late in 2010, American interest was attracted by a mysterious compound with high walls in the quiet, leafy Pakistani garrison town of Abbottabad, 190 kilometres (120 mi.) from the Afghan border, after they intercepted a mobile phone call from one of bin Laden's most trusted couriers (though there are also claims that a former Pakistani intelligence officer tipped off the Americans about the compound in return for a very big reward). Because of the high walls and screens on every balcony, it was hard to see inside. The building had no phone or Internet connection, and any rubbish was burned inside. The only way in was through two big metal security gates. As the cia began covert investigations, setting up a safe house nearby, local people told them the occupants rarely ventured out, and if they did, they quickly sped off in a vehicle. It is not clear whether the Pakistani authorities knew about bin Laden's whereabouts, but the compound was close to a number of military sites. Even if they did, they would have had to tread carefully. Bin Laden was a hero to many in the country. For their part, the Americans deployed an advanced drone that could fly high over the compound taking photographs and shooting video without being detected. This enabled them to spot a man who often walked up and down inside the compound, but they were not able to positively identify him as bin Laden. President Obama, who was one of the very few people in the u.s. government and military who knew about the compound, later said that they were only about 55 per cent sure it was the arch-terrorist, though again some claim Pakistani sources provided DNA evidence of his identity. Anyway, the president authorized a raid on the moonless night of 2 May 2011.

Two helicopters flew a team of two dozen Navy Seals special forces, drafted in from Afghanistan, to the compound. The plan had been for the aircraft to drop the Seals directly inside, but one got into difficulties and had to crash-land. The other helicopter then deposited its complement outside the building, leaving the Seals to fight their way in. They had to blast their way through a perimeter wall and an inner wall protecting the house where bin Laden lived with his family. As one of bin Laden's close confidants opened fire on them from a guard house, they killed him and his wife. When they got into the main building, they were confronted by the confidant's brother and shot him too. A similar fate met one of bin Laden's grown-up sons whom they encountered on the stairs. It took twenty minutes from entering the building before they finally sighted bin Laden. He took refuge in a bedroom, as two women tried to protect him. Accounts differ as to where exactly he was shot or how many times, but what is clear is that he was killed. What remains unclear is how much the Pakistani authorities knew about the raid.

Forty minutes after the Seals arrived, with the terrorist leader dead, a helicopter appeared and picked them up along with bin Laden's body and documents and computer hard drives. Before leaving, the Seals blew up the damaged helicopter. Soon they were back in Afghanistan while bin Laden's body was buried at sea from a u.s. aircraft carrier to make sure his followers had no shrine to visit. So was this a deliberate assassination or had the plan been to capture him? The military commander in charge of the operation, Admiral William McRaven, said the terrorist could 'absolutely' have been taken alive, and that killing him was not the objective, but that the operation did not go completely to plan because of the helicopter crash. President Obama expressed his disappointment that it was not possible to arrest bin Laden and put him on trial, so 'preventing him from appearing as a martyr', but in reality, an attempt to capture him in a foreign country where many people supported him, then carry him back to American-controlled territory, would have been a very high-risk enterprise.

According to a former director of the cia, the killing of General Qassem Suleimani, a senior figure in Iran's Republican Guard, in 2020 was even more 'consequential' than the elimination of Osama bin Laden. By then Donald Trump was president, and he also angrily rejected suggestions that Suleimani, who was struck down by a drone at Baghdad airport, had been 'assassinated'. The killing was part of a decades-long great game of reprisal and retaliation between the u.s. and Iran. The immediate spiral of violence that accounted for Suleimani, who coordinated the activities of pro-Iranian militia outside the country's borders, began in late 2019. As Iran's economy tottered under crippling u.s. economic sanctions, some of its sympathizers in Iraq attacked a military base there, killing an American contractor. Three days later, America retaliated by killing two dozen or more members of the militia responsible. The next day demonstrators besieged the u.s. embassy in Baghdad and set fire to its gates. President Trump tweeted that Iran would pay a 'BIG PRICE' if it carried on like this. In response, a Twitter account associated with Iran's supreme leader, Ayatollah Ali Khameini, retorted: 'You can't do anything.'

If it all sounded more like the playground than international diplomacy, any possibilities for humour were eliminated in the early hours of 3 January 2020 when Suleimani was killed along with a senior Iraqi militia leader. America initially justified the action on the grounds that the general was planning an attack that posed imminent danger to u.s. citizens. Then when the government was challenged to provide evidence, the grounds switched to a complaint that Suleimani had been responsible for killing a lot of Americans in the past, while critics claimed President Trump had mounted the operation to divert attention from his impeachment by congress. Though Iran was by now a bitterly divided country (November 2019 had seen big demonstrations against the regime that had brought a savage response), hundreds of thousands turned out to pay their respects to the general, even in regions hostile to the government. In Suleimani's home town more than fifty mourners were killed in the crush. Iran's leaders vowed revenge for the general's death, and five days after the drone strike, they fired missiles at u.s. bases in Iraq, though they seem to have gone out of their way to minimize casualties. The Iranian Foreign Minister even appeared to try to draw a line under this episode in the long-running feud, tweeting that the country had 'concluded proportionate measures in self-defence'. Then the law of unintended consequences struck. Four hours after Iran's 'proportionate' response, a Ukrainian airliner crashed as it took off from Tehran airport, killing all 176 people on board. At first the Iranians said it was an accident, but after three days they admitted they had shot it down, mistakenly believing it was an incoming u.s. cruise missile. The regime faced more protests, which were put down with a heavy hand, while newspapers and a prominent television presenter apologized for lying to the Iranian people for years.

Assassination and the Mass Media

There are photographs of the arrest of Gavrilo Princip after the assassination of Archduke Franz Ferdinand, and of the motorcade before the shooting. Images of this kind, of course, might be a considerable boost for 'propaganda of the deed'. The first assassination to be caught as moving picture was the murder of King Alexander I of Yugoslavia (incidentally the last European monarch to be assassinated) while he was in Marseilles in 1934 on a state visit to France. Having survived the assassination attempt for which Dragutin Dimitrijević was executed in 1917, Alexander became the first king of Yugoslavia. He had grown increasingly autocratic as he tried to fuse its disparate nationalities into a single country, banning political parties based on ethnic groupings in the process. Barely five minutes after he arrived in Marseilles, a gunman leapt on the running board of his open-top car and shot and killed the king, the French foreign minister, Louis Barthou, who was riding beside him, and the driver. The cameraman was not rolling at the precise moment when the fatal shot was fired, but he was only a few feet away from the action, and filmed the king's dead body in close-up and the mêlée in the crowd as the assassin, a Macedonian separatist, was himself killed.

Inejiro Asanuma, murdered with a samurai sword during a Japanese television debate, 1960.

Then came television. On 12 October 1960 the Japanese socialist leader Inejiro Asanuma was speaking in a televised election debate when a seventeen-year-old right-wing extremist, Otoya Yamaguchi, leapt on stage and ran him through with a traditional samurai sword. Unlike the death of Alexander I, Inejiro's was captured on camera. The debate was not being transmitted live, but the footage was shown on television later that evening. It is clear that the victim does not realize anything is amiss until the last moment, but then his terrified glance to his left, apparent in slow motion, is particularly horrifying. The killer was said to have been smiling when he was arrested. He followed in a long tradition of political murder by the far right in the country. As we saw, they were very active during the Age of Revolution, and in the five years after 1931 three Japanese prime ministers were murdered. Within a month of Inejiro's assassination, Otoya had torn up a sheet in his juvenile detention cell and improvised a rope which he used to hang himself from the light fitting.

President John F. Kennedy

In fact, the victim of the first assassination to be captured live on television was himself an assassin or, some would say, an alleged assassin. In the years after 22 November 1963, 'Where were you when you heard President Kennedy had been shot?' was a standard question, and nearly everyone could tell you the answer. The assassination of John F. Kennedy was one of history's most resonant events. On the last day of his life, he was visiting Texas to shore up Democrat support in what was expected to be a key battleground in the following year's presidential election. The youngest man ever to be elected u.s. president, Kennedy was still only 46 and he and his wife Jackie personified youth and glamour. He was about to push through controversial civil rights legislation designed to end racial segregation, and Texas's National Democratic Committeeman Byron Skelton had urged the president not to come to Dallas, arguing that it was not safe. There had been nearly a hundred murders in the city already that year, but JFK insisted he and Jackie travel through it, like the Archduke Franz Ferdinand and his wife and like Alexander I of Yugoslavia, in an open-top car. The Kennedys would be accompanied by the governor of Texas, John Connally, and his wife. The American Nazi Party had been distributing 'Wanted for Treason' leaflets in the city bearing the president's face, and on the morning of 22 November, the ultra-conservative *Dallas Morning News* had carried a full-page advertisement from the self-styled American Fact-Finding Committee denouncing Kennedy as a communist sympathizer. Jackie was alarmed, and her husband had wryly remarked: 'we're heading into nut country.' Still, their reception had been warm and enthusiastic as the motorcade, travelling at about eleven miles an hour, reached Dealey Plaza thirty minutes after noon.

Shots rang out. Abraham Zapruder, an amateur cameraman who was filming the spectacle with his little 8mm model, saw Kennedy grab his chest and thought at first that he was playing to the crowd, but it was soon clear he had been wounded. The president was hit in the back, the throat and the back of his head. Connally was also wounded. The car rushed them to hospital, but the president was pronounced dead shortly after. Witnesses said the shots had come from the Texas School Book Depository. By a window on the sixth floor, police found a cheap mail order rifle with three spent cartridges. Lee Harvey Oswald, who worked there as a shipping clerk, was missing. After the shooting, he took a bus to his rooming house, and then went out again with a handgun with which he killed a police patrolman in broad daylight in front of plenty of witnesses. It is thought the officer had spotted that Oswald matched the description of the man police were looking for in connection with the shooting of the president, and witnesses speak of the two men exchanging words, though the policeman did not seem to be making any clear attempt to arrest Oswald. Then the suspect ducked inside a cinema where he was arrested after a brief struggle, though with what some saw as suspicious ease, eighty minutes after the assassination. The following day he was charged

The assassination of President John F. Kennedy, Dallas, Texas, 22 November 1963.

with both murders. He denied both, saying he was a 'patsy', a fall guy. A police tip-off to the media ensured there was mayhem when Oswald was moved from the city to the county jail on 24 November. In the crowd was a night-club owner, Jack Ruby, said to have links with the mob. He stepped forward and shot the prisoner in the stomach from point blank range as television viewers watched. It was the first assassination to be transmitted live on television. (Zapruder had been filming at the moment Kennedy was shot, but the footage was not shown on television until 1975 because it was thought too graphic.) Oswald died at the same hospital as Kennedy. Ruby claimed he had killed him to spare Jackie Kennedy the ordeal of testifying in court.

On the day after Oswald's murder, Kennedy's funeral was televised all over the world. More than half a century later, seeing three-year-old John Kennedy Jr saluting his dead father's coffin, in particular, remains deeply poignant. Even though the moment of Kennedy's murder had not been broadcast live, this was the first assassination to be caught up in the full glare of modern mass media. Did that play a part in the doubts and questions that soon arose and have remained to this day? To some, the police seemed to have decided who the culprit was with extraordinary haste, and before he could answer any questions, he was dead. Could Oswald really have hit the president from so far away? The suspect seemed to have fired only three shots, so why did so many witnesses think they had heard a fourth? The worry that any vacuum would be filled by conspiracy theories was addressed even before the president was buried, with the deputy attorney general writing in an internal memo: 'It is important that all the facts surrounding President Kennedy's assassination be made public in a way that will satisfy people.' Within ten days, a commission set up by the new president, Lyndon Johnson, and headed by u.s. Chief Justice Earl Warren, held its first meeting.

Oswald was 24. His father had died before he was born and he had had a rootless childhood, being moved from house to house,

The first assassination transmitted live on television. Jack Ruby shoots Lee Harvey Oswald, 24 November 1963.

while his mother switched from husband to husband. He was a loner, sulking and playing truant from school, though he was also an avid reader. At the age of fourteen he told a psychiatrist: 'I dislike everybody.' Petty crime led him to a spell in a correctional facility. He dropped out of school and joined the Marines, getting training with a gun, but it is not clear how good a shot he was. In one test, he just achieved the top 'marksman' grade, but in another he managed only the lesser 'sharpshooter' rank. At the same time, he learned Russian and openly voiced his support for communism. He was court-martialled twice, and defected to the Soviet Union in 1959, where he married a Russian woman. In June 1962, with what to the suspicious seemed surprisingly little difficulty, he was able to return to America with his wife and baby daughter. He flitted between a variety of jobs and flirted with various anti-communist groups, as well as with some that supported Castro's regime in Cuba, but a couple of months before the assassination he may have been think- ing about trying to return to Russia. It is also possible that he had tried to assassinate a propagandist for the extreme right-wing John Birch Society. His wife said he was desperate to be famous, to go down in history 'by any means, good or bad'.

Warren's commission submitted its report, backed up by 26 volumes of evidence, in September 1964. It made a number of criticisms of law enforcement agencies, including the Secret Service, whose job it was to protect the president, complaining, for example, about its failure to do proper checks on buildings along the route of the motorcade. The commission concluded that Oswald was a loser and political malcontent who acted alone, though as to his motive, they could not 'make any definitive determination'. So, dreadful though the assassination had been, it was surely comforting that the killer was a one-off misfit and not a symptom of

Lee Harvey Oswald (1939–1963) photographed with a rifle in Dallas, March 1963, eight months before Kennedy's assassination.

some widespread malaise in American society, and equally that Kennedy was not the victim of a political conspiracy. But the report did not end speculation. The Russians believed Kennedy had been killed by the far right. In America there were theories that he had been killed by the Russians, or by pro-Castro elements, or the far right, or the CIA or the Mafia. For some, Oswald just seemed too insignificant a character to have perpetrated this cataclysmic deed. Still, at first, the vast majority of Americans appeared to accept Warren's verdict, but then came the Watergate scandal of the early 1970s, and confidence in politicians plummeted. After Zapruder's film was finally transmitted, Congress re-opened the inquiry into Kennedy's death. In 1979 the House of Representatives Select Committee on Assassinations endorsed the conclusion that Oswald was the killer, but thought it likely that a fourth shot had been fired, though they came to no conclusion about who might have been responsible, and some experts had argued that echoes in the Dealey Plaza made it hard to be sure about the number of shots people had heard. Crucially, the committee concluded the president had 'probably' been the victim of a 'conspiracy', though it delivered no view about who was involved, only a long list of who was not, including the Russians, Castro, anti-Castro groups, the security services and organized crime. Then there was the matter of Jack Ruby. He was initially sentenced to death for Oswald's murder, but his conviction was overturned on appeal. In front of the Warren Commission, he seemed to hint there was more to his motive than the line about trying to spare Jackie from having to testify. In response to this tantalizing tit-bit, the chief justice appeared uncharacteristically obtuse. Ruby died of lung cancer in prison in 1967, aged 55, just a month after being diagnosed. He was awaiting a retrial and was convinced he had been injected with cancer cells. The commission had accepted he might be involved in some 'shady' dealings, but dismissed the suggestion he was connected with organized crime.

To this day, the conspiracy theories have never been demolished as more than 1,000 books poured over the evidence. As late as 54 years after the shooting, fresh material was being released by the U.S. government. In 2017 we learned that Oswald was in touch with a senior KGB official who handled 'sabotage and assassinations' (the KGB was the main Soviet security organization). We also discovered that Jack Ruby had told an FBI informant to 'watch the fireworks' as Kennedy was driven through Dallas, and that the FBI had warned the Dallas police there was a plot to kill Oswald. Intriguingly, at the last minute, President Trump blocked the release of hundreds of other documents relating to the assassination on the grounds of 'potentially irreversible harm' to national security.

In spite of his film-star good looks, JFK was a sick man, suffering severe problems with his spine and his adrenal glands, so even if he had been re-elected in 1964, he might not have seen out a second term. His death probably gave a push to civil rights legislation, which was being determinedly obstructed in Congress. Lyndon Johnson was able to argue that pressing on with it was the best way of honouring Kennedy's legacy, and in 1964 the Civil Rights Act was passed. JFK's death may also have swung America more determinedly behind the space programme, enabling his ambition to put a man on the moon by the end of the decade to be fulfilled. Whether Kennedy would have become mired in Vietnam as disastrously as Johnson did is harder to say. What is clearer is that his presidency became idealized as a golden age of lost innocence (in spite of the president's many extramarital affairs) that was lost to an assassin's bullet in Dallas on 22 November 1963. His accomplishments in his short time in office were limited, but he was perhaps the first celebrity president as the glamour and charisma of Jack and Jackie coalesced with new media technology. Lightweight cameras made television more nimble, allowing apparently spontaneous Kennedy moments to be transmitted into everyone's home. The family seemed to be people ordinary Americans knew personally.

Martin Luther King

One of the key campaigners who had helped push JFK behind civil rights reform was Martin Luther King. Inspired by the example of Mahatma Gandhi, he wanted to use non-violent protest to defeat racism in America. Having followed in his father's footsteps and become a pastor, King had cut his campaigning teeth in Montgomery, Alabama, in 1955 when he was in his mid-twenties, supporting black people boycotting local buses in a year-long protest against segregation of passengers. The following year the Ku Klux Klan bombed his house. Then, in 1958, he was almost killed by a black woman who stabbed him in the chest with a letter opener when he was signing books in Harlem. He would say later that the blade went so close to his heart that if he had sneezed it would have killed him. The woman was committed to an institution for the criminally insane. As King continued his anti-racism protests, his enemies carried on targeting him. In 1963 they tried to bomb his motel room and his brother's home. The following year, he became the youngest ever winner of the Nobel Peace Prize, and a beach cottage he had rented was riddled with bullets.

Then King began to widen his protests, condemning the Vietnam War and poverty in the USA. In 1968 black refuse workers in Memphis went on strike to protest at dangerous working conditions and at being paid less than their white colleagues. Even though he had received death threats, King went to the city to support them on 3 April. That night he delivered one of his most famous speeches, declaring to a packed audience:

> Like anybody, I would like to live a long life; longevity has its place. But I'm not concerned about that now . . . I've seen the Promised Land. I may not get there with you. But I want you to know tonight that we, as a people, will get to the Promised Land. So I'm happy, tonight . . . I'm

not fearing any man. Mine eyes have seen the glory of the coming of the Lord.

At six o'clock the following evening, King was shot dead as he left his room at the Lorraine Motel, one of the few in the city that welcomed black people. The police found a rifle and various personal items nearby, from which they recovered the fingerprints of James Earl Ray, aged forty, a not very competent petty criminal then on the run from prison, who had been staying at a boarding house a block from the motel. The FBI believed King had been shot from a bathroom window in the building, though it was claimed it provided a poor view of the place where he was hit by the fatal bullet. If the bureau was right, this would be one of the relatively few successful assassinations by a sniper. According to some of Ray's fellow prisoners, if ever he saw King on television, the convict would fly into a rage and vow: 'If I ever get to the streets, I am going to kill him.' A Federal warrant charged Ray and others unknown with conspiracy to kill King, and he was arrested at London's Heathrow Airport on 8 June.

Tens of thousands turned out for King's funeral, and a week later, the Memphis refuse workers' strike ended as they were given a pay rise and better working conditions. In March 1969 Ray avoided the death penalty by pleading guilty to King's murder. He was sentenced to 99 years in prison, but he leapt to his feet in court to protest when the defence and prosecution both agreed that no one else was involved in the assassination. Three days later, he wrote to the judge to try to retract his confession. Echoing Lee Harvey Oswald, he described himself as a 'patsy', and soon the kind of suspicions and conspiracy theories that had surrounded JFK's assassination began to cluster around King's. While he was on the run, Ray had gone to Canada and Portugal before he was arrested in England. It was reckoned he must have spent about $9,000 in spite of having virtually no means of his own. So where had the money come from? Ray claimed a mysterious blond-haired Cuban named 'Raoul' had bankrolled him. 'Raoul' had got him to buy a rifle and book into the boarding house. The Cuban or an accomplice had then shot King, and dumped the rifle where it would be discovered with Ray's fingerprints. 'Raoul' was never found.

Then there was other food for suspicion. It was never established that the rifle with Ray's fingerprints had fired the bullet that killed King, and witnesses spoke of a mysterious figure fleeing on foot from shrubs opposite the motel, who was never found either. The FBI were not admirers of the civil rights leader. The director J. Edgar Hoover called him 'the most notorious liar' in the U.S. and claimed he had 'communist ties', while some FBI agents are supposed to have celebrated his death. In 1964 the bureau had sent King a tape purporting to be a recording of adulterous flings with women, and threatened to release it unless he killed himself. When he made his fateful trip to Memphis, the local police had assigned a couple of its small contingent of black detectives to keep a protective eye on the civil rights leader, but soon after his arrival, they were put on other duties by the city's police commissioner, a former FBI agent. Reviewing the evidence in 1979, the House of Representatives' Select Committee on Assassination concluded that Ray had shot King, but that there was a 'likelihood' of a conspiracy between the killer and his two brothers (though neither was ever charged) and that the motive was to collect a substantial price put on the civil rights leader's head by two rich white racists, who were both by then dead. The committee expressed regret that evidence of a conspiracy had not been properly examined immediately after King's murder.

Other theories were advanced: that the Ku Klux Klan were behind the assassination, for example, and evidence was produced of some links Ray had with the organization. Or that there was a right-wing plot to kill King in order to foment riots in black ghettos and so help a conservative win the forthcoming presidential election. Following the civil rights leader's murder, there was indeed serious disorder in more than a hundred cities, and Richard

After Martin Luther King's murder, there was rioting in more than a hundred American cities. This is some of the damage in Washington, DC.

Nixon became the new president. Or was it the Mafia, who had interests in the waste disposal business and were angry at King's meddling? There were even claims the assassination was a government contract killing. Certainly King's family did not accept that Ray was the killer, and in 1998 they launched a civil lawsuit naming a man called Lloyd Jowers along with 'unknown conspirators'. Jowers owned a diner on the ground floor of the boarding house where the rifle and other items carrying Ray's fingerprints were discarded. He had appeared on television saying he had been paid $100,000 by a Memphis businessman with links to the Mafia to arrange King's killing and that the gunman was a Memphis policeman who had since died, though many believed Jowers was just spinning a yarn in the hope of making some money. Still, the jurors found he was responsible for King's death, but added that unspecified 'government agencies' were also involved, and they awarded no payment to the family. The Justice Department did investigate Jowers, but said he kept making conflicting statements. They considered the evidence produced in the case 'consisted of either inaccurate and incomplete information or unsubstantiated conjecture', and said that none of the various conspiracy theories advanced about King's death had 'survived critical examination'. Jowers died in 2000. Two years later, a pastor in Florida said his father, a Klansman called Henry Clay Wilson, who was an acquaintance of Ray's, was the assassin, working with three other Klan members. Wilson had died in 1990, and if Ray had further secrets to reveal, he took them with him to the grave in 1998. King's widow described his death as a 'tragedy', saying America had never learned the truth about her husband's assassination.

Bobby Kennedy

When President Kennedy's younger brother, Bobby, heard about Martin Luther King's assassination, he put his head in hands and lamented: 'Oh, God. When is this going to stop?' He then made a speech eloquently condemning what he saw in the U.S. as 'a rising level of violence that ignores our common humanity and our claims to civilization . . . We glorify killing on movie and television screens.' He complained it was too easy for people to get hold of weapons, but he also attacked the 'violence of institutions . . . that afflicts the poor, that poisons relations between men because their skin has different colours'. Two months later, at ten past midnight on the morning of 5 June 1968, he was celebrating victory in the California Democratic Party Presidential Primary. With America torn apart by the Vietnam War, Lyndon Johnson had announced he would not be running for re-election, and though Kennedy was still behind Vice-president Hubert Humphrey in the race for the Democratic nomination, many believed he would win. After a speech at a Los Angeles hotel celebrating his victory in California, his team was easing him through the kitchen to get him to a press conference. The area was packed with journalists and supporters, and he shook hands with staff as he passed. Then a young man managed to fire eight bullets while he was being wrestled to the ground. In addition to shooting Kennedy, he hit five other

Pamphlet from Bobby Kennedy's ill-fated election campaign of 1968.

On May 7, Indiana can choose the next President of the United States. Make your vote count.

Kennedy for President Committee
2000 L STREET · WASHINGTON, D.C. · CHAIRMAN, JOSEPH CARGAN · TREASURER, HELEN KEYES

people. All of them survived. The candidate just managed to ask: 'Is everybody else all right?' Then a Catholic among the bystanders administered the last rites, and Kennedy was rushed to hospital where he died 26 hours later.

The man who fired the shots was Sirhan Sirhan, a 24-year-old Palestinian who had lived through the dispossession of his people as the state of Israel was founded. He had come to the u.s. at the age of thirteen, and worked in a number of small-time jobs like grocery boy and labourer, though a police officer would later say he was 'one of the most alert and most intelligent persons' he had ever questioned. Sirhan had wanted to become a jockey, but a blow to his head when he fell from a horse put an end to that and also seemed to change his personality. He became solitary and reserved, and developed an interest in the occult. In March 1968 he bought a gun, and started to write repeatedly in his diary that Kennedy must die before 5 June – the first anniversary of the Six-day War in which the Arabs had been heavily defeated by Israel. He was angry with Kennedy because of his support for the Israelis. On 4 June Sirhan did some target practice. Then he went to the candidate's hotel. Although he did not usually drink alcohol, he downed four cocktails. He claimed not to remember much else after that, though under hypnosis, he said he recalled meeting a girl who wanted a coffee, and going down into the kitchen with her.

At his trial Sirhan admitted killing Kennedy 'with twenty years of malice aforethought'. He was found guilty of murder and sentenced to the gas chamber, but he escaped the death penalty because California outlawed capital punishment before the execution could be carried out. Kennedy was no saint. He had thrown himself enthusiastically into Senator Joseph McCarthy's anti-communist witch hunt and had been serially unfaithful to his wife, but his death, like that of his brother, brought a huge outpouring of national grief and disappointment. Many saw him as a man who could bring a bitterly divided America back together, someone who seemed genuinely committed to making life better for those bypassed by the country's prosperity. His death represented the death of hope, and ushered in the corrupt presidency of Richard Nixon, but at least there seemed no doubt this time about who was the killer. Sirhan Sirhan had been caught with a smoking gun in front of dozens of witnesses.

In fact, in no time at all questions were being raised. There was evidence that thirteen shots had been fired in the kitchen, though Sirhan had been responsible for only eight. The coroner reported that all the shots that struck Kennedy came from behind him, and that the one that killed him, hitting him behind his right ear, was fired no more than an inch from his skull, but eyewitnesses were virtually unanimous that the Palestinian stood in front of Kennedy and was never closer than three feet from him. A leading criminologist swore an affidavit that a bullet that hit one of the survivors could not have come from the same gun as one that was removed from Kennedy's neck, and a panel of ballistics experts said it was possible there was a second gunman. Then there were the reports of a well-built young woman in a polka-dot dress running from the kitchen shouting: 'We shot Senator Kennedy!' and the stories that police tried to bully people into saying they had not seen her. Some witnesses believed they had spotted a uniformed security guard draw a pistol behind Kennedy. So if someone other than Sirhan killed the candidate, what would be the motive? There was the far right. According to one media investigation, three members of the CIA's covert anti-Castro operation were at the hotel that night, and one was later reported to have boasted: 'I was in Dallas when we got the son of a bitch [President Kennedy] and I was in LA when we got the little bastard.' According to another theory, the CIA hypnotized Sirhan into shooting Kennedy, which explained why he had no proper memory of the event. Then there was organized crime. Kennedy had pursued mobsters with great energy when he was attorney general, and Sirhan had links with the underworld. He had worked for a time at a race track owned by a mob associate, and one of his defence attorneys had represented a leading Mafioso. Later Sirhan complained the attorney was 'crooked' and that he had been chosen 'to make sure I was convicted'. As the fiftieth anniversary of Kennedy's death approached in 2018, his son Robert F. Kennedy Jr said he was sure Sirhan Sirhan, still serving his life sentence, had not killed his father, and demanded a fresh investigation.

Celebrity Assassinations

As we saw, President Kennedy was regarded as the first celebrity president, and in the Modern Age, the celebrity emerged as a new class of assassination victim. By killing a celebrity, an assassin could piggy-back on the victim's fame and become famous, or at least notorious, him- or herself. One of the first celebrity victims was movie star Sharon Tate, wife of the controversial film director Roman Polanski, whose *Rosemary's Baby*, about a woman who is raped by the Devil and gives birth to his child, came out in 1968. Tate herself had played a beautiful witch in a horror movie called *Eye of the*

Devil. The year after *Rosemary's Baby* appeared, on 9 August 1969, the star, who was aged 26 and eight-and-a-half months pregnant, was at home in Los Angeles with four friends including a coffee heiress and a celebrity hair stylist. (Polanski was away working in London.) They were all savagely butchered: shot, stabbed and hanged. The following night, a middle-class Los Angeles couple were murdered in their home in a similar way, and slogans including 'pig' and 'Helter Skelter' were daubed in blood on the walls of the house. The killers were two young men and three young women from the so-called Manson 'family'. Petty criminal Charles Manson, then aged 34, had assembled a commune around him in the California desert. Sometimes calling himself Satan or Jesus, he exercised power over them by controlling their access to drugs and deciding who should be allowed to have sex with whom. One of his group declared: 'I am the Devil and I'm here to do the Devil's business.' Such ideology as Manson could concoct was based on psychobabble and mumbo-jumbo about everyone being a part of everyone else, so murder did not matter as you were just erasing a part of yourself. He was convinced America was on the verge of an apocalyptic race war between black and white, which he described as 'Helter Skelter', a name he appropriated from a raucous, bitter love song by the Beatles that he claimed had a special message just for him. Manson imagined killing a swathe of 'Beautiful People' such as Elizabeth Taylor, Frank Sinatra and Tom Jones. A woman in the gang who killed Sharon Tate dismissed her as a 'store mannequin', though it may be that Tate and her friends were actually murdered because they were unlucky enough to be in a house which had once been the home of a producer who had rebuffed Manson's attempts to get a record contract. (Manson had musical aspirations. He made one unsuccessful album and the Beach Boys recorded a version of one of his songs.)

After a media circus of a trial, the five were all sentenced to death. Manson was convicted of ten murders, though some believe the 'family' was responsible for up to 35. Then in 1972 the California

Charles Manson on his way to arraignment on conspiracy to murder charges, Los Angeles, 1969.

Supreme Court declared the death penalty unconstitutional, so, like Sirhan Sirhan, they had their sentences commuted to life imprisonment. Manson died in prison in 2017, aged 83. To some, he and his followers emphasized the danger of Bakunin's nihilism: 'recognise no other activity but the work of extermination' – that it would provide philosophical cover for any misfit, loner or psychopath to take revenge on the society they felt had wronged them. But the left-wing American radical group the Weathermen celebrated Manson's killings and imagined themselves following him in a campaign of chaotic violence. Shortly after the murders, they set off bombs in Chicago.

Eleven years after Sharon Tate's murder, the co-writer of 'Helter Skelter', John Lennon, then aged forty, was one of the most famous people in the world. His use of drugs had got him on the wrong side of the authorities in the u.s., and he was arrested in 1972, but later it was his activism for world peace and various left-wing causes that alarmed them and he was allegedly kept under surveillance by the FBI and the CIA. Late on the afternoon of 8 December 1980, a group of fans were waiting outside New York's Dakota apartment block where Lennon lived with his wife Yoko Ono. When they emerged, a 25-year-old former security guard named Mark Chapman, who had been hanging around for a couple of days, asked the ex-Beatle to sign a copy of his new album. 'He took his time,' said Chapman. 'He asked me if I wanted anything else. His wife had come out with him and she was waiting in a limo and that's something I often reflect on how decent he was to just a stranger. He signed the album and gave it back to me. He got in the limo.'

John and Yoko went off to a recording studio, and six hours later they returned. Again Chapman was waiting. This time, as the couple entered the building, the former security guard pumped four bullets into Lennon's back. The ex-Beatle was rushed to hospital, but was dead on arrival. Chapman sat quietly at the scene reading J. D. Salinger's classic novel of adolescence, *The Catcher in the Rye,* until police arrested him. The killer was married, plump, bespectacled, brooding. An average student, he had played for a time in a rock band. Andy Warhol, who perhaps did more than anyone to create the cult of celebrity and who was himself the victim of an assassination attempt, said: 'If you're a crook . . . you can write books, go on TV, give interviews – you're a big celebrity . . . more than anything people want stars.' In an age of celebrity Mark Chapman was, like Lee Harvey Oswald, a nobody, but he was not reconciled to this fate. On his last day at work, he signed himself out as 'John Lennon'. The idea of killing the singer had come to him when he first read *The Catcher in the Rye.* Its hero, Holden Caulfield, is always castigating 'phoneys'. Chapman now began to believe he was Caulfield and that Lennon was a terrible phoney for singing 'imagine no possessions' (in his famous song 'Imagine') when he was so rich. Above all, though, Chapman wanted to be famous. If he could not get Lennon, he had back-up plans to kill JFK's widow, by now Jackie Onassis, or the actor George C. Scott, or the television compere Johnny Carson. When he murdered the singer: 'It was like I was in a movie.' He told a parole hearing that in the last hour before he killed Lennon: 'I did talk to myself. I sent up a prayer and said please help me turn this around. I couldn't do it . . . there was no feeling towards his son or his wife or himself. I was obsessed on one thing and that was shooting him so that I could be somebody.' In 2016 his request for release was turned down, partly because of what the parole board called the 'celebrity-seeking nature of the crime'. As with JFK's assassination, conspiracy theories sprouted: that Lennon was a victim of the security services, who were worried that he was just one month away from becoming an American citizen, and that his killer was a trained hitman programmed by the CIA. Perhaps Mark Chapman, like Lee Harvey Oswald, simply seemed too minor a character to have brought down such a world-famous figure.

As we saw, Mark Chapman had a number of other potential celebrity victims in mind if he failed to kill John Lennon, and Canadian ice hockey star turned sports presenter Brian Smith was

Police mugshot of John Lennon's assassin, Mark Chapman, 1980.

Memorial to John Lennon, Central Park, New York City.

gunned down simply because he was the first person his killer recognized as he waited outside an Ottawa television station on 1 August 1995. Jeffrey Arenburg, a 38-year-old paranoid schizophrenic, had been hearing voices in his head and decided the world had to know. He said he had nothing against Smith or his family, but he had to shoot him 'to draw attention to all this . . . bullshit that was messing up my life'. The next day he turned himself in to police. Arenburg was found to be 'not criminally responsible' for the killing and was remanded to a mental health centre from which he was released after nine years to considerable furore. He later served two terms of imprisonment after brushes with the law, and went on to die of a heart attack aged sixty, never having expressed any remorse for killing Smith.

At first, another misfit got the blame for the murder of British television star Jill Dando in April 1999. Aged 38, she was shot dead on the doorstep of her home in a quiet London street a few months before she was due to be married. The killing had all the hallmarks of a professional hit. The assassin had coolly walked up behind her in broad daylight as she was about to open her front door, and killed her with a single shot, pressing the pistol firmly against her head to silence the noise and protect him- or herself against any spattering of blood. A month later, police charged a local man named Barry George with the murder. George was once found hiding in the grounds of Kensington Palace, wearing a balaclava and combat fatigues while carrying a poem for Prince Charles and a knife. A note found in his messy flat read: 'I have difficulty handling rejection. I become angry . . . it starts a chain of events which is beyond my control.' He once told a woman friend: 'The me they know is not the real me. Perhaps I have another face.' He suffered from epilepsy and had attended a school for 'maladjusted children'. Unable to get a job, he invented fictitious companies and said he worked for them. He claimed to be friends with or related to top rock stars, changing his name to Bulsara, Freddie Mercury of Queen's real name, and pretending to be the star's cousin. On another occasion he masqueraded as a karate champion. George was in the territorial army for a time and had some training in the use of firearms, in which he showed considerable interest. He had been convicted of indecent assault and attempted rape, and more than a dozen women gave evidence to the police that he had stalked them. In 2001 he was convicted and sentenced to life imprisonment, but many believed the authorities had the wrong man. After a number of appeals, George was retried seven years later. His defence counsel described the accused as the 'local nutter', and said he was not capable of carrying out such a meticulously planned assassination. The jury agreed, and he was released. So who did kill Jill Dando? There are plenty of theories. She had presented a programme called *Crimewatch* which helped convict many criminals. Had one of them or one of their associates borne a grudge? Or was the motive prevention? There were rumours that at the time of her death she was working on trying to expose a paedophile ring. Was she the victim of a deranged fan? Or was it a crime of passion, and the killer an ex-lover? Or, famous though Dando was, could it have been mistaken identity? The cool, professional nature of the murder led to speculation that Serbian terrorists might have been involved, and that it was in retaliation for NATO's cruise missile strike on Serbian television headquarters, but terrorists usually make some kind of claim of responsibility. Otherwise, the propaganda value of the killing is wasted.

Journalists as Targets

Journalists are often targets for assassins. In 2016 more than ninety met violent ends. In 2017 more than eighty. Mexico had the highest number of victims, at thirteen. Most of the murders there were unsolved, but it is believed the main culprits were crime gangs or corrupt officials angered by what the journalists had written. Next came Afghanistan with twelve deaths. An independent watchdog, the Afghan Journalists' Safety Committee, said the Taliban and so-called Islamic State were responsible for most attacks, but it also reported that the security services and people affiliated to the government were behind some. On a single day in April 2018, nine journalists perished in bombings while a tenth was shot dead. The third worst blackspot was Iraq, with ten victims. An Iraqi human rights organization, 17Shubat for Human Rights, said journalists were under threat from armed groups, political parties and the authorities. In Europe, too, journalists have been targeted. In Spain the Basque terrorist group ETA made dozens of attempts. According to the international Committee to Protect Journalists, between 1992 and 2018, 37 were murdered in Russia. Perhaps the best known was Anna Politkovskaya, who was found shot dead by the lift of her Moscow apartment building in 2006. She had received numerous death threats after denouncing President Putin's government for corruption and human rights abuses, particularly during the war in Chechnya. Eight years later, five men were imprisoned for the killing, two of them for life, but the European Court of Human Rights criticized the Russian government for failing to properly investigate who was behind it, and Politkovskaya's relatives blamed the security services.

And it is not just in Mexico that organized crime has targeted journalists. In Ireland drug lords murdered the celebrated investigative reporter Veronica Guerin in 1996. In Malta in 2017 Daphne Caruana Galizia, who specialized in exposing corruption, was killed by a car bomb. After a local tycoon with alleged ties to government ministers was charged with being involved in 2019, the country's prime minister resigned, though he said he had done nothing wrong. In Italy, in addition to politicians, judges, prosecutors, police officers, and trade union leaders, the Mafia murdered at least ten journalists between 1970 and 1993, while in 2018, nearly two hundred were under police protection. The same year, a 27-year-old Slovak reporter, Jan Kuciak, was shot dead at his home along with his fiancée, while he was investigating links between the country's government and the Italian Mafia. The killings led to street protests that brought down the Slovak government. In January 2020 a former soldier admitted being the hit-man, while another man admitted hiring him. A Slovak businessman was charged with having ordered the murder.

Sometimes the burgeoning mass media became not a victim of, but a participant in assassinations. On 14 February 1922 Finland's Minister of the Interior, Heikki Ritavuori, was shot dead at his front door in Helsinki. His killer, a nobleman named Ernst Tandefelt, said he had been motivated by articles in the right-wing press condemning the minister as a danger to his country. It is the only political assassination in Finnish history, and came four years after a bitter civil war between left- and right-wing forces had cost 36,000 lives before the left was defeated. Ritavuori had incensed the right by working to get pardons for left-wing prisoners of war after the conflict. Tandefelt was initially sentenced to life imprisonment, but was then declared 'partially insane'. He died in an asylum in 1948.

New Technology

We have noted that over several hundred years methods of assassination changed surprisingly little, in spite of major technological innovations such as the gun and the bomb, and the old-fashioned ways survived into the modern era. As we saw, in 1960 the Japanese politician Inejiro Asanuma was killed with a traditional samurai sword. Slipping poison to the victim was a favourite method in ancient Rome, and in 2004 leading Indonesian human rights activist Munir Said Thalib met his end when his coffee was spiked with arsenic at Singapore's Changi Airport. Munir was en route from Jakarta to Amsterdam to take up a scholarship to study international law. Witnesses said that on the leg from Jakarta to Singapore, he was sitting next to an off-duty Indonesian civil airline pilot named Pollycarpus Budihari Priyanto. Pollycarpus left the flight at Singapore, but he was seen giving Munir a coffee at the airport. The civil rights activist died of arsenic poisoning on the next leg of the journey to Amsterdam. It was suspected that Pollycarpus worked for Indonesia's intelligence service, and evidence was given at his trial that he often went to meetings at its headquarters. The airline pilot served six years in prison for Munir's murder, but a top intelligence official was cleared of any involvement amid claims that the Indonesian government had been less than enthusiastic in pursuing the case. The same year, the Russian journalist Anna Politkovskaya, who would be assassinated in 2006, survived after drinking poisoned tea given to her by an Aeroflot flight attendant.

But although the old methods continued, the last century has seen some major innovations in assassination. More and more things have become doable at a price, and because governments tend to have more money than insurgents, it is not surprising that they have often made the running. One new development was better training and organization. We have seen how meticulously Mossad assassinations are planned, but there are earlier examples. During the Second World War, Reinhard Heydrich, dubbed 'the hangman', was the Nazi governor of the occupied Czech Republic, and had been personally responsible for the execution of hundreds of Czechs. He had also organized the mobile killing squads that murdered nearly a million Polish and Soviet Jews. In 1941 the Czech government in exile in London began to plan his assassination. After a rigorous selection process, it chose two men from about 2,500 Czech soldiers who had escaped to the UK. With the help of Britain's Special Operations Executive, they were trained in parachuting, commando and anti-interrogation techniques, and taught to know the area where they were to strike like the backs of their hands. The pair, Jan Kubiš and Josef Gabčik, both in their mid-twenties, were friends. Gabčik had won the Croix de Guerre while fighting alongside the French, and both were excellent shots and spoke fluent German. General František Moravec, who was organizing the operation from London, planned an escape route for them, but warned them their fate was almost certainly 'death – perhaps a very painful and degrading death'. Moravec told them they were completely on their own. They must have no contact with the Czech underground, which was riddled with Heydrich's agents.

On 15 April 1942 the two assassins were parachuted into occupied Czech territory. They had no means of keeping in touch with London, and for six weeks no one heard anything from them. Gabčik and Kubiš discovered that Heydrich took the same route every day from his residence to his office in Prague. As with Walter Rathenau, his journey included a bend at which his car, an open-top Mercedes, had to slow right down. On 27 May, as it reached the turn, Gabčik leapt in front of it armed with a sub-machine gun, but, as we have seen, assassination is often difficult. The gun jammed. The assassins were also armed with pistols and a bomb, but they needed a stroke of luck too. Heydrich made the same mistake as Michael Collins. Instead of getting the hell out of the danger zone, he ordered his driver to stop, and drew his pistol. That gave Kubiš the chance to throw his bomb. It exploded near the car, wounding the Nazi, who still made a brief attempt to pursue his assailants before going back to his vehicle and collapsing. Eight days later, Heydrich died of septicaemia from his wounds. Hitler organized two huge state funerals for him, one in Prague and one in Berlin, but privately he was furious at what he considered Heydrich's 'stupidity' in travelling without an armed escort in a car without armour plating. Kubiš and Gabšik got away but after three weeks on the run, they were betrayed by a traitor tempted by an enormous reward, and cornered in a church where they had been hiding. After a fierce firefight with ss and Gestapo troops, they killed themselves using the cyanide pills they had been issued with at the start of their mission. The Nazis then launched a merciless campaign of reprisals. The assassins' families were rounded up and shot, and two villages were razed to the ground. According to some estimates, 15,000 people were murdered.

As we shall see, governments also played an important role in the development of new technologies of assassination, but this does not mean they had a monopoly in innovation. There is a theory that as states became less squeamish about the civilian casualties they caused in, for example, air raids, assassins followed their example and worried less about the collateral damage that is one of the drawbacks of bombs. When a car bomb was used to murder the Lebanese prime minister Rafiq al-Hariri in 2005, another 21 people were killed and two hundred injured. Sometimes a bomb produces only collateral damage. In London in 1975 the Provisional IRA planted one under a car belonging to Conservative MP Hugh Fraser, but one of his neighbours, Professor Gordon Hamilton Fairley, a world-famous Australian cancer specialist, spotted it as he walked his dog. When he moved in to investigate, the bomb went off. He was killed. Fraser, still safely in his home, was unscathed. The bomb nearly caused another piece of collateral damage which might have been very costly for the IRA. At the time of the explosion, JFK's daughter, Caroline Kennedy, was staying with the MP and his family, and when the bomb went off they were just about to take her out in the car. If Miss Kennedy had been killed or injured, it might have seriously damaged the IRA's standing with its sympathizers in America who were an important source of funds.

Whether growing callousness was the reason or not, assassins certainly started to use bombs more. New technology meant more sophisticated triggering devices became available which gave the perpetrators a better chance of escape. Alfred Herrhausen was a captain of German industry and the boss of the mighty Deutsche Bank. A key advisor to Chancellor Helmut Kohl, he also served on the boards of companies such as Xerox and Daimler-Benz, but he had liberal views on easing the burden of debt on Third World countries and supporting emerging East European economies as the Berlin Wall came down in November 1989. Less than a month later, on 1 December 1989, he was killed, and his driver seriously injured, when a bomb demolished his armoured Mercedes-Benz on a busy street less than a mile from his home in a fashionable suburb of Frankfurt. The force of the blast threw the car into the air and set it on fire.

Herrhausen's Mercedes was in the middle of a convoy accompanied by two security vehicles. The bomb was hidden behind a

The bombed car in which German businessman Alfred Herrhausen met his end in 1989.

bicycle and triggered when the banker's car bisected an infrared beam shone across the road. Police said it was controlled by a cable run from a park about 200 metres (200 yd) from the blast, and that the assassins had let the first car in the convoy go past before activating the beam. This had called for split-second timing. A note left at the scene suggested the Red Army Faction were responsible. They had been focusing their attacks on what they called the military-industrial complex, and it is not clear whether Herrhausen had been chosen because of the extreme left's habitual fear of the more moderate practitioners of capitalism or whether he was simply a victim of his own prominence. Three years earlier the group had used a remote-controlled bomb to murder Karl-Heinz Beckurts, director of research and technology at Siemens, while he was driving to work near Munich. The Red Army Faction also murdered prominent politicians and legal figures. Rather than fighting for any masses who might be downtrodden in Germany, they believed their task was to 'destroy the islands of wealth in Europe' on behalf of the oppressed Third World. They also hoped to provoke a violent reaction from the German government, so sparking a broader revolutionary movement. One of the co-founders of the group, Andreas Baader, was a high school drop-out, and he and Ulrike Meinhof were both children of academics. After the collapse of Communism in Europe, it was discovered that the East German secret police had provided training, shelter and supplies to the gang.

The last years of the twentieth century saw the emergence of a new kind of assassin with explosives, the suicide bomber, and as Machiavelli noted five centuries before, the killer who is not afraid of being killed is perhaps the hardest to stop. The bomber who assassinated Czar Alexander II in 1881 also killed himself, but there is no evidence that suicide was his intention. The first politician to be murdered by a classic suicide bomber was Rajiv Ghandi in 1991. A woman working for the Sri Lankan separatist Tamil Tigers hid her device in a basket of flowers and rushed up to greet the former

Indian prime minister while he was campaigning in the Indian state of Tamil Nadu. The assassin, who herself died in the blast, was clearly not worried about collateral damage, as she killed another fourteen people in addition to the politician.

A suicide bomber also claimed the life of Pakistan's former prime minister, Benazir Bhutto, in 2007. In 1988 Bhutto became the first woman ever to lead a Muslim country, but Pakistan's politics are rough and tough, and its conservative president, Ghulam Ishaq Khan, was soon at work with senior army officers trying to smear her with fabricated charges of corruption. The media exposed the plot, and a number of army officers were sent to gaol, but Khan did not give up and he finally got rid of Bhutto in 1990. By the time she had become premier, she had seen her father, Zulfikar Ali Bhutto, deposed in a military coup after he became prime minister, then executed on what some believed were manufactured charges of conspiring to kill an opponent. Benazir spent years under house arrest, and her brother was mysteriously poisoned.

She got elected prime minister again in 1993 and survived an attempted military coup in 1995, then saw another brother killed, before she was sacked by another Pakistani president, Farooq Leghari, in 1996 on charges of corruption. She took refuge in Dubai and stayed there until 2007 when President Pervez Musharraf, who had seized power in a military coup and survived a number of assassination attempts, dismissed all outstanding criminal charges against her. Bhutto came back in time to campaign in a general election. After she arrived at Karachi's international airport on 18 October, her motorcade was targeted by two bombs. She survived, but around 150 other people, mainly her supporters and fifty security guards from her Pakistan People's Party, were killed. Al-Qaeda field commander Saeed al-Masri claimed responsibility for the attack, but the government blamed Taliban leader Baitullah Mehsud. Bhutto's family and her political party rejected both accounts, and said her opponents in the military and intelligence services were behind it. Musharraf proclaimed a state of emergency and put Bhutto under house arrest, but a public outcry made him free her. Both al-Masri and Mehsud would be killed by U.S. drones. The bombers were never found.

And so it was that on 27 December 2007, a fortnight before the election, Bhutto was campaigning in Rawalpindi. On the spot where an earlier prime minister was assassinated 56 years before, she was waving to the crowd out of the sunroof of her bullet-proof car when a fifteen-year-old suicide bomber approached, shot at her, then detonated his explosive vest, killing more than twenty people. Bhutto was rushed to hospital for emergency surgery, but died soon after. If we examine who was behind the killing, we enter very deep waters. Musharraf, who fled Pakistan in 2009, and ended up, like Bhutto, in Dubai, was charged with murder and criminal conspiracy to murder, amid allegations that he warned the former prime minister not to come back to her home country. The ex-president denied the charges and pointed the finger at other, unnamed figures in the Pakistani establishment. Within weeks of the assassination, five people had admitted to helping the suicide bomber, but they later withdrew their confessions, and though there was some forensic evidence, the case against them collapsed. Some in Pakistan accuse Bhutto's widower, Asif Zardari, who won the 2008 presidential election following his wife's assassination and served for five years. He has angrily rejected the allegations, but he was also criticized for allowing the inquiry into his wife's killing to be pursued with so little enthusiasm that those responsible were bound to escape. A BBC investigation found evidence that two men who had helped the suicide bomber were later shot at a military checkpoint. A number of other people allegedly involved also met violent deaths. When Bhutto was killed, one of her security guards, Khalid Shahenshah, who was within a few feet of her, was seen raising his eyes towards the politician while at the same time drawing his fingers across his throat. In July 2008 he was shot dead outside his home, while state prosecutor Chaudhry Zulfikar was gunned down in 2013 just after telling friends he was making real progress on the case.

We have already seen how another piece of new technology, the drone, has become an assassination weapon, with governments at the forefront of this innovation. Apart from the United States, at least another nine countries have used them to kill, including the UK and Israel, while the militant Shia group Hezbollah has also deployed them for surveillance, though, at least until 2019, not for assassination. Another new weapon, the guided missile, was used to bring down the aircraft of Juvénal Habyarimana, the president of Rwanda, in 1994. For decades the country had been riven by enmity between two tribes – the majority Hutu and the Tutsi. Habyarimana, a Hutu army officer, seized power in a coup in 1973. He ruled with a rod of iron, but refrained from stirring up persecution of the Tutsis. Then in the mid-1980s, drought and a global fall in the price of coffee, one of the mainstays of the Rwandan economy, brought hardship, and a rebel organization, the Rwanda Patriotic Front (RPF), made a botched attempt to overthrow him. Though some of the group's supporters were Hutu, it was mainly made up of Tutsis, and within Rwanda, hundreds from the minority tribe were murdered. Under pressure from the West, Habyarimana was forced to make a deal with the rebels, bringing some of them into his government.

This enraged Hutu supremacists, who launched a 'Hutu Power' movement, winning plenty of support among the unemployed and the disappointed, while Hutu hate sheets – pamphlets and newspapers – said the Tutsi were planning to massacre them. Hutu paramilitary 'self-defence' units armed with machetes began to spring up. On 3 April 1994 a radio station well-known for its vicious anti-Tutsi propaganda broadcast that 'a little something' was about to happen. Three days later, Habyarimana was on his way back from an African leaders' summit in Dar es Salaam in his private jet, a present from President Mitterand of France, with seven members of his government and the president of neighbouring Burundi, who was hitching a lift. As the aircraft approached the Rwandan capital Kigali, two missiles hit it, bringing it down and killing everyone aboard. Who exactly fired them remains a mystery, but there is no doubt about the aftermath of President Habyarimana's assassination. At once roadblocks sprang up all over the country, and Hutus began massacring Tustis. In a hundred days at least 800,000 people were killed: the fastest mass murder in history, though the Hutu supremacists were then defeated by the RPF, who formed a government that has held power in the country ever since.

The poisoning of Indonesian human rights activist Munir Said Thalib may have used a method that dated back to the earliest days of assassination, but poisoning saw major technological changes in the Modern Age, with Russia playing an important role. In 1957 and 1959 a KGB hitman named Bogdan Stashinsky killed two leading Ukrainian anti-communists who were in exile in Munich, using a custom-built poison spray-gun that fired cyanide. When Stashinsky shot it directly into his victims' faces, it killed them quickly, leaving no visible traces, making it look as though they had died of a heart attack. The episode inspired Ian Fleming's James Bond novel *The Man with the Golden Gun* (1965). Two years after the second assassination, Stashinsky fled to the West on the day of his baby son's funeral. He was put on trial in West Germany for the murders, but it emerged that the Soviet secret police had recruited him by threatening his family. He served four years in prison after one of his judges described him as 'a poor devil who acted automatically under pressure of commands'.

If being killed by a deadly face spray sounds a bit like spy fiction, then what about being jabbed with a poisoned umbrella on a London street? That was the fate of Georgi Markov, a Bulgarian dissident working for the BBC's Bulgarian Service. Markov was a very prickly thorn in the side of Todor Zhivkov's communist regime in what was then a Soviet satellite. An eminent writer, once his plays were banned, Markov fled in 1969 to the UK, where he started making scathing satirical broadcasts, describing Zhikov as a 'paltry mediocrity who has proclaimed himself a demi-god'. Not surprisingly, this did not go down well in Sofia. On 7 September 1978,

Zhikov's birthday, Markov was waiting for a bus on Waterloo Bridge to take him home from the BBC when he felt a sting in his thigh. A man passing by with an umbrella muttered an apology in a foreign accent, and then leapt into a taxi. The only sign of injury was a red pimple, but soon Markov fell into a fever and four days later he was dead. A tiny pellet of the deadly poison ricin was found in his body. It had been coated in a wax that would melt once it had entered his leg. High-level Soviet defectors confirmed that the Bulgarians approached the KGB for help with the operation, but the identity of the umbrella killer has never been discovered.

The fall of the Soviet Union did nothing to diminish Russia's interest in poisons. In London in 2006 a former KGB officer, Alexander Litvinenko, was assassinated with radioactive polonium. After the Soviet Union collapsed, Litvinenko had worked for the KGB's successor, the Federal Security Bureau (FSB). He claimed he had fallen out with his bosses in 1997, when he was ordered to kill the Russian businessman Boris Berezovsky, a vocal critic of President Putin. Instead of carrying out his instructions, he told Berezovsky about it, and the businessman announced the news to the world, provoking a major scandal. The FSB then sacked Litvinenko and he was imprisoned for a month for 'abusing duties'. Released on condition that he leave the country, the Russian moved to London and started working for MI6. He also publicly attacked Vladimir Putin. On 1 November 2006, shortly after becoming a naturalized British citizen, he had lunch with two other former KGB agents, Dmitri Kovtun and Andrei Lugovoi. Soon after, Litvinenko fell ill, then three weeks later he died in hospital. Pathologists said he was killed by radiation poisoning from polonium added, it is believed, to a cup of tea. By then, the two suspects were safely back in Russia. The UK applied for their extradition, but President Putin refused, denying any Russian involvement, and Lugovoi got himself elected to the Russian parliament. One particularly chilling aspect of the affair was the assassins' contemptuous carelessness about potential collateral damage from the highly poisonous polonium, as traces were found in various places including a hotel, a restaurant, taxi cabs and commercial airliners. Berezovsky, incidentally, was found hanged in mysterious circumstances at his Berkshire home in 2013.

Another example of Russian assassination by innovative poison exhibited an even more reckless attitude to collateral damage. In 2018 a nerve agent from the Novichok family was used on a former Russian spy, 66-year-old Sergei Skripal, and his daughter Yulia in Salisbury. Sergei had been a colonel in Russian military intelligence, and was gaoled for thirteen years in 2006 for revealing the identities of undercover agents to MI6. Four years later he was freed in a prisoner exchange and came to the UK. Yulia came to see him on one of her regular visits from Russia on 3 March 2018. The next day they went to a restaurant in Salisbury. Later that afternoon, the pair were found slumped on a bench outside the restaurant in 'an extremely serious condition'. Yulia was frothing at the mouth. Police inquiries suggested the Novichok had been smeared on a door handle at Sergei's house. An officer who went there also fell seriously ill. Yulia spent more than a month in hospital and her father two and a half months before they were both released and taken to secure locations, though it was not known what long-term effects they and the policeman might suffer. Another 48 people had to go to hospital for checks, up to five hundred more were told to wash clothes and possessions, while more than four hundred counter-terrorism and military personnel were deployed, and parts of the city and surrounding area were put on lockdown. Incidentally, a number of Skripal's other relatives seem to have been unlucky with their health. His wife, elder brother and son all died in the previous six years; some, the family believe, in suspicious circumstances.

The targets may have survived, but a woman from Amesbury, about 10 miles away, was killed, and her partner was seriously ill in hospital for three weeks. They were exposed to the Novichok when the man found a perfume bottle in a charity bin. The bottle, which had a specially modified nozzle, contained the nerve agent. He got some of the contents on himself while the woman spread it on her wrists. Police identified two suspects: Alexander Petrov and Ruslan Boshirov. The pair had flown into London on 2 March, come to Salisbury for a quick recce, then smeared Skripal's door handle before flying back to Moscow on the night of 4 March. They were caught on a series of closed-circuit television cameras. In a bizarre interview on Russian television, the two men claimed they were tourists visiting the UK to see the 'wonderful town' of Salisbury with its famous cathedral, even though they spent remarkably little time there. Investigative journalists found both men were using assumed names and that the one who called himself Boshirov was actually a highly decorated military officer, while 'Petrov' was a doctor working for Russian intelligence who had made three visits to the UK over the previous eighteen months. The UK applied for their extradition, with Prime Minister Theresa May declaring the attack was 'almost certainly' approved at the highest levels, but once again the Russians sarcastically denied any involvement, and dismissed May's allegation as 'insane'. Noting that the UK's Porton Down defence research establishment was only eight miles away, the Russians suggested that might be the source of the Novichok, and accused the UK of obstructing investigation of the crime. Some felt the Russian denials were actually meant to be implausible in the tradition of Stalin's contempt for any criticism or reproaches. The UK retaliated against the attack by sending home more than twenty Russian diplomats and their families, and Britain's allies expelled another 150. The Russians responded in kind.

But perhaps the most bizarre poisoning was one involving the isolationist communist dictatorship of North Korea. Since television began, celebrities have been part of its staple diet, but from around the end of the twentieth century, our screens began increasingly to be populated by unknown people trying to become celebrities, as 'reality' shows took over. So when two young women were accused of murdering Kim Jong-nam, brother of the North Korean leader Kim Jong-un, at Kuala Lumpur airport in 2017, their defence was that they had believed they were taking part in just such a programme. Siti Aisyah from Indonesia and Doan Thi Huong from Vietnam said that while they were working as escorts, they had been approached by men believed to be North Korean state agents, and told they would be taking part in a Japanese YouTube show in which they would smear lotion on people's faces as a prank. Kim had been pointed out to them as the target, but they said they had no idea who he was or that they were about to smear him with toxic vx nerve agent.

They were charged with conspiring with the state of North Korea to kill Kim. The prosecution said Doan came up behind Kim and smeared his face. She then ran off to the bathroom to wash her hands. Within twenty minutes, the North Korean was dead. Kim had originally been the favourite to succeed his father Kim Jong-il as North Korean leader, but he severely blotted his copybook in 2001 by trying to escape from his country's privations to visit Disneyland. His father then banished him, and he settled in Macau. When his younger brother took over, Kim Jong-nam dismissed him as a 'joke'. The court was told that Kim lived in fear of being assassinated and was carrying an antidote to vx in his bag at the time he was killed. Charges against Siti were dropped in March 2019, while Doan was freed a couple of months later after pleading guilty to 'causing injury'. An Interpol warrant remained out against four men, believed to be North Koreans, who had fled Malaysia on the day of the killing and were still at large.

So new technology in missiles, drones, bombs and poisons all made it easier for assassins to strike from distance, as did more accurate firearms. In 2003 the Serbian prime minister Zoran Djindjić, who had helped to bring down Slobodan Milošević, was shot by a sniper as he was going into a government building. Twelve men, with links to ultranationalist paramilitaries and to the criminal underworld, were later convicted of his assassination. In 2010 Thailand was bitterly divided between the yellow-shirts, largely supported by royalists and the urban middle class, and the red-shirts, whose members were mainly rural workers. On 13 May the red-shirts' head of security, Major-General Khattiya Sawasdipol, was killed by a sniper, probably a soldier, while he was being interviewed by a reporter. Sawasdipol's insistence on always wearing his green military uniform among his red-shirted supporters made him an easy target. But even in the Modern Age, snipers remained a rarity and getting up close and personal with the victim continued to be the favourite method.

New Ways of Combatting Assassination

So if the technology of assassination has developed, what about measures to combat it? We saw how, during the Age of Revolution, victims such as Abraham Lincoln or Lord Frederick Cavendish or the Spanish prime minister José Canalejas y Méndez appear to have behaved with surprising carelessness. Did things tighten up in the Modern Age? On 28 February 1986 a man walked up to Swedish prime minister Olof Palme in a Stockholm street and shot him dead as he walked home from the cinema with his wife. There was no bodyguard with them, but Palme was very much the exception, and most important figures have made sure they are well guarded. One consequence of this has been that terrorists have tended to switch from hard, well-protected targets, such as prominent politicians, to soft targets like ordinary people attending concerts or working in offices. One analysis looking at more than 12,000 attacks across the world from 1968 to 2005 concluded that nearly three-quarters had been aimed at soft targets. When the G8 summit was held in the UK in July 2005, terrorists ignored it. After all it was protected by 1,500 police and security personnel (many of them diverted from London). Instead, suicide bombers killed more than fifty rank-and-file Londoners travelling to their jobs on tube trains and buses. Terrorism expert David Capitanchik from Aberdeen University described the assailants' philosophy as: 'Why attack a tiger when there are so many sheep?'

India, 1962. A year before JFK's murder, his wife, Jackie, sits with Indira Gandhi, who would herself be assassinated 22 years later.

One of the new technologies deployed to try to combat assassination saved the president of Georgia, Eduard Shevardnadze, in 1998. He escaped thanks to the armour-plating in his limousine, when at least ten heavily armed men attacked his motorcade with machine guns and rocket-propelled grenades, though three of his entourage were killed. But, as we saw, armoured cars did not save Anastasio Somoza in 1980 or Alfred Herrhausen in 1989, and most defences against assassination still involve more traditional methods. One is to keep potential assassins out of the way. Under authoritarian regimes, this can be done by locking them up, but in democratic societies more subtle means are required. In France in the 1950s, for example, when Soviet dignitaries were due to arrive on official visits, potential troublemakers among Russian emigrés would be strongly invited to take themselves off for the duration of the visit to pleasant country mansions at the government's expense. Then there are bodyguards. Most modern leaders and lots of other prominent folk ensure they have them, sometimes plenty of them. In 2018, for example, it was revealed that South Africa's Presidential Protection Unit employed 1,382 people. There are many instances of bodyguards sacrificing their own lives to protect those in their charge, such as those working for the Mexican revolutionary Pancho Villa. Similarly, five of the Chechen president Akhmad Kadyrov's bodyguards were killed when a woman suicide bomber tried to blow him up in 2003. (A year later Kadyrov met his end in another explosion.) Then there were the fifty guards killed in the failed bomb attack on Benazir Bhutto in 2007. However, as we have seen, body-guards have sometimes constituted an assassination risk, ever since the Egyptian pharaoh Teti was killed by his more than 4,300 years ago. In the modern age Rajiv Gandhi's mother, Indira, then prime minister of India, was murdered by two of her Sikh bodyguards in 1984. Sikhs were incensed when she had ordered a raid on the Golden Temple to expel separatists who had taken refuge there, and in Pakistan in 2011 the governor of the Punjab, Salman Taseer, was killed by his bodyguard because of his support for the repeal of the country's blasphemy laws.

If one defence is to remove from circulation people who might be assassins, another is to keep possible targets out of reach of any potential killer. Especially in democracies, this is not always easy. In election campaigns, in particular, politicians have to get close to potential voters. In the run-up to elections in Mexico in 2018, more than a hundred candidates were murdered, including one shot in the head from behind as he was taking a selfie with a supporter. As we saw, Bobby Kennedy was assassinated while campaigning, as were Rajiv Gandhi and Benazir Bhutto.

A FORENSIC ANALYSIS of 83 people involved in 74 assassinations and assassination projects in the USA in the fifty years leading up to 1999 was carried out by an agent and a psychologist from the Secret Service. The 74 projects resulted in 34 actual attempts. It found that handguns were the most popular weapons, used in half of the cases, while knives were chosen eleven times, sometimes because the would-be killers could not get hold of a gun. Explosives featured in only six. The study also revealed other intriguing insights: those involved were mainly men (71) and mainly white (63). Half were single, and 47 of the 83 had no children. Only twenty were involved with militant groups at the time of the project, but 53 had been involved with or had had an interest in extreme organizations. Sixteen had been arrested for at least one offence involving violence, while 44 had been arrested for non-violent offences, but 52 had never been in prison. Most had experience of using weapons, but not formal training. Although 80 per cent had planned their attacks, few approached the task 'with the technical expertise that has been presented in popular culture', and fewer than a quarter had an escape plan. Indeed, fourteen of the sample quoted 'suicide' as a motive, while 29 had at some point threatened to kill themselves, 27 had a history of substance abuse and 29 were described as 'delusional' at the time of the attack. Winning attention or gaining notoriety was a motive for 25, while others quoted revenge, hopes of bringing about political change, or wanting to establish a 'special relationship' with the person they targeted. The ages of the would-be assassins ranged from 16 to 73, and the researchers warned that they exhibited 'no single profile', but said they were often 'social isolates' with 'histories of mobility and transience', adding that almost all were 'persons who had – or believed themselves to have had – difficulty coping with problems in their lives' and noting that those 'who see themselves as doing well in life rarely attempt assassinations'.

So, does assassination work? As we saw in the case of Reinhard Heydrich, it can provoke fearful reprisals. It can also have the opposite effect to the one intended. Benigno Aquino was the main opposition leader in the Philippines when President Ferdinand Marcos had the country under martial law. Aquino spent eight years in jail and in 1977 was sentenced to death, only to be reprieved and allowed to go to America for a heart operation. While he was away, martial law was lifted and he returned to the Philippines, but almost as soon as he landed at Manila airport in

1983, he was shot in the head and killed. This does not appear to have been too much of a surprise to Aquino. On the flight, he had warned reporters to have their cameras ready because something might happen 'very fast', after which, he said: 'I may not be able to talk to you again.' Far from making Marcos safe, though, the assassination triggered his downfall. There were widespread demonstrations followed by an inquiry that found the chief of staff of the country's armed forces was behind the killing. When the case came to trial, he and 25 others were acquitted by judges appointed by the president, but Aquino's widow, Corazon, took up her husband's torch and defeated Marcos in the election of 1986, after which he resigned and went into exile.

In 2007 two American academics at the National Bureau of Economic Research found one respect in which assassination did seem to work after analysing nearly three hundred attempts on national leaders since 1875, of which 59 had been successful. They concluded that killings of democratic leaders brought little change, but that with autocratic regimes a transition to democracy is 13 per cent more likely if an assassination attempt succeeds than if it fails.

I analysed one hundred assassinations from the modern age, involving 103 victims. I have generally assumed that the accepted storyline is correct, that, for example, Lee Harvey Oswald shot President Kennedy. Of the victims, 47 were leading politicians, including nine presidents, one former president, six prime ministers and four former prime ministers. Royalty continued to suffer too, but in much smaller numbers – just four victims, including two kings and one heir to an empire. On the other side of the fence, 26 revolutionaries, national liberationists or civil rights activists were murdered. Four of the 103 were attacked because they were celebrities. There were also two figures from the arts, along with six journalists or writers and two propagandists. At least three of the victims fought back – Michael Collins, Trotsky and one of the Kurds murdered by the Iranians in 1989 – while at least four had survived earlier assassination attempts. Six victims were women.

As to where the assassinations happened, nearly half, 48, were in Europe – 38 of them in Western Europe – with twelve in the Middle East, ten in the Indian sub-continent, and eight in North America; but a note of caution: the figures may be skewed because we have better information about Europe and North America than we do about other parts of the world such as Africa and Latin America. The countries with the highest number, seven in each, were Germany and the United States. Next come France and Ireland, each with six. The globalization of assassination took off, as twenty of the episodes had an element of extra-territoriality; in other words, the victims were killed away from their own countries, or the assassins were operating abroad.

A quarter of the assassinations were done by people fighting for national liberation or, in one case, against apartheid. Another fourteen killers were right-wing activists, with eight coming from the left. Religion was a motive in seven assassinations, while three were perpetrated by organized crime. On the other hand, at least eighteen killers, and perhaps as many as 26, were agents of governments. The most murderous government was the Soviet Union, involved in four, or possibly five assassinations, plus another as Russia, after the USSR fell. Then came the USA, Iran and Israel with three each. Four killers were bodyguards, while, as dynastic ambition declined as a motive, so did the number of assassins from within the family – just one nephew and one niece, and she had been radicalized by the Islamic fundamentalist group Al-Shabaab to carry out a suicide bombing against her uncle, a leading Somali politician. A further three or four killings were also carried out by suicide bombers. At least a dozen, and perhaps as many as nineteen of the murders were perpetrated by lone assassins, and four were committed by Jackal-style hired killers. The youngest assassin was the fifteen-year-old suicide bomber who killed Benazir Bhutto, while three others were aged seventeen. Only seven of the assassinations involved women, including the only one featuring killers who appear to have been duped into their crime – the poisoning of the North Korean Kim Jong-nam in 2017. At least four were committed by killers who were mentally disturbed, while another two assassins, Lee Harvey Oswald and Mark Chapman, were social misfits. Sometimes in addition to ideological motives, 25 of the assassinations were prompted by revenge, anger or resentment. At least a dozen gave rise to conspiracy theories, and three people who queried the official story about Soviet politician Sergei Kirov's murder in 1934 were executed.

A technological revolution in assassination was completed, with stabbing, once the favourite method, now used in only two of the one hundred killings. Guns were by far the most common, employed in 66 (including one poison gun), though only four assassins were snipers in *Day of the Jackal* style. After guns, bombs were the next most favoured weapon, featuring in eighteen cases. Then came the time-honoured method of poison, with seven. In spite of the technological changes, of the 94 assassinations where we can be sure, the vast majority, 77, were committed at close quarters. Two that were not involved the drastic step of shooting down aeroplanes, the ones carrying President Juvenal Habyarimama of Rwanda, and the Japanese admiral Isoroku Yamamoto, the architect of the attack on Pearl Harbor, killed in 1943 by the Americans. With more bombs being used, not surprisingly there was much more collateral damage. This happened in 32 assassinations, with a total of nearly three hundred other people killed in addition to the targets. The most bloody murder was the car bomb attack on an Iraqi Shia religious leader, Ayatollah Mohammad Baqir al-Hakim, in 2003, which cost up to another 120 lives.

So what was the fate of the assassins? I have identified 206 people involved in the one hundred killings; 26 were executed, though it took 45 years for justice to catch up with one of those involved in the murder of President Mujibur Rahman of Bangladesh. Thirteen were killed or fatally wounded at the scene, and another eleven were killed or assassinated later. In addition to six suicide bombers, five other assassins killed themselves, including one of the young German ultra-nationalists who murdered Walter Rathenau, and the mentally disturbed man who killed a Canadian singer, Christina Grimmie, in 2016. A total of 77 were imprisoned. Thirteen died in gaol, while 42 completed terms of fifteen years or more; three served five to fifteen years and eleven were incarcerated for five years or less. In 2019 another eight of the 77 were still in prison, serving sentences of twenty years or more. A further four assassins were sent to psychiatric institutions, where three of them died. The fourth, the killer of sports presenter Brian Smith, was released after nine years. In seven cases assassins were rewarded, including the murderers of the Mexican revolutionaries Emiliano Zapata and Pancho Villa, while more than fifty escaped without punishment.

Of the victims, more than twenty became national heroes, with towns, districts, airports, universities and streets named after them, while Zapata's face appeared on banknotes. Trotsky became an international hero to some, and some assassins became heroes or martyrs for particular groups, so Jaurès' murderer became a hero for the right in France and Sadat's for jihadists in Egypt. The enduring nature of the passions that stir assassinations is illustrated by the story of leading Irish politician Kevin O'Higgins. In 1927 he was murdered, like Michael Collins, because of his support for the peace treaty with the British. It took 85 years to put up a memorial to him, and within a week it had been defaced, while a suicide bomber killed four people at the memorial service for Afghan politician Ahmed Karzai, who was assassinated in 2011.

Working out the consequences of assassinations is often difficult, but two at least played a part in momentous events that followed – the murder of Archduke Franz Ferdinand in sparking the First World War and that of President Habyarimana in fomenting the Rwandan genocide. Seven were followed by increased disorder or instability, including demonstrations that brought down the government in Slovakia after the murder of the journalist Jan Kuciak in 2018. Five led to fearful reprisals, notably by the Nazis after the murders of Reinhard Heydrich and an ss leader in Poland, while six brought security crackdowns, including Stalin's reign of terror after Kirov's murder and a state of emergency in Egypt after Sadat's assassination that lasted for 31 years. Five assassinations misfired, as they helped to advance the causes the victim had promoted, with the civil rights programme in the United States, for example, probably aided by the murders of President Kennedy and Martin Luther King. In five, the status quo the killing was designed to disturb continued. Apartheid, for example, lasted for another 28 years after the murder of President Verwoerd in South Africa, u.s. support for Israel was not shaken by the assassination of Robert Kennedy, and the murder of the Russian ambassador to Turkey in 2016 did not get Russian troops withdrawn from Syria. On the other hand, the assassination of Rajiv Gandhi in 2006 did lead to India virtually ending its involvement in Sri Lanka, while the furious response to the murder of former Lebanese prime minister Rafiq al-Hariri the previous year, in which Syria was suspected of being involved, led to the withdrawal of Syrian soldiers from the country.

On some occasions, it is fairly easy to say whether an assassination succeeded or failed. So the killing of a South African anti-apartheid activist, David Webster, in 1989 by the security services seems a clear failure, as apartheid began to be dismantled the following year, while the Israeli murder of Gerald Bull in 1990 seems to be a clear success in that it stopped the development of the Iraqi super-gun. With many other assassinations, it is less easy to give a definitive answer as to whether the perpetrator would have been satisfied with the outcome or not, but my assessment is that we can count 41 as successes, with a further eight as possible successes, while fourteen were clear failures and eighteen more possible failures.

7

THE ONES THAT GOT AWAY

Perhaps the most famous assassination attempt in fiction is meticulously planned. The man who wants to kill President de Gaulle in Frederick Forsyth's *The Day of the Jackal* equips himself with a collection of passports under different names. He commissions a specially designed extremely thin rifle plus mercury-tipped explosive bullets, kills a number of people who threaten the success of his enterprise, disguises himself as a wounded war veteran and hides his rifle in his crutch. Then he chews cordite so he will look old and sick to smooth his way through security checks. He has already identified the perfect window from which to shoot the president as he presents decorations to commemorate the Liberation of Paris during the Second World War. The Jackal gets into the room with a stolen key. Now the president is in his sights, but just like more than four in five of the assassinations examined by the analysts from the National Bureau of Economic Research, this one too fails. The Jackal's shot is perfectly aimed, but at the last split second De Gaulle bows his head to kiss the cheek of one of the veterans. The bullet just misses its target and there is no second shot, as the police who are hot on the assassin's heels burst in and kill him. In real life, De Gaulle had angered elements of the right in France by giving independence to Algeria, which they considered a betrayal. There were at least thirty attempts to kill him, and *The Day of the Jackal* begins with the execution of a real person, Jean-Marie Bastien-Thiry, who was involved in a number of them.

History is littered with the stories of giants who narrowly escaped being assassinated long before they completed the deeds that brought them fame or infamy, and it is hard to resist speculating on what might have happened if, say, JFK had not been killed. One of the most momentous escapes involved the Prophet Muhammad, who came close to being murdered in Mecca in 622. He had made plenty of enemies with his message about the vanity of riches and the need to share with the poor, and one day he discovered there was a plot to kill him involving the city authorities, so he asked his cousin Ali ibn Abu Talib to sleep in his bed, while he slipped away to Medina, shunning the paths travellers normally used. When the conspirators entered Muhammad's house with daggers drawn, they found Ali instead. Incensed, they were all set to kill him, but he confronted them so bravely they decided to spare his life. The Islamic calendar begins from the day the prophet arrived in Medina. In that city, he created a theocratic state, and by the time he died ten years later, most Arab tribes had converted to Islam.

Adolf Hitler

One of the most fascinating might-have-beens in history is the question of what would have happened if Hitler had been killed before he could instigate mass murder and plunge the world into its most destructive war. There were at least seven attempts on his life before he came to power in 1933. The earliest was in November 1921, when he was still a fairly obscure young extremist. In the audience for his speech at Munich's famous Hofbräuhaus beer hall were plenty of members of the new Nazi party, but also lots of leftist opponents. A brawl broke out, and in the mêlée, a group of unknown assailants started firing in Hitler's direction. The future Führer was unhurt; indeed he carried on ranting for another

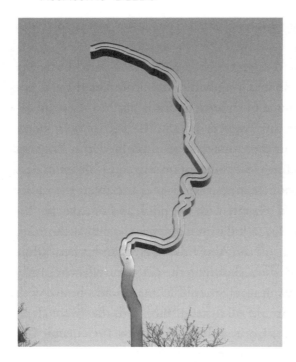

A distinctive memorial in Berlin to Georg Elser, who tried to assassinate Adolf Hitler in 1939.

twenty minutes until police arrived. Two years later, there was a similar episode in Thuringia, and also in 1923, shots were fired at his car in Leipzig. In 1932 a gunman shot at his train between Munich and Weimar.

During the years after he took power, there were more than 25 further attempts on his life. One of the most ingenious was planned by a communist carpenter named Georg Elser. From late 1938 he started making a time bomb, and once he had finished, night after night he would steal into Munich's Bürgerbräukeller, the site of Hitler's failed Beer Hall Putsch of 1923, to make a hidden cavity in a stone pillar next to the speaker's platform, knowing that Hitler would come to speak there on 8 November 1939. This was a big day in the Nazi calendar because it was the anniversary of the attempted coup. Finally the carpenter had the bomb installed and primed to go off halfway through the dictator's speech. It worked perfectly. The device exploded exactly as planned and brought a section of the roof down on the speaker's podium. Dozens of people were injured and eight were killed, but Hitler was not among them. The war had made him change his schedule and end his speech earlier than planned, so by the time the bomb went off, he had been gone for thirteen minutes. Elser was captured and put in a concentration camp before being executed during the last days of the war.

The most celebrated of all the plots against Hitler was von Stauffenberg's on 20 July 1944. An injured war hero as well as a scholar and aristocrat, Claus von Stauffenberg led a group of disgruntled army officers who wanted to kill the Führer, overthrow his regime, then make peace with the Allies. As a senior military figure, he had regular meetings with Hitler. This time he packed a briefcase with plastic explosives. Having placed it as close to the Führer as possible, von Stauffenberg left the room ostensibly to make a phone call. Minutes later, the bomb exploded, killing four people, but once again the dictator escaped, though this time he did have minor injuries. An officer had happened to move the briefcase behind a thick table leg just before it went off. The conspirators were rounded up and executed along with hundreds of other dissidents. Even if von Stauffenberg's plot had worked, of course, Hitler would by then have performed most of his terrible deeds, and in August 1944 Churchill warned the British parliament not to put too much trust in assassination plans, telling them there was more to the Nazi war machine than the Führer. The UK's Special Operations Executive had its own schemes but they were never put into effect over fears they might fail or that they might make Hitler a martyr. Some even believed his removal might make Germany a more formidable enemy if someone more sane took over. As it was, von Stauffenberg's plot seems to have given a morale boost to Hitler, who kept repeating after the explosion: 'I am invulnerable! I am immortal!'

But what if one of the assassination plots before Hitler came to power had been successful? Would that have spared the world the horrors he unleashed? There is a theory that the assassination of a democratic leader rarely changes the course of history. Whether it is Abraham Lincoln, Spencer Perceval or Olof Palme, there will be great distress, perhaps a tightening of security, but soon a new leader will come along not much different from the one who was killed, and the government will continue much as before. When it comes to dictators, as we saw from the National Bureau of Economic Research figures, there is more chance of things changing, and when you get a gigantic, monstrous figure like Hitler, it is hard to believe that everything would have gone on just the same without him. Yes, Germany would have had the same grievances: the humiliation of Versailles, the myth that the army was stabbed in the back by politicians in 1918, the economic collapse of the 1920s. But Hitler had the ideal portfolio of dark gifts to exploit them – the charisma, the ruthlessness, the cunning – so without him, even if there had been a chapter of horrors in Europe's history, perhaps it would not have been so terrible.

Benito Mussolini

Hitler's fascist ally, the Italian dictator Benito Mussolini, also survived a series of assassination attempts, including four in just seven months in 1926. In April of that year, Violet Gibson, the daughter of the Lord Chancellor of Ireland, nearly shot off his nose, but (shades of *Day of the Jackal*) he turned his head at the crucial moment and ended up with just a 'slight' wound. Mussolini was horrified that he should have been shot at by a woman, especially one he considered 'ugly and repulsive'. At the time, the UK did not see Mussolini as an enemy, and Gibson was sent to a mental hospital in England where she died in 1956. Six months after her attempt, a fifteen-year-old anarchist tried to shoot the dictator, but missed. The boy was lynched by a mob, and Mussolini used the attack to abolish civil liberties and close down opposition parties. Il Duce was plainly much better at organizing assassinations than those who were trying to kill him, as his thugs murdered a series of political opponents,

Dictator with injured nose: Mussolini showing the scars of a failed assassination attempt, 1926.

but when his fascist regime lost the war, and he tried to flee with his mistress in 1945, he was caught by communist partisans, who shot the pair of them. The mob were then as unkind to him as he once was to his opponents, hanging the corpses of the couple upside down from meat hooks in a public square.

King Zog

In 1939 Mussolini had declared Albania an Italian protectorate and driven its ruler, King Zog, into exile. Zog is perhaps the only king to have foiled an assassination attempt by opening fire on the would-be assassins, but then he was not your average monarch. Handsome, courteous, ruthless and a chain-smoker, he was born into the family of a feudal chief, when the country was still part of the Ottoman Empire. After independence, he became president, but decided to make himself king in 1928 – Europe's only Muslim monarch. Two years later, two disgruntled army officers ambushed Zog and his party while they were coming out of Vienna's Opera House. As gunfire rang out, music lovers ran for cover, and Zog's aide-de-camp was shot dead, falling on the king he was protecting. Zog pushed his body out of the way, pulled a gun from the waistband of his dress trousers and started shooting back. The gunmen, also in evening dress, surrendered. Zog survived dozens of assassination plots, and got rather blasé. After one left him wounded and bleeding, he just sat down at his desk and got on with his work. He survived them all to live a fairly pleasant life in exile, some of it at the Ritz in London, financed by the gold bars his retinue carried around in trunks. He died peacefully in Paris in 1961.

Kaiser Wilhelm II

Just as Hitler survived assassination attempts, so did the man usually blamed for the First World War, Kaiser Wilhelm II of Germany, though the attempts against him were less well planned. At the turn of the twentieth century there was a spate of attacks on royal figures in Europe, with the Empress Elizabeth murdered in 1898 and King Umberto I of Italy in 1900. A few months after Umberto's assassination, a woman said to be 'mentally deranged' threw an axe at the Kaiser's carriage but did no damage. In 1901 in Bremen, a young workman of 'unsound mind' got closer, cutting Wilhelm's cheek with an iron buckle. The chief of the naval cabinet noted: 'On the temple or in the eye the blow could have been devastating.' As we saw in Chapter Six, there are those who believe the First World War was inevitable, but it is still tantalizing to wonder what would have happened if Wilhelm had been killed. He would have been succeeded by his eldest son, also named Wilhelm. In fact, there are no clear indications that things would have been much different. Some feel the Crown Prince might have been more level-headed than his father, but he too seems to have been keen on German expansion. He played an active role in the First World War, and flirted with extreme right-wing politics in Germany in the 1930s.

Even during a world war, we have seen the British government was not very keen on trying to assassinate Hitler, and he was just an upstart corporal! How much more reluctant must they have been to contemplate killing Kaiser Wilhelm, the cousin of George v, king of England? In fact, evidence is emerging of a British plot to assassinate the Kaiser in June 1918. Allied intelligence had discovered his secret headquarters in France – a chateau close to the Belgian border. A dozen RAF bombers were dispatched to attack it. They dropped thirty bombs, but the chateau escaped virtually unscathed. The main damage was to cars parked outside, and anyway, the Kaiser had left nineteen hours before. The same day, a British aircraft spotted the German imperial train on the private railway line that led to the chateau, and strafed it with machine-gun fire. It is believed that a number of people were killed, but the Kaiser was not on the train either.

Lenin

The other great cataclysmic event in the second decade of the twentieth century was the Russian Revolution of 1917. It had barely got into its stride when a 28-year-old woman named Fanya Kaplan fired three shots at its leading architect, Vladimir Ilyich Lenin, from close range on 30 August 1918. One passed through his coat without hitting him, another wounded him in the arm, and the third went through his neck, puncturing his left lung. The attack happened as a crowd milled around the revolutionary hero after he had delivered a speech at an armaments factory in Moscow. Kaplan was arrested immediately. She was a Jew from what is now Ukraine, the daughter of a teacher. As a teenager, she went off to learn to be a hatmaker, but by the time she was sixteen she had joined up with anarchist terrorists. In 1906 she was sentenced to life in a Siberian labour camp after a maid was killed by a bomb that went off in her flat. There she had a terrible time, until the revolution came along and she was released.

Kaplan joined the Socialist Revolutionary Party, a rival of Lenin's Bolsheviks. When the Soviet leader banned them, she decided he was a 'traitor to the revolution'. After shooting him, she quickly signed a statement saying: 'Today I shot Lenin. I did it on my own. I will not say from whom I obtained my revolver.' On 3 September she was executed with a bullet to the head. Kaplan had gone blind because of the ill-treatment she had suffered in the labour camp, and, although doctors were able to restore some sight, there are doubts as to whether she was actually up to firing the shots that injured Lenin, or whether her confession was designed to protect someone else. Some of the consequences of the failed assassination are clear. On 30 August 1918 not only did Kaplan try to assassinate Lenin, but Moisei Uritsky, chief of the Petrograd secret police, was murdered, and whether because of genuine fear or out of opportunism, the Bolsheviks launched a reign of terror. The secret police were ordered to carry out mass executions of thousands of suspected opponents. Supporters of the tsar's regime and the well-to-do were taken hostage, to be executed if required. It is estimated that 140,000 were killed. Lenin never really recovered from being shot, and following a stroke four years later, he died in 1924. If he had been killed in 1918 things might have been very different. Would the Bolsheviks still have prevailed, would another party of the left have taken over, or might the Royalist

White Army even have been victorious? Would Russia have been spared Stalin's terror in which tens of millions perished? The ailing Lenin had warned his comrades against the Georgian, but he still rose to the top. If the maker of the revolution had died as early as 1918, Stalin would probably not have been in a position to grab the reins of power.

Napoleon

Like Hitler, Napoleon was charismatic, ruthless, with the ability to think very big, but mercifully, he lacked the German leader's enthusiasm for mass murder, and he was one of the greatest of all military commanders. It is true that he had advantages that any French leader of the time might have exploited – a country with the biggest population in Europe, twice as big as that of his arch-enemy Great Britain, and energized by a revolution that had swept away an inefficient ancien regime – but it is hard to believe that anyone else would have mobilized them quite as effectively, or built such an empire. It is estimated that he survived up to thirty assassination plots. Some would-be killers tried poisoned snuff. Others plotted to stab him to death at the opera or set fire to cottages close to his house so his minders would run out to extinguish the flames, leaving him unprotected. In 1809, after he had occupied Vienna, a German medical student tried to knife him, but was arrested before he could get his weapon out. Napoleon offered to spare his life if he would apologize, but the student said he had no regrets and would try to kill the emperor again if he got the chance. He went to the firing squad.

Perhaps the most intriguing conspiracy was the one involving a so-called 'infernal machine' on Christmas Eve 1800. The attack was planned for when Napoleon was on his way to the opera. Inspired by an explosive device designed by their ideological opposites, the extreme-left Jacobins, a group of royalists decided to blow him up. They acquired blue uniforms similar to those worn by Paris's water carriers and made a bomb in a water barrel, which they put

Napoleon Bonaparte in an early 19th-century engraving.

on a horse-drawn cart. Then they drove it onto the route Napoleon would be taking. The conspirators' leader, known as Saint-Réjant, waited by it for a sign from one of his comrades that Bonaparte had left the Tuileries palace. When the signal did not come, Saint-Réjant became worried and went off to investigate, paying a fourteen-year-old girl to hold the horse for him. The emperor (who was then first consul) had been late leaving because his wife Josephine had changed her outfit at the last minute. Suddenly Saint-Réjant spotted Napoleon's coach approaching behind a detachment of grenadiers and raced to the cart, which was partially blocking the street. As the man at the head of the patrol pushed by it, Saint-Réjant lit the fuse and ran for cover.

A few seconds later there was a huge explosion, breaking windows, throwing people into the air and showering them with glass, tiles and masonry. The girl, who was still holding the horse, was killed, as were perhaps a dozen other people. Napoleon's coach leapt off the ground but he was unhurt. His wife was in another coach, but unlike Alexander II of Russia, Napoleon did not hang around to check on any wounded, instead ordering his driver to hurry on to the theatre. In fact, his family escaped uninjured, apart from his step-daughter whose arm was cut when the window in her coach broke. Saint-Réjant was knocked out and buried under rubble. As soon as he came round, he discovered Bonaparte had escaped, but, though he was seriously injured, he coolly melted away from the scene and managed to get himself treated by a doctor. Then he took to his bed, hoping to keep out of the way of the police investigation.

Inside the theatre the explosion was heard clearly. Was it cannon fire to celebrate some new triumph of the French army? Or was it something more ominous? When Napoleon appeared, he was calmness itself, though Josephine was more frazzled, but after a quarter of an hour, Bonaparte left to see his chief of police, Joseph Fouché. Blaming the Jacobins, he ordered Fouché to arrest more than a hundred of them, who were promptly transported without trial to Cayenne and the Seychelles. When the police chief realized the attack had been organized by royalists, he asked Napoleon to rescind the Jacobins' punishment, but Bonaparte was not going to miss out on such a good opportunity to get rid of dozens of his enemies, saying they deserved to be exiled 'for all that they have done, for all that they might yet do'. In fact, only three people had played an active role in setting up the explosion, but another twenty went on trial with them. Saint-Réjant and the bomb maker were executed, eight of the defendants were acquitted, while the others, including the doctor who had treated Saint-Réjant, got varying gaol terms.

While the British government seemed lukewarm about assassinating Hitler, they do appear to have been actively involved in plans to kill Napoleon. This may not have gone down well with the victor of Waterloo, the Duke of Wellington, who, when told that his gunners had Bonaparte in their sights, exhibited no interest, saying it was 'not the business of commanders to be firing upon one another', but recent research suggests the British government was behind a failed royalist plot in 1804 to kill the emperor by throwing a bomb at his coach.

Napoleon III

An assassination attempt on Napoleon's nephew, the French emperor Napoleon III, had an unusual outcome. On 14 January 1858 an Italian nationalist named Felice Orsini with his accomplices threw three bombs at the coach carrying the emperor and his wife to the opera in Paris. The explosions killed eight people, but the royal couple were unhurt. Orsini was arrested and executed. Two of his comrades were also condemned to death, though one had his sentence commuted, escaped from Devil's Island, and went on to join the U.S. cavalry, fighting at, and surviving, Custer's Last Stand. At the time of the attack on Napoleon III, Italy was divided into a number of different states, with much of the north ruled by Austria. For fifteen years Orsini had been fighting for Italian unification, and was a well-known figure because of the popular

Orsini's failed attempt to kill Napoleon III in 1858, from a history of Paris published 24 years later.

accounts he had written of his adventures. He believed that if he killed Napoleon that would foment revolution in France, which would then spread to Italy. The attack seems to have jogged the memory, or perhaps the conscience, of the emperor who allowed the publication of a letter Orsini had sent to him: 'Set my country free!' Recalling that he too had fought for Italian unity in his youth, Napoleon started secret talks with the leaders of the unification movement and in 1859 he invaded Austria's Italian territories, scoring some notable victories. Nationalist heroes like Garibaldi joined in the fray and by 1861 Orsini's dream had come true, with Italy unified. Napoleon was rewarded by being handed Nice and other Italian territory, but his triumph was relatively short-lived as defeat and capture in the Franco-Prussian War of 1870 cost him his throne.

Gunpowder, Treason and Plot

Plenty of English monarchs have met violent deaths. Edward II, Richard II, Henry VI and probably Edward V, one of the 'princes in the Tower', were all murdered by enemies who were holding them captive, while Charles I was beheaded, but since the Norman Conquest, there was only one who might have been assassinated, according to the definition we have used in this book. William II, often known as William Rufus, was killed in a hunting 'accident' in the New Forest in 1100. He was hit by a supposedly stray arrow from a crack archer, who was then handsomely rewarded by the new king, William's brother, Henry II. But if assassinations were rare or non-existent, it does not mean there were no attempts. The most spectacular, surely, was the infamous Gunpowder Plot of 5 November 1605, now synonymous with the Roman Catholic Guy Fawkes who is still burned in effigy on thousands of bonfires every year on its anniversary.

Fawkes, in fact, was not the leader of the conspiracy. That was another Roman Catholic, Robert Catesby, and the aim was to free

Catholics in England from the persecution they were suffering. Remember, this was the era of the Wars of Religion. The proposed remedy was drastic: to kill King James I, his queen, his eldest son and a large number of MPs by blowing up the Houses of Parliament. In the chaos they hoped Catholics would take over the country. In March 1605 the conspirators managed to hire a vault directly beneath the Lords. By May they had brought in up to 36 barrels of gunpowder which they hid under coal and firewood. Fawkes and others went to Catholic countries on the continent to drum up support, while in England, selected members of the Catholic gentry were alerted to be ready to rise up after the great bomb went up at the opening of parliament on 5 November.

One of the problems the plotters faced was that the explosion would kill Catholic lords as well as Protestants, some of them related to, or friends of, the conspirators. One Catholic lord got an anonymous letter warning him to steer clear of Westminster on the appointed day, and showed it to some of the king's ministers. Exhibiting considerable nerve, they decided not to search the cellar immediately so as not to alert the conspirators. For their part, some of the plotters got wind that the government had seen the letter and begged Catesby to call the whole thing off, but he was reassured when no search was mounted, and decided the authorities must be sceptical about the document. Fawkes was guarding the gunpowder when the authorities finally came to search the cellar on the night of 4 November. He was arrested and, under torture, named the other conspirators, some of whom had fled from London, still hoping there might be a Catholic rising against the king. There was none, and on 8 November they were cornered in Staffordshire. As they tried to shoot it out, Catesby and two others were killed. Fawkes and seven more were executed. As far as English Roman Catholics were concerned, after the plot, they were persecuted more severely than before.

King George III

George III reigned longer than any other king in English history – sixty years. In 1786, when he had been on the throne for 26 years, a woman named Margaret Nicholson tried to stab him with a penknife. The Privy Council examined her and declared her insane. Eight years later James Hadfield suffered serious head wounds

Contemporary engraving produced 'In Commemoration of the Providential Escape of his Most Sacred Majesty King George the Third' from an assassination attempt at London's Drury Lane Theatre, 1800.

fighting for his country against the French. After leaving the forces, he was taken in by a millennial cult who persuaded him to assassinate the king. Hadfield believed Christ was communicating with him and that killing George would advance His Second Coming. At the same time, the ex-soldier said he was tired of life and hoped to be executed. In 1800 he fired his pistol at the king while he was standing for the national anthem in a London theatre, but, you have guessed it, at the crucial moment George bowed to the audience, and the bullet missed. When the king called him over, Hadfield said: 'God bless your royal highness; I like you very well; you are a good fellow.' Charged with treason, he was found not guilty on grounds of insanity and sent to Bedlam, where he died four decades later in 1841. Ironically, George himself had periodic bouts of mental illness, culminating in his son being appointed Prince Regent, though some modern scholars have suggested that really he was suffering from the genetic blood disorder porphyria.

Queen Victoria

On hearing about Abraham Lincoln's assassination, Queen Victoria remarked: 'One never heard of such a thing. I only hope that it will not be catching elsewhere.' In fact, the queen, who enjoyed the second longest reign in English history, had already survived a number of assassination attempts. Over her whole reign, she faced at least eight. On 10 June 1840, while she was pregnant, she and Prince Albert had just left Buckingham Palace in their carriage when the prince noticed 'a little mean-looking man holding something towards us'. Edward Oxford was a baby-faced eighteen-year-old barman and the 'thing' he pointed was a duelling pistol. From about six yards he fired, but missed. He took a second shot with another pistol, but the queen ducked and he missed again. A crowd of people pulled Oxford to the ground, and the royal couple carried on with their ride as though nothing had happened.

Albert wrote that their aim was to demonstrate they had not 'lost all confidence' in their people. When police searched Oxford's rooms they found papers apparently relating to a secret society called 'Young England', but there is no evidence that such a group really existed. The young man's trial heard that he drank too much and was prone to erratic and sometimes threatening behaviour, that his mother suffered from delusions, and that his father was mad and had once ridden a horse around his parlour. When asked whether he knew it was wrong to shoot at the queen, he replied: 'I might as well shoot at her as anybody else.' Oxford was found to be insane and sent to a lunatic asylum before eventually being deported to Australia where he worked as a house painter.

Two years later as Victoria and Albert were returning from church one Sunday, at almost exactly the same spot Oxford had fired from, Albert saw 'a little, swarthy, ill-looking rascal' pointing a small flintlock pistol at them. The man pulled the trigger, but nothing happened. Then he hid the gun under his coat and wandered off into Green Park. Victoria refused to be intimidated and

Surely the most shot-at of all British monarchs, Queen Victoria, survives the attentions of Edward Oxford near Buckingham Palace in 1840.

the next evening they went out for another drive in their open coach. 'You may imagine that our minds were not very easy,' wrote Albert. 'We looked behind every tree, and I cast my eyes round in search of the rascal's face.' The royal couple had drawn a crowd as usual, and plain-clothes police mingled as they searched for the gunman, but he still managed to fire at the carriage yet again from just a few metres away. He missed, and this time a policeman grabbed him. The assailant was a carpenter named John Francis, who claimed his gun was not loaded and that the whole affair was just a prank. Sentenced to death, his punishment was commuted to transportation for life at the queen's request.

Just five weeks later, in the same area, a seventeen-year-old hunchback tried to shoot at Victoria, but his gun failed to go off. That night police reportedly rounded up all of London's hunchbacks and found the culprit, William Bean. His father said he wanted to be famous and had been inspired by Edward Oxford. Bean claimed his pistol had been loaded mainly with tobacco and that the queen's life had never been in danger. He was sentenced to eighteen months' hard labour. In 1849 Victoria was fired on by an Irishman who had fled the potato famine and wanted to go to prison because he was tired of being out of work. He said there had been no bullet in his gun, which was loaded only with powder. He was transported for seven years, as was a former army officer who managed to hit Victoria on the head with the brass top of his cane in another attack. In 1872 an Irishman with a pistol got right up to the queen before being wrestled to the ground by her famous servant John Brown. He said he was trying to secure freedom for Irish political prisoners. His gun did not work.

Edward VIII

If Queen Victoria had one of the longest reigns in English history, her great-grandson, Edward VIII, had one of the shortest – just ten months until his abdication – but that was still time to fit in an assassination attempt. On 16 July 1936 he was riding on horseback in a parade by Buckingham Palace when a man in the crowd pointed a gun at him. A special constable dashed it out of his hand and arrested him. The gun flew into the road and landed at the feet of the king's horse. According to Edward's official biography, he assumed it was a bomb and braced himself for the impact. His equerry, John Aird, who had always thought he was a bit of a coward, was impressed by Edward's coolness as he 'rode on in complete calm, not even quickening his horse's pace'.

Witnesses said that earlier the gunman had been seen talking to a well-dressed man some distance away. Identified as George Andrew McMahon, the gunman said he had no intention of harming the king and that he 'only did it as a protest'. After brief inquiries, Scotland Yard told the palace that McMahon was a frustrated Irish journalist who had managed to persuade himself the UK government was hampering his career and that this was his way of trying to draw attention to the perceived injustice. It later emerged that McMahon was a caretaker whose real name was Jerome Bannigan, and that he was suspected of being a Nazi sympathizer. At his trial, he told a rather complicated story about being in contact with 'a foreign power' who said they would pay him £150 to assassinate the king, but that he had alerted MI5. Bannigan hinted that the 'foreign power' was Nazi Germany, but the names of the contacts he gave did not match any known Germans associated with the regime or living in Britain. He was sentenced to twelve months' hard labour. Edward had been furious that Bannigan's antics got all the newspaper headlines, and that the speech he had delivered that day, on the horrors of war, was virtually ignored. One of the first telegrams the king had received on his safe return to Buckingham Palace was from Adolf Hitler, saying: 'I have just received the news of the abominable attempt on the life of your Majesty, and send my heartiest congratulations on your escape.' Later Edward himself would be widely suspected of harbouring Nazi sympathies.

Elizabeth II

Those who shoot at British monarchs do not generally seem to have very effective guns. In 1981 a seventeen-year-old named Marcus Sarjeant fired a series of blank shots at Queen Elizabeth II as she rode down the Mall during a Trooping the Colour ceremony. The judge said Sarjeant had wanted to use a real gun, but that he could not get hold of one. He had apparently been inspired by assassination attempts on Pope John Paul II and President Reagan during the previous three months. In his diary, in an echo of John Lennon's killer, Mark Chapman, Sarjeant wrote that he was 'going to stun and mystify the whole world' and 'become the most famous teenager in the world'. He was sentenced to five years in prison, and on his release changed his name to start a new life.

Another plot against the queen remained secret for nearly forty years. It happened in 1970 at the small Australian town of Lithgow in New South Wales, as the royal train carrying the queen and Prince Philip was passing through. In the short interval between a security train checking the track and the royal train itself appearing, someone placed a log on the rails, designed to derail the train. The front wheels hit the log, which got caught under them, but the driver managed to keep the carriages on the track, and no one was hurt. Experts said if the train had been going any faster, it would have been derailed and then crashed into an embankment. The story came to light only in 2009, with a local reporter claiming police had asked the media to observe a news blackout. No one was ever arrested.

British Prime Ministers

Spencer Perceval remains the only British prime minister to have been assassinated, but if the IRA had had their way, there would have been at least two more, not to mention plenty of cabinet ministers. In 1984 they set off a bomb at the Grand Hotel in Brighton where Prime Minister Margaret Thatcher and many other leading Conservatives were staying during their party conference. Nearly a month before, the bomber had hidden the device, timed to go off during the conference, in a bathroom directly above Thatcher's suite. It exploded just before three in the morning on 12 October, when the prime minister was still working on her speech to be delivered later that day. The blast caused a large part of the building to collapse, and severely damaged Thatcher's bathroom, but she was unhurt. Five people were killed, none of them cabinet members, though one was a Conservative MP, and trade secretary Norman Tebbit was seriously injured. The prime minister was urged to return to Downing Street at once for her own safety, but she refused and instead delivered a rousing speech to the conference, declaring: 'This attack has failed. All attempts to destroy democracy by terrorism will fail.' She got a standing ovation. The IRA responded: 'Today we were unlucky, but remember we only have to be lucky once. You have to be lucky always.' The bomber was caught and served fourteen years in prison before being released under the Good Friday Agreement.

Destroying the evidence: the van from which the IRA fired mortar shells at John Major and his cabinet, set on fire after the attack, London, 1991.

The IRA tried its luck again on the snowy morning of 7 February 1991. They abandoned a van close to the Ministry of Defence in the heart of Whitehall, having primed a home-made mortar inside to fire three shells at 10 Downing Street, where Thatcher's successor, John Major, was chairing the War Cabinet to consider the latest developments in the first Gulf War. One shell exploded in number 10's garden, thirty yards from the meeting. Members of the cabinet ducked under the table and were saved from injury by bomb-proof netting on the windows. Four people, including two police officers, suffered minor injuries from flying debris. If the shell had hit the building, John Major and his cabinet would certainly have been in grave danger. After the last shell had been fired and before police could examine it, the van was destroyed by a pre-set incendiary device. A leading member of the police Anti-Terrorist Branch said of the IRA operation: 'Technically, it was quite brilliant.'

American Presidents

Only four U.S. presidents have been assassinated, but it is estimated that at least thirty were targeted by would-be killers. The one who mounted the first attack – on Andrew Jackson in 1835 – got more than he bargained for. Richard Lawrence, an unemployed house painter, tried to shoot the president as he left the Capitol building after a funeral, but his gun misfired. Jackson, aged 67 and a national hero thanks to his victory over the British at the Battle of New Orleans in 1815, gave him a beating with his walking cane. Lawrence managed to pull a second gun, but that one misfired too. Among those who then helped to grab the gunman was 'King of the Wild Frontier' turned congressman Davy Crockett. Jackson believed his political opponents were behind the attack, but Lawrence was found to be insane and was sent to a mental institution for the rest of his life. A century later, researchers tested Lawrence's two pistols. Each of them fired successfully at the first attempt.

In all the failed assassination plots against U.S. presidents, the only one to be injured was Ronald Reagan. On 30 March 1981 he had been giving a speech at the Washington Hilton. Among the crowd outside was a 25-year-old Beatles fan, John Hinckley Jr, who had been wondering how the world could keep turning after the assassination of John Lennon three months before. As Reagan emerged, Hinckley fired six shots from a distance of about 3 metres (10 ft). In a well-rehearsed routine, one secret service agent bundled the president into a car, while another spread his body to take the bullets. He was wounded in the abdomen. A policeman was also wounded, while Reagan's press secretary, Jim Brady, was hit in the head and suffered serious injuries. One shot ricocheted off the limousine, hit the president, and lodged in his lung less than an inch from his heart. As people in the crowd grabbed Hinckley, another secret service agent leapt on to him to ensure he did not suffer the same fate as Lee Harvey Oswald, while yet another grabbed a submachine-gun to cover Reagan's escape in his car.

Reagan, then aged seventy, was rushed to hospital, and made a remarkable recovery to complete two terms as U.S. president, and to

Said to be 'drawn from a sketch by an eye witness', an etching depicts the attempted assassination of President Andrew Jackson in 1835, Washington, DC.

end the Cold War with the Soviet Union. As he was being wheeled in for surgery, he lifted his oxygen mask and said to his wife: 'Honey, I forgot to duck!' He also joked with the operating team, saying he hoped they were all Republicans. Reagan later confided that he had prayed for the man who shot him as a 'lost sheep', and within two weeks he was back at work, with considerably enhanced popularity that may have helped him get through Congress some of his more controversial policies, such as increasing defence spending at the expense of social programmes. But probably none of that bothered the man who tried to kill him, who appears to have been one of those would-be assassins for whom the deed is simply part of their own psychodrama.

Hinckley was the youngest child of a Denver oil executive, part of a 'fine Christian family'. He did pretty well at school, but at university he found it hard to settle to his studies. Becoming withdrawn, he started doing menial jobs in restaurants and bars, before dropping out and going to Hollywood to try to make it as a songwriter. That failed, and he ended up living on the street and

The aftermath of John Hinckley Jr's assassination attempt against President Ronald Reagan, Washington, DC, 1981.

had to get his parents to bail him out. He became obsessed with the film *Taxi Driver* (1976) and particularly its female lead, Jodie Foster, and started modelling himself on its hero, who plots to kill a presidential candidate. He invented a fictitious girlfriend and a fictitious right-wing party of which he was 'National Director'. He bought a gun and started taking Valium and anti-depressants. In 1980 he was arrested with three firearms at Nashville Airport when President Jimmy Carter was passing through.

Then Hinckley took a drug overdose and toyed with the idea of killing himself at the site of John Lennon's assassination, while at the same time reading up on assassination and starting to stalk Ronald Reagan, who had succeeded Carter as president. On 29 March 1981 he found Reagan's itinerary for the next day in a news-paper, and resolved to kill him, after sending a last note to Jodie Foster, whom he had inundated with letters, postcards and poems, asking her to 'give me the chance with this historic deed to gain your respect and love'. After the assassination attempt, Hinckley was tried but acquitted on grounds of insanity. He was finally freed from psychiatric care, under strict conditions, in 2016. It is esti-mated that when he shot Reagan, the u.s. security services were monitoring four hundred people as serious potential assassins, plus another 25,000 who were considered lesser risks. Hinckley was not among them.

Among the other presidents to be targeted by assassination plots were Herbert Hoover, Richard Nixon, Gerald Ford, the two Bushes, Bill Clinton and Barack Obama. One of America's most important leaders, Franklin D. Roosevelt, the architect of the New Deal and of victory in the Second World War, might have been killed before he really got started. On 15 February 1933, when he had been elected but had not yet taken office, Roosevelt was visiting Miami. Thousands turned out, including a contingent of Democratic Party bigwigs. Just after Roosevelt made an impromptu speech from his car, shots rang out. They were fired by Italian immigrant Giuseppe Zangara, an unemployed bricklayer who suffered from chronic

Sang-froid: President Harry Truman delivers a speech at Arlington National Cemetery shortly after surviving an assassination attempt, 1 November 1950.

abdominal pain, using a gun he had bought for $8 from a pawn shop. Quickly the crowd wrestled him to the ground, but not before one of his shots had mortally wounded Anton Cermak, the mayor of Chicago. Four other people were also wounded, but Roosevelt was unhurt. When he was taken to gaol, Zangara, a self-styled 'anarchist', declared: 'I kill kings and presidents first and next all capitalists.' Tried and found guilty, on 20 March he went to the electric chair, apparently furious that there were no newsreels present to capture the moment. If Roosevelt had been killed, history might have been very different. His vice-president, John Nance Garner, was much less enthusiastic about the New Deal which helped America to recover from the Great Depression.

Almost as significant a figure as Roosevelt was his successor Harry Truman, who ordered the use of nuclear weapons against Japan and saw through final victory in the Second World War, who helped create NATO and who implemented the Marshall Plan to rebuild Western Europe. In 1950, while the White House was being extensively refurbished, Truman was staying at Blair House in Washington. On 1 November two Puerto Rican nationalists, Oscar Collazo and Griselio Torresola, tried to shoot their way into the building. The noise woke the president who came to a window, but a guard shouted at him to take cover. In the gunfight, Torresola was killed and Collazo wounded along with three policemen, one of whom died the same day from his injuries. The two would-be assassins were the opposite of the Jackal. They had never visited Washington before, and Collazo had never fired a gun. He said they were not trying to kill a man, but a symbol of the system, hoping to trigger a revolution in America that would bring freedom for Puerto Rico. Half an hour after the attack, Truman was at a ceremony in Arlington Cemetery, saying: 'a president has to expect these things.' Collazo was sentenced to death, but Truman had his punishment commuted to life imprisonment, and he was released in 1979.

Pope John Paul II

Marcus Sarjeant, who fired a gun at the queen, said he had been inspired by attacks on Ronald Reagan and Pope John Paul II. In the Dark Ages, at least four popes were murdered. After that, there were no confirmed killings, but that does not mean no one tried. John Paul II, perhaps the most famous pope of modern times, was the first ever pontiff from a Slavic nation and the first non-Italian in more than 450 years. His time as head of the Church coincided with his native Poland's attempts to free itself from Soviet domination. On 13 May 1981, a 23-year-old Turkish man, Mehmet Ali Agca, shot him twice at close range while he was being driven around St Peter's Square in Rome in an open-top vehicle. John Paul was critically injured as one shot just missed his heart. The attack happened on the feast day of the Virgin of Fátima, and the pope said she had saved his life by guiding the bullet away from his vital organs.

Agca's motive remains a mystery. In Turkey, he had been a member of the Grey Wolves right-wing ultra-nationalist organization, but some believed he was hired to attack the pope by an East European Communist intelligence service, perhaps the Bulgarians, for giving too much support to the anti-communist Solidarity movement in Poland. KGB head (and later Soviet leader) Yuri Andropov, had described John Paul as 'our enemy . . . Due to his uncommon skills and great sense of humour he is dangerous,' but no communist link with Agca was ever proved. In 1983 John Paul went to visit the Turk in prison and forgave him for the attack. Agca spent nineteen years behind bars in Italy before the pope secured his pardon. He was then extradited to his native country where he was wanted in connection with the murder of a human rights activist and imprisoned again. Agca had frequently claimed to be the messiah, and when he was released from prison in Turkey in 2010, he wrote a statement proclaiming 'the end of the world. All the world will be destroyed in this century. Every human being will die . . . I am the Christ eternal.' On the first anniversary of Agca's attack, John

Rome, 1983: Pope John Paul II meets Mehmet Ali Agca, the man who tried to kill him.

Paul had made a pilgrimage to Fátima's shrine in Portugal, where an anti-reform Belgian priest who believed the pope was a Soviet agent tried unsuccessfully to stab him with a bayonet. The assailant served three years in gaol. John Paul lived until 2005 and was beatified in 2011.

Fidel Castro

'If surviving assassination attempts were an Olympic event,' said Fidel Castro, 'I would win the gold medal.' Confirmation of this claim comes, among other places, from a television documentary, *638 Ways to Kill Castro*. That is the number of attempts on the Cuban leader's life according to the head of his secret service, and U.S. Secretary of Defence Robert McNamara admitted: 'we were hysterical about Cuba.' In 1959 Castro swept aside the corrupt dictatorship of Fulgencio Batista. At first the USA was fairly sympathetic, but then the new Cuban leader started nationalizing American-owned land and businesses, as well as closing down casinos and brothels owned by American gangsters. As the U.S. grew more hostile, Castro moved closer to the Soviet Union. This led to a panic in Washington that communism might spread from Havana and infect the whole of Central America. By December 1959 CIA director Allen Dulles was instructing that 'consideration be given to the elimination of Castro', though there were suggestions that President Eisenhower was even keener on killing the Cuban leader than Dulles. There followed a succession of plots with exotic names – 'Mongoose', 'ZR/Rifle', 'AM/Blood' – involving perhaps even more exotic methods: exploding cigars, a poisoned handkerchief, a radio full of poison gas, a bomb in a seashell in Castro's favourite snorkelling spot, infecting his breathing apparatus for diving with tuberculosis bacteria, and so on. At one point his mistress was supplied with poison pills. She tried hiding them in a jar of cold cream, but they dissolved. So then she thought about forcing the cream into his mouth while he was asleep. Instead, overcome with remorse, she confessed to him.

He offered her his gun to do the deed, but she burst into tears and said: 'I can't do it, Fidel.'

At first, the u.s. government's view was that it made sense to assassinate Castro only if there was also an invasion of Cuba. Otherwise he might be replaced by someone they considered even worse, such as his brother Raul (who eventually did succeed him) or Che Guevara. Then, after JFK had moved into the White House, came the fiasco of the Bay of Pigs invasion of 1961. It cost Dulles his job, but the disappearance of an invasion option did not bring an end to the assassination plots. Sometimes the agency hired figures from the criminal underground. A Mafia leader supplied poison to Castro's personal secretary Juan Orta, but Orta was exposed and imprisoned. In 1962 inter-agency rivalry in the u.s. took a hand, as FBI director J. Edgar Hoover blew the whistle about CIA plots against Castro to Attorney General Bobby Kennedy. This revelation was particularly embarrassing for Kennedy because of his high-profile campaign against organized crime, leading to the Attorney General telling off the CIA for colluding with 'hoodlum elements'. Still the assassination plots continued. On 7 September 1963 Castro was asked in an interview about the conspiracies against him, and replied: 'we are prepared to . . . answer in kind.'

On the very day that JFK was assassinated, an attempt on Castro's life involving a poisoned pen failed. Perhaps this incorrigible American plotting was the reason why Lyndon Johnson continued to believe Castro was responsible for Kennedy's assassination in spite of the Warren Commission's findings. In 1975 the Church Committee said it had found 'concrete evidence of at least eight plots' to assassinate Castro involving the CIA between 1960 and 1965. The last known attempt was in 2000 while the Cuban leader was on a visit to Panama, when a Cuban ex-CIA agent placed 200 lb of high explosives under a podium he was due to speak from, but his security team found and defused it.

Andy Warhol

Castro's revolutionary colleague Che Guevara was one of the many famous people Andy Warhol featured in his works, along with Elvis Presley, Marilyn Monroe, Jackie Kennedy, Mao Zedong and so on. In the course of helping create the cult of celebrity, he became a celebrity himself – by far the best-known artist in America, and an *enfant terrible* immediately recognizable way beyond artistic circles. Openly gay, he hung out with drag queens and assorted bohemians in a fashionably edgy atmosphere. In 1968 he died at the hand of an assassin – for a minute and a half anyway.

Warhol's works were churned out at The Factory in Manhattan. Of his way-out hangers-on, the artist remarked: 'Crazy people had always fascinated me because they were so creative.' And it seemed to work. It was clear to everyone that Warhol was no starving artist. He was plainly making a lot of money. The art was edgy too – with his silkscreen paintings of soup cans, a film version of Anthony Burgess's violent and controversial novel *A Clockwork Orange* six years before Stanley Kubrick's adaptation, and another about the assassination of JFK. He was sometimes described as 'the most hated artist in America'. One day in 1967 a 31-year-old woman named Valerie Solanas walked into his life and tried to persuade him to stage a play she had written entitled *Up Your Ass*. He was intrigued, but the script was 'so dirty', he was suspicious, afraid she might be 'a lady cop'. Solanas described herself as a 'man-hater'. She had been abused by her father, borne a child at fifteen and had it taken away from her, then financed her psychology degree by prostitution before falling in with the lesbian community. She founded an organization called SCUM, the Society for Cutting Up Men, of which she was the only member, an advertisement for followers in the *Village Voice* having produced no response.

On the streets she sold her SCUM Manifesto, which proclaimed: 'males can't love and all the evils of the world emanate from this male incapacity to love.' Elimination of the male sex, therefore, was essential for world peace. During the implementation phase, some males would be spared to form a Men's Auxiliary – a group of 'sympathetic' members of the sex who would work 'diligently to eliminate themselves'. Among those who would specifically not be invited to join were '"Great Artists", liars and phonies'. In spite of this, she asked Warhol to be a member. Babies would be created in the lab, so men would not be needed for reproduction, and once ageing and death had been eliminated, even laboratory babies might no longer be required. The SCUM female would have many characteristics including being 'nasty, violent, selfish'.

When Warhol showed no sign of putting on her play, she asked for her manuscript back. He replied that he had 'lost' it. The artist got proposals the whole time, and most ended up in a great slush pile of unanswered correspondence in his office. Solanas, who was always broke, began demanding money, so Warhol offered her a part in one of his films for a no doubt very welcome $25. The movie *I, A Man* is a sexual odyssey of a man who seduces eight women, but it was Solanas who caught the eye of some critics as she delivered a sassy performance as a 'tough lesbian' who stole the show, never letting the hero get beyond the staircase outside the flat she shared with her girlfriend. For all her revolutionary zeal, Solanas was desperate to be famous, declaring: 'I want a piece of a groovy world.' She managed to get a contract from Maurice Girodias of the controversial Olympia Press to write an autobiographical novel. He represented one admission ticket to the 'groovy world' while Warhol seemed to be another, but by the end of 1967, Solanas was destitute and homeless. She complained to Warhol about Girodias, and to Girodias about Warhol. She said the artist was a vulture and a thief, and kept pestering him, demanding to know where her play was and issuing threats. In response, he stopped taking her calls.

The summer of 1968 was a turbulent time. Martin Luther King had been assassinated in April. The Vietnam War was tearing America apart, and the newsreels were reporting student riots across Europe. On 3 June Solanas headed off to Girodias's office with two handguns in a laundry bag. The publisher was away, so she went and hung around outside Warhol's headquarters. When he appeared in the late afternoon, she buttonholed him and then accompanied him into the building. People noted that she seemed very on edge, and while the artist was on the phone, she suddenly fired at him twice, missing each time. Warhol begged her not to shoot again and hid under a desk, but she walked up to him and aimed more carefully, hitting him in the abdomen. The bullet went right through his body. She also shot one of Warhol's visitors and would have shot his business manager in the head, except that her gun jammed. He then persuaded her to leave. A few hours later, she gave herself up to a policeman, saying she had shot Warhol because he had 'too much control over my life'. When reporters asked her about her motives, she told them to read her manifesto.

In hospital, Warhol was clinically dead, but the doctors managed to revive him after ninety seconds. For the rest of this life, he had to wear a surgical corset, and was never the same again. His health was permanently damaged, he was more fearful and less adventurous, less 'creative' according to his own assessment. Although he lived on until 1987, it was often said that really he died the day he was shot. The attack also left him with a fear of hospitals which may have shortened his physical as well as his artistic life. He died aged 58 from cardiac arrest suffered after a gallbladder operation which he had delayed for years, allowing his condition to worsen. After Solanas had handed herself in to the police, Girodias asked her if she would shoot him if she got the chance. She giggled and said she would not: 'I'm over it now . . . I don't have to do it again.' She was given bail and sent for psychiatric tests, but was locked up again when she threatened Warhol and Girodias. Despite being diagnosed as a paranoid schizophrenic, she stood trial, admitting assault on Warhol but claiming she was only trying to attract his attention. She was gaoled for three years. The police told Warhol that if he testified, she would get a very long sentence, but the artist, still very ill, decided not to. The apparent leniency of the sentence horrified the singer Lou Reed, from the experimental rock group the Velvet Underground that Warhol managed: 'You get more for stealing a car . . . but the hatred directed towards him by society was obviously reflected in the judgment.' Solanas was hailed as a hero by some radical feminists and revolutionary hippies. Ti-Grace Atkinson of NOW, the National Organization for Women, said she would go down in history as an outstanding champion of women's rights.

Girodias published Solanas's SCUM Manifesto, but after her release she wrote nothing of note, though she continued to utter apparently frivolous but murderous threats against people. She out-lived Warhol by a year, dying of pneumonia in 1988. Her shooting of the artist was a huge story, and the issue of *Life* magazine that came out following it was meant to include an eight-page spread on him, but just over a day later there was an even huger event, the assassination of Bobby Kennedy, and the feature was squeezed out. In the febrile atmosphere of 1968, some said Warhol's shooting was his greatest work of art, others, like *Time* magazine, that he had reaped what he had sown: 'for years he celebrated every form of licentiousness . . . photographing depravity and calling it truth.' Warhol himself was philosophical: 'I realized that it was just timing that nothing terrible had ever happened to any of us before now . . . I guess it was just being in the wrong place at the right time. That's what assassination is all about.'

SELECT BIBLIOGRAPHY

BOOKS

Ahmed, Dr Nazeer, *Islam in Global History*, vol. 1 (Bloomington, IN, 2001)

Aiton, William, *A History of the Rencounter at Drumclog, and Battle at Bothwell Bridge* (Hamilton, 1821)

Antiphon, *On the Murder of Herodes*, www.perseus.tufts.edu, accessed 2 February 2020

Aristotle, *The Athenian Constitution* [330 BC], www.onemorelibrary.com

Armstrong, Karen, *Islam: A Short History* (London, 2001)

Azoulay, Vincent, *Pericles of Athens*, trans. Janet Lloyd (Princeton, NJ, 2014)

Barker, F., and P. Jackson, *London: 2000 Years of a City and Its People* (London, 1983)

Barrett, Anthony A., *Agrippina* (London, 1996)

Boardman, John, and I.E.S. Edwards, eds, *The Cambridge Ancient History*, vol. III, pt 2 (Cambridge, 1991)

Bockris, Victor, *Warhol* (London, 1990)

Breasted, J. H., ed., *Ancient Records of Egypt*, vol. IV (Chicago, IL, 1906)

Briant, Pierre, *From Cyrus to Alexander: A History of the Persian Empire*, trans. Peter T. Daniels (Winona Lake, IN, 2002)

Burstein, Stanley, *Outpost of Hellenism: The Emergence of Heraclea on the Black Sea*, University of California Publications: Classical Studies, vol. XIV (Berkeley, CA, 1974)

Cassius Dio, *Roman History*, http://penelope.uchicago.edu, accessed 2 February 2020

Constantino, Renato, with Letizia R. Constantino, *A History of the Philippines* (New York, 1975)

Cook, David, *Martyrdom in Islam* (Cambridge, 2007)

Crompton, Louis, *Homosexuality and Civilization* (London, 2006)

Deutscher, Isaac, *Stalin* (Harmondsworth, 1966)

Donald, David Herbert, *Lincoln* (New York, 1995)

Duka, Cecilio D., ed., *Struggle for Freedom* (Manila, 2008)

Dumas, Alexandre, *Celebrated Crimes* [1841], www.gutenberg.org

Falk, Avner, *Franks and Saracens: Reality and Fantasy in the Crusades* (London, 2010)

Fletcher, Catherine, *The Black Prince of Florence: The Spectacular Life and Treacherous World of Alessandro de' Medici* (Oxford, 2016)

Forsyth, Frederick, *The Day of the Jackal* (London, 1975)

Garmonsway, G. N., trans. and ed., *The Anglo-Saxon Chronicle* (London, 1975)

Gascoigne, Bamber, *A Brief History of the Dynasties of China* (London, 2003)

Geyl, Pieter, *The Revolt of the Netherlands* (London, 1966)

Gibbon, Edward, *The Decline and Fall of the Roman Empire* (London, 1912)

Grimal, Nicholas, *A History of Ancient Egypt* (London, 1992)

Henderson, Peter V. N., *Gabriel García Moreno and Conservative State Formation in the Andes* (Austin, TX, 2008)

Hibbert, Christopher, *The French Revolution* (London, 1988)

Hillsborough, Romulus, *Samurai Assassins: 'Dark Murder' and the Meiji Restoration, 1853–1868* (Jefferson, NC, 2017)

John of Fordun, *Chronicle of the Scottish Nation* [1872], www.archive.org

Josephus, Flavius, *The Wars of the Jews or The History of the Destruction of Jerusalem*, trans. William Whiston, 2009, www.gutenberg.org

Kanawati, Naguib, *Conspiracies in the Egyptian Palace: Unis to Pepy I* (London, 2002)

Kautilya, *Arthashastra*, trans. R. Shamasastry (Bangalore, 1915), www.archive. org

Kee, Robert, *The Green Flag*, vol. III: *Ourselves Alone* (London, 1976)

Keeley, Lawrence H., *War Before Civilization: The Myth of the Peaceful Savage* (New York, 1996)

Keene, Donald, *Emperor of Japan: Meiji and His World, 1852–1912* (New York, 2002)

—, *Yoshimasa and the Silver Pavilion: The Creation of the Soul of Japan* (New York, 2003)

Kitto, John, *Palestine: The Bible History of the Holy Land* (London, 1841)

Knecht, Robert J., *Hero or Tyrant? Henry III, King of France, 1574–89* (Abingdon, 2016)

Laqueur, Walter, *Terrorism* (London, 1978)

Lauderbaugh, George M., *The History of Ecuador* (Santa Barbara, CA, 2012)

Lewis, Kevin James, *Sons of Saint-Gilles: The Counts of Tripoli and Lebanon in the Twelfth Century* (Abingdon, 2017)

Love, Dane, *Scottish Covenanter Stories: Tales from the Killing Times* (Glasgow, 2000)

Lynch, Michael, *Scotland: A New History* (London, 1992)

Lynn, John A., *Battle: A History of Combat and Culture* (Philadelphia, PA, 2003)

Machiavelli, Niccolò, *The Prince*, www.gutenberg.org, accessed 2 February 2020

McKisack, May, *The Fourteenth Century* (London, 1959)

Malraux, André, *La Condition humaine* (Paris, 1946)

Manetho, *The Fragment of Manetho*, http://penelope.uchicago.edu, accessed 28 February 2020

Marsden, P., *Roman London* (London, 1980)

Meredith, M., *The State of Africa* (London, 2006)

Montefiore, Simon Sebag, *Monsters: History's Most Evil Men and Women* (London, 2008)

Mookerji, Radha Kumud, *Chandragupta Maurya and His Times* (Delhi, 1988)

Motley, John Lothrop, *The Rise of the Dutch Republic* (London, 1883)

Myers, J.N.L., *The English Settlements* (Oxford, 1998)

Newton, Michael, *Age of Assassins: The Loners, Idealists and Fanatics who Conspired to Change the World* (London, 2012)

Newton, Michael, *Famous Assassinations in World History: An Encyclopedia*, 2 vols (Santa Barbara, CA, 2014)

Nicholas, David M., *Medieval Flanders* (Abingdon, 2014)

Onon, Urgunge, trans., *The History and the Life of Chinggis Khan* (Leiden, 1990)

Plutarch, *The Parallel Lives*, vol. VII: *The Life of Julius Caesar*, http://penelope. uchicago.edu, accessed 2 February 2020

Poe, Edgar Allan, *Hymn to Aristogeiton and Harmodius* [1903], https://etc.usf. edu

Porter, Lindsay, *Assassination: A History of Political Murder* (London, 2010)

Poulsen, C., *The English Rebels* (London, 1984)

Prebble, John, *The Lion in the North: A Personal View of Scotland's History* (London, 1981)

Prescott, William H., *History of the Conquest of Peru* (Mineola, NY, 2005)

Robinson, John J., *Dungeon, Fire and Sword: The Knights Templar in the Crusades* (Lanham, MD, 2009)

Röhl, John C. G., *Wilhelm II: Into the Abyss of War and Exile, 1900–1941*, trans. Sheila de Bellaigue and Roy Bridge (Cambridge, 2014)

Roskam, Geert, *Plutarch's 'Maxime cum principibus philosopho esse disserendum': An Interpretation with Commentary* (Leuven, 2009)

Runciman, Steven, *A History of the Crusades* (Harmondsworth, 1971)

Salmon, Edward T., *A History of the Roman World from 30 BC to AD 138* (London, 1972)

Salway, P., *Roman Britain* (Oxford, 1988)

Schama, Simon, *Citizens: A Chronicle of the French Revolution* (London, 2004)

Scobbie, Irene, *The A to Z of Sweden* (Lanham, MD, 2006)

Smedley, E., *The History of France: From the Final Partition of the Empire of Charlemagne, AD 843, to the Peace of Cambray, AD 1529* (London, 1836)

Sommerstein, Alan H., *The Tangled Ways of Zeus: And Other Studies In and Around Greek Tragedy* (Oxford, 2010)

Stenton, F. M., *Anglo-Saxon England* (London, 1971)

Suetonius, *The Lives of the Twelve Caesars*, http://penelope.uchicago.edu, accessed 2 February 2020

Sun Tzu, *The Art of War*, www.suntzusaid.com, accessed 2 February 2020

Tacitus, *The Annals*, http://penelope.uchicago.edu, accessed 2 February 2020

Taylor, A.J.P., *The First World War: An Illustrated History* (Harmondsworth, 1966)

Thant Myint-U, *The Making of Modern Burma* (Cambridge, 2012)

Thucydides, *The History of the Peloponnesian War*, http://classics.mit.edu accessed 2 February 2020

Vaughan, Richard, *John the Fearless: The Growth of Burgundian Power*, vol. II (London, 1966)

Vieusseux, André, *The History of Switzerland: From the Irruption of the Barbarians to the Present Time* (London, 1840)

Walsh, Michael, and Don Jordan, *The King's Revenge: Charles II and the Greatest Manhunt in British History* (London, 2012)

Watson, J. Steven, *The Reign of George III, 1760–1815* (London, 1960)

Whitehorne, John, *Cleopatras* (London, 2001)

Williams, Anne, and Vivian Head, *Terror Attacks* (London, 2006)

Withington, John, *A Disastrous History of the World: Chronicles of War, Earthquake, Plague and Flood* (London, 2008)

Worthington, Ian, ed., *Alexander the Great: A Reader* (London, 2011)

Ziegler, Philip, *King Edward VIII: The Official Biography* (London, 1990)

ARTICLES AND PAMPHLETS

Alberge, Dalya, 'Plot to Kill Napoleon Linked to British Cabinet Minister', 27 September 2014, www.theguardian.com

Alexander, Harriet, 'John Lennon's Killer Revealed Details of Shooting as He Was Denied Parole for the Ninth Time', 16 September 2016, www.telegraph.co.uk

'Alleged Assassination Plots Involving Foreign Leaders: An Interim Report of the Select Committee to Study Governmental Operations with Respect to Intelligence Activities', United States Senate, 20 November 1975, intelligence.senate.gov

'Anarchist Kills Spain's Premier', *New York Times*, 13 November 1912

Andrews, Evan, '6 Assassination Attempts on Adolf Hitler', 29 April 2015, www.history.com

'Armoured Cars: Essential Kit for Presidents', 18 November 2003, www.bbc.co.uk

'The Assassination of Reinhard Heydrich', CIA Historical Review Program, 22 September 1993, www.cia.gov

'The Average Number of Bodyguards the President and Deputy President Have – 81 Each,' 11 July 2018, www.mybroadband.co.za

'Barry George Not Guilty of Jill Dando Murder', 1 August 2008, www.belfasttelegraph.co.uk

Black, Ian, 'Rise and Kill First: The Secret History of Israel's Targeted Assassinations – Review', 22 July 2018, www.theguardian.com

Brincat, Shannon K., '"Death to Tyrants": The Political Philosophy of Tyrannicide', academia.edu, accessed 2 February 2020

Bronner, Ethan, 'Intelligence Correspondent Ronen Bergman Persuades Mossad Agents, Shin Bet and Military Personnel to Disclose their Stories on State-sponsored Killings', 28 January 2018, www.independent.co.uk

Brown, Adrian, 'Osama Bin Laden's Death: How it Happened', 10 September 2012, www.bbc.co.uk

Burnett, Amy Nelson, 'Randolph C. Head. *Jenatsch's Axe: Social Boundaries, Identity, and Myth in the Era of the Thirty Years' War*. Changing Perspectives on Early Modern Europe', *Renaissance Quarterly*, LXII/1 (2009), www.cambridge.org

Cameron, Rob, 'Czech Pride in Jan Kubis, Killer of Reinhard Heydrich', 27 May 2012, www.bbc.co.uk

Campbell, Duncan, Richard Norton-Taylor and Conal Urquhart: 'They Say Why Attack a Tiger When There Are So Many Sheep?', 8 July 2005, www.guardian.com

—, '638 Ways to Kill Castro', 3 August 2006, www.theguardian.com

Cavendish, Richard, 'Claudius Died on October 13th, AD 54: Roman Opinion Was Convinced that Agrippina Had Poisoned Him', *History Today*, 10 October 2004

—, 'The Duke of Orleans Was Assassinated on November 23rd, 1407', *History Today*, 11 November 2007

'Chilean Agent Convicted over Prats' Killing', 21 November 2000, www.bbc.co.uk

Cook, Andrew, 'The Plot Thickens', 3 January 2003, www.theguardian.com

Corera, Gordon, 'Licence to Kill: When Governments Choose to Assassinate', 17 March 2012, www.bbc.co.uk

Dall'Aglio, Stefano, 'History's Coldest Case: The Assassination of Lorenzino de' Medici', 29 October 2015, http://blog.yalebooks.com

Dash, Mike, 'The Ottoman Empire's Life-or-death Race', 22 March 2012, www.smithsonianmag.com

David, Dr Saul, 'Mary, Queen of Scots, and the Earl of Bothwell', 17 February 2011, www.bbc.co.uk

Dearden, Lizzie, 'Osama Bin Laden could "Absolutely" Have Been Captured Alive, says U.S. Military Commander', 18 July 2017, www.independent.co.uk

Ekinci, Ekrem Buğra, 'The History of Fratricide in the Ottoman Empire', pts 1 and 2, 6–7 August 2015, www.dailysabah.com

'The Empress of Austria Assassinated', *Los Angeles Herald*, 11 September 1898

Everitt, Anthony, '*Empress of Rome: The Life of Livia*, by Matthew Dennison', 23 April 2010, www.independent.co.uk

Fawthrop, Tom, 'Major-General Khattiya Sawasdipol Obituary', 17 May 2010, www.theguardian.com

Fein, Robert A., and Bryan Vossekuil, 'Assassination in the United States: An Operational Study of Recent Assassins, Attackers, and Near-lethal Approachers', *Journal of Forensic Sciences*, March 1999, www.secretintelligenceservice.org

'Findings of the Select Committee on Assassinations in the Assassination of President John F. Kennedy in Dallas, Tex. November 22, 1963', www.archives.gov

Fisk, Robert, 'My Conversation with the Son of Soghomon Tehlirian, the Man who Assassinated the Organiser of the Armenian Genocide', 20 June 2016, www.independent.co.uk

Fitterman, Lisa, 'Troubled Loner Killed Ottawa Sportscaster', 8 July 2017, www.theglobeandmail.com

Gallagher John, review of '*Killers of the King: The Men Who Dared to Execute Charles I*', 31 October 2014, www.theguardian.com

Green, David B., 'This Day in Jewish History 1948: Stalin's Secret Police Murder a Yiddish Actor', 13 January 2013, www.haaretz.com

Harding, Colin, 'Enrique Gorriaran Merlo: Argentine Revolutionary', 26 September 2006, www.independent.co.uk

'He Took a Shot at a President-elect, and Could Have Changed History', 6 February 2017, miamiherald.com

Hersh, Seymour M., 'The Killing of Osama bin Laden', 21 May 2015, www.lrb.co.uk

Holder, Eric H. Jr, Letter to Patrick Leahy, 22 May 2013, www.justice.gov

Holmquist, Kate, 'Dallas Then: "Nut Country"', 22 November 2013, www.irishtimes.com

Hopkins, Nick and Steven Morris, 'Obsessive Whose Life of Fantasy Ended in Deadly Reality', 3 July 2001, www.theguardian.com

Hosken, Andrew, 'The Mafia Murders that Brought Down Slovakia's Government', 22 July 2018, www.bbc.co.uk

Hoyle, Ben, 'Reopen Bobby Kennedy Case File, Urges Son', *The Times*, 29 May 2018

Huggler, Justin, 'Tamil Tigers Apologise for Suicide Bomber's Murder of Rajiv Gandhi', 28 June 2006, www.independent.co.uk

Hughes-Hallett, Lucy, '*The Woman Who Shot Mussolini* by Frances Stonor Saunders', 27 February 2010, www.theguardian.com

'Istanbul Court Orders Release of Two Suspects in Murder of Turkish-Armenian Journalist Hrant Dink', 21 December 2018, www.dailysabah.com

Jacobson, Gavin, '"By Now, There Was No Way Back for Me": The Strange Story of Bogdan Stashinsky', 19 January 2017, www.newstatesman.com

'Japan Socialist Party Leader Assassinated at Political Rally – Archive', 13 October 2016, www.theguardian.com

Jernigan, Kelly Diane, 'Political Conspiracy in Napoleonic France', PhD Thesis, Louisiana State University and Agricultural and Mechanical College, 2015, digitalcommons.lsu.edu

Jones, Benjamin F., and Benjamin A. Olken, 'Hit or Miss? The Effect of Assassinations on Institutions and War', National Bureau of Economic Research, May 2007

Jones, Owen Bennett, 'Benazir Bhutto Assassination: How Pakistan Covered Up Killing', 27 December 2017, www.bbc.co.uk

Keys, David, 'Britain Tried to Kill Kaiser Wilhelm II in 1918 with Secret RAF Bombing Raid, Reveals Archives', 30 May 2018, www.independent.co.uk

Klein, Christopher, '8 Times Queen Victoria Survived Attempted Assassinations', 30 May 2017, www.history.com

Knapton, Sarah, 'Face of Lord Darnley Revealed – Mary Queen of Scots' "Lusty and Well Proportioned" Husband', 15 August 2016, www.telegraph.co.uk

Kubie, Jiri, 'How to Foil an Assassin', 3 April 1993, www.newscientist.com

Leitenberg, Milton, 'Deaths in Wars and Conflicts in the 20th Century', 2003, www.clingendael.org

Lennon, Troy, 'Blind Female Anarchist Executed for Lenin Assassination Plot', 30 August 2018, www.themorningbulletin.com.au

'*The Life and Legend of the Sultan Saladin* by Jonathan Phillips', *The Economist*, 1 June 2019

Lucas, Peter, 'King Zog Not Afraid to Open Fire', 23 November 2012, www.lowellsun.com

Lunacharsky, Anatoly, 'Revolutionary Silhouettes: Comrade Volodarsky' [1965], www.marxists.org

Lusher, Adam, 'Martin Luther King Jr Assassination: Did James Earl Ray Really Kill the Civil Rights Leader in Memphis?', 4 April 2018, www.independent.co.uk

Lynch, Patrick, '10 Brilliant Military Commanders You've Probably Never Heard Of', 18 March 2018, www.historycollection.com

Lynch, Suzanne, 'JFK Files: Seven Things We Now Know after Secret Papers Released', 27 October 2017, www.irishtimes.com

Macdonald, Cheyenne, 'The Gruesome Murder of Ramesses III', *Daily Mail*, 22 March 2016

Macintyre, Donald, 'Israel's Forgotten Hero: The Assassination of Count Bernadotte – and the Death of Peace', 18 September 2008, www.independent.co.uk

McKeown, Rory, 'Shock Claim: "John Lennon Murdered by the CIA"', 9 October 2017, www.dailystar.co.uk

Maclean, William, 'Dubai Cameras Shine Light on Killers' Dark Arts', 26 February 2010, www.reuters.com

MacNamee, Terence, 'DNA Tests Aim to Identify 17th Century Figure', 17 April 2012, www.swissinfo.ch

McPhee, Rod, 'Was Lee Harvey Oswald's Killer Jack Ruby Injected with Cancer to Stop Him Revealing Who Really Shot JFK?', 6 January 2017, www.mirror.co.uk

Malkin, Bonnie, 'Plot "to Kill Queen and Duke of Edinburgh" Kept Secret by Media for 38 Years', 28 January 2009, www.telegraph.co.uk

Manzoor, Novo, '5 Absurdly Hard to Kill Historical Figures', 8 October 2015, www.thedailystar.net

Martin, Paul, 'Lincoln's Missing Bodyguard', 7 April 2010, www.smithsonianmag.com

Milton, John, 'The Tenure of Kings and Magistrates' [1650], www.dartmouth.edu

'No Safe Haven: Iran's Global Assassination Campaign', Iran Human Rights Documentation Center, 2008, www.iranhrdc.org

Noyes, C. Lee, 'Custer's Conspirator Charles DeRudio led a Stranger-than-fiction Life', 6 April 2018, www.truewestmagazine.com

O'Neil, Des, 'Mercenary Conduct – An Irishman's Diary on Two Wild Geese and the Murder of Albrecht von Wallenstein', 20 February 2017, www.irishtimes.com

Osborne, Samuel, 'Lee Harvey Oswald's Killer Jack Ruby told FBI Informant to "Watch the Fireworks" Hours before JFK's Assassination', 19 November 2017, www.independent.co.uk

Partos, Gabriel, 'Analysis: Marathon Djindjic Trial', 23 May 2007, www.bbc.co.uk

Persio, Sofia Lotto, 'How the Mafia's Murder of an Italian Prosecutor Became a Turning Point in Italy's Fight Against the Mob', 23 May 2017, www.newsweek.com

Petersen, Daniel C., and William J. Hamblin, 'Who Were the Sicarii?', 7 June 2004, www.ldsmag.com

Preston, Richard, 'First World War Centenary: The Assassination of Franz Ferdinand, As it Happened', 27 June 2014, www.telegraph.co.uk

Protzman, Ferdinand, 'Head of Top West German Bank Is Killed in Bombing by Terrorists', 1 December 1989, www.nytimes.com

Pruitt, Sarah, 'Andy Warhol Was Shot By Valerie Solanas. It Killed Him 19 Years Later', 31 May 2018, www.history.com

'Revenge of the 47 Ronin', www.historychannel.com.au

Rodgers, Garry, 'Five Ways the JFK Assassination Changed the World', 20 November 2015, www.huffingtonpost.com

'Russian Spy Poisoning: What We Know So Far', 8 October 2018, www.bbc.co.uk

Ryan, Jason, 'ACLU Sues U.S. Government Over Awlaki's Hit List Designation', 19 July 2010, abcnews.go.com

Saha, Abhishek, 'The Politics of an Assassination: Who Killed Gandhi and Why?', 28 May 2017, www.hindustantimes.com

Schindler, John R., 'Who Murdered Olof Palme?', 16 November 2016, www.observer.com

'Sheikh Mujibur Rahman had Ignored RAW Alert Ahead of Bloody 1975 Coup', 12 July 2018, www.economictimes.indiatimes.com

'Slovak Officials say Ex-police Officer Killed Reporter Jan Kuciak', 1 October 2018, www.dw.com

Sofaer, Abraham D., 'Responses to Terrorism: Targeted Killing is a Necessary Option', 26 March 2004, web.archive.org

'The St Neots Assassin', www.bbc.co.uk

'This Day in History: 30 January 1835: Andrew Jackson Narrowly Escapes Assassination', www.history.com

Thomas, Gordon, 'Mossad's Licence to Kill', 17 February 2010, www.telegraph.co.uk

Timm, Leo, 'Desperate Measures in Ancient China: Assassins of the Eastern Zhou Dynasty', 5 February 2015, www.theepochtimes.com

Tran, Mark, 'Man who Shot Pope John Paul II Gets Out of Prison', 18 January 2010, www.theguardian.com

'Trump Blocked Release of Hundreds of JFK Records at Last Minute', 27 October 2017, www.irishtimes.com

Turak, Natasha, 'More than 100 Politicians Have Been Murdered in Mexico Ahead of Sunday's Election', 26 June 2018, www.cnbc.com

'Turkish Ambassador to Vatican is Slain', 10 June 1977, www.nytimes.com

'Turkish Court Hands Prison Sentences for 9 Suspects in Dink Assassination', 17 July 2019, www.ahvalnews.com

'Turkish Police Chiefs on Trial Over Murder of Journalist Hrant Dink', 19 April 2016, www.theguardian.com

'U.S. Secretary of State Honors Slain Activist Munir Said Thalib', 8 September 2014, www.jakartaglobe.id, accessed 2 December 2019

van Rensburg, Alet Janse, 'The Man who Killed Apartheid: New Book Sheds Light on Verwoerd's Assassin', 5 November 2018, www.news24.com

Warren Commission Appendix 7: A Brief History of Presidential Protection, www.archives.gov/research

Weaver, Matthew, 'Poisoned Umbrellas and Polonium: Russian-linked UK Death', 6 March 2018, www.theguardian.com

Welch, Frances, 'The Sexual Obsession that Drove Rasputin to his Death', 7 February 2014, www.dailymail.co.uk

'Who Killed Georgi Markov?', www.yesterday.uktv.co.uk, accessed 3 February 2020

'Who Murdered Jill Dando? Six Theories on the Killing', 23 August 2018, www.theweek.co.uk, accessed 19 September 2018

Withington, John, 'Prime Minister Assassinated!', *Scottish Portrait*, May 1984

Withington, John, 'Sarajevo', *London Portrait*, August 1984

'The World's Most Unusual Assassinations', 16 February 2017, www.bbc.co.uk

Zink, Dr Albert, 'Study Reveals that Pharaoh's Throat Was Cut during Royal Coup', *British Medical Journal*, 17 December 2012, www.bmj.com

PHOTO ACKNOWLEDGEMENTS

The author and the publisher wish to express their thanks to the below sources of illustrative material and/or permission to reproduce it.

Alamy: pp. 74 (Heritage Image Partnership Ltd), 77 (Chronicle), 246 (Archive PL), 248 (Niday Picture Library), 263 (Mugshot); British Library: p. 174; © The Trustees of the British Museum, London: pp. 67, 133, 200, 307; Condé Museum, Chantilly: p. 107; Danish State Archives: p. 89; Gallica Digital Library: pp. 73, 108, 302; Getty Images: p. 220 (Apic); Getty Museum, Los Angeles: p. 21; Leopold Museum, Vienna: p. 130; Library of Congress, Washington, DC: pp. 122, 170, 171, 195, 197, 313; National Archives and Records Administration (NARA), Washington, DC: pp. 218, 314, 316; National Gallery of Modern and Contemporary Art, Rome: p. 36 top; National Library of Ireland on The Commons: p. 215; National Palace Museum, Taipei: p. 99; National Portrait Gallery, London: p. 109; Portland Art Museum, Oregon: p. 126; Rätisches Museum, Chur: p. 132; Royal Museums of Fine Arts of Belgium: p. 145; Shutterstock: pp. 228 (Tolga Bozoglu/EPA), 244, 261, 295 (AP), 271 (Udo Weitz/AP), 311 (Tele-Search), 318 (SIPA); Stockholm City Museum: p. 147; Tokyo National Museum: p. 151; Victoria and Albert Museum, London: p. 305; Wikipedia: pp. 28 (Shakko CC BY-SA 3.0), 36 bottom (Marie-Lan Nguyen (2006)), 51 (VladoubidoOo CC BY-SA 4.0), 54 (Twlywyth Eldar), 64 (Ablakok CC BY-SA 4.0), 96 (Karl-Heinz Meurer – Charlie1965nrw CC BY-SA 3.0 DE), 212 (Cassowary Colorizations CC BY-SA 2.0), 222 (Allan Warren CC BY-SA 3.0), 264 (Ingfbruno CC BY-SA 3.0), 292 (Lienhard Schulz CC BY-SA 3.0).

INDEX